HIJACKED MINDS

How Addiction Rewires The Soul

By

Muhamad Aly Rifai, MD

FORWORD

Darrin Mangiacarne, DO, MPH, CPE, DFASAM, DFAOAAM

As a physician with more than 15 years of experience in addiction medicine, I have worked across medical detoxification, residential treatment, outpatient programs, and long-term recovery support. In that time, I have witnessed how substance use disorders can completely upend lives—physically, emotionally, and spiritually. Addiction does not merely disrupt behavior; it fundamentally changes the brain and deeply impacts the human spirit.

It is with great enthusiasm that I introduce HIJACKED MINDS: How Addiction Rewires The Soul, written by one of my trusted colleagues and a dedicated physician with whom I have had the privilege of working closely. I have witnessed his clinical expertise, compassion, and genuine commitment to holistic healing. Dr. Rifai brings that same thoughtful, patient-centered perspective to these pages, blending rigorous medical insight with a profound understanding of the spiritual and emotional dimensions of recovery.

The title captures a painful truth: addiction literally hijacks the brain's reward pathways, rewiring neural circuits in ways that make continued use feel like survival itself. What begins as a search for relief or pleasure, or simple experimentation can evolve into a chronic disease that overrides logic, relationships, and self-worth. Yet the subtitle reminds us that the impact goes even deeper—it reaches the soul, affecting meaning, identity, and our sense of connection to others and to something greater.

In today's landscape of rising overdose deaths and co-occurring mental health challenges, this book arrives at a critical time. It offers readers a clear-eyed yet hopeful exploration of how addiction takes hold and, more importantly, how healing and rewiring toward recovery are possible. Drawing from extensive front-line clinical experience, Dr. Rifai helps demystify the science while honoring the very human—and often spiritual—journey of reclaiming one's life.

Our shared approach to care emphasizes evidence-based medical treatment, including detoxification and medication-assisted options when appropriate, alongside therapies that address the whole person—mind, body, and spirit. We have seen how individualized, comprehensive care can restore hope and support lasting recovery. The insights in HIJACKED MINDS reflect this same philosophy: recovery is not just about stopping use; it is about healing the rewiring that has occurred and rediscovering a life of purpose and connection.

Whether you are struggling with addiction yourself, supporting a loved one, or working in the helping professions, this book provides valuable clarity and encouragement. It reduces stigma, counters myths, and illuminates practical pathways forward.

I am proud to collaborate with dedicated professionals like Dr. Rifai n this field. May HIJACKED MINDS serve as a trusted companion for those seeking understanding and a beacon of hope for everyone impacted by addiction.

Recovery is possible. Healing is possible. A rewired soul can find its way home.

With optimism and gratitude for every reader's journey,

CONTENTS

PROLOGUE

> *"All of our minds can be hijacked.*
> *Our choices are not as free as we think they are."*
>
> – TRISTAN HARRIS.

The Announcement

The first announcement doesn't sound like destiny. It sounds like housekeeping.

A hospital corridor at 2 a.m.—fluorescent lights buzzing, monitors sighing, a janitor pushing a bucket that smells faintly of bleach. My shoes squeak against the tile. I am thinking about discharge summaries, not danger, when the intercom snaps open and speaks my name.

"Doctor Rifai, you have a new order to enter."

The voice is flat, neutral, bureaucratic. The kind of voice that asks nothing of you—except everything.

I tell myself it's routine. Routine is the spine of medicine. Routine keeps people breathing. So I walk, half-awake, toward the workroom, white coat billowing like a flag of surrender, ID badge tapping my chest like a metronome. Pen already in hand. Reflex, not intention.

A new order. A minor adjustment. A click. A number. A dosage.

This is how many catastrophes begin—so small they look harmless.

The computer screen blinks to life, illuminating my face like an interrogation lamp. The cursor waits inside the little box that decides how much chemical enters a human bloodstream. Pain. Anxiety. Insomnia. Agitation. Trauma. The chart lists wounds the way war lists casualties—without emotion.

I know the right move. Years of training built the safe path. Dozens of teachers, hundreds of patients, endless nights inside textbooks and guidelines—all pointing to the same restrained decision.

But my fingers drift toward the other option. The stronger one. The faster one. The one that promises silence.

A voice rises—not loud, not commanding, but coaxing. My own voice, softened by nostalgia and sandstorms.

"Habibi... just this once. He's suffering. You're exhausted. A kinder dose. A quicker fix. No one will question compassion."

That voice knows me intimately—my childhood, my secrets, the places where my armor never fully hardened. It grew up with me in Aleppo, memorized the sound of mortars, learned my fear before I learned language. It sat beside me in exam rooms, courtrooms, prayer rooms. It knows exactly which guilt to press and when.

The order in front of me looks harmless: increase here, add there, change the timing. A prescription, not a prophecy. But the whisper sketches a road—one paved with good intentions and tiny compromises.

Addiction rarely kicks the door open. Addiction slips in wearing your coat.

It doesn't threaten. It reasons.

It flatters.

It empathizes.

You're a healer.

You hate watching people hurt.

You deserve relief too.

So the brain hands over the keyboard—not with a dramatic surrender, but with a weary shrug.

It never starts with a needle on a bathroom floor. It starts with a small permission. A drink to quiet the shift. A pill from a friend. An early refill. A late-night scroll. A secret. A tiny lie. A boundary moved half an inch.

Each step feels insignificant—until the map no longer resembles home.

Here lies the brutal genius of a hijacked mind: the intruder never introduces itself. The intruder already knows your passwords, your history, your weak joints. It speaks in your cadence. It calls you by your childhood nickname. It knows exactly when your willpower sleeps.

"Today doesn't count. You've earned this."

No weapon needed—only memory, shame, and exhaustion. The attacker is internal, a familiar ghost reaching for the controls.

I have seen this takeover thousands of times—in parents, surgeons, teenagers, CEOs, grandmothers, veterans, college students, refugees. People who survived unspeakable trauma, and people whose trauma was simply being alive in a body that never felt safe.

No alarms. No dramatic music. Just a series of reasonable decisions that slowly tilt a life off its axis.

This book begins in that dim control room—the cockpit of human behavior—where impulses argue with values, where biology negotiates with biography, where trauma bargains with reason.

We will stand together in the moment before the click—the moment where a life can still turn.

I write as a physician, yes—but also as a defendant, a witness, a son of war, a man whose nervous system learned to expect disaster and seek escape. I have felt the whisper in my own skull. I have watched my own hand hover over the wrong choice.

Recovery does not arrive like a parade. It arrives like a correction—small, stubborn, unglamorous. A redirected finger. A breath taken. A phone call made instead of a pill swallowed. A truth spoken instead of swallowed.

No heroism. Just course adjustment.

This book will not lecture you. It will not shame you. It will not pretend your cravings contradict logic. Craving is logic—logic written by experience, chemistry, fear, memory, and survival.

Instead, we will learn navigation—how dopamine pushes, how cortisol blinds, how trauma rewires safety, how culture and law and family shape temptation, how to rebuild a nervous system that has forgotten what calm feels like.

If you know the quiet terror of almost choosing the wrong thing, this book is yours.

If you love someone whose mind has shifted out of their own reach, this book is yours too.

We will chart a new flight path—not toward perfection, but toward agency. Toward a voice that sounds like yours again.

Place your hands on the controls.

The next decision approaches.

We take it together.

INTRODUCTION

> "*Genes Do Not Cause or Maintain Addiction.*"
>
> — GABOR MATÉ, MD

The Barrymore Family: Breaking a Cycle

John Barrymore woke before call time at Kelley's Rest Home, the personal care home MGM had chosen to keep him steady, and slipped a small bottle into his coat as if tucking away a secret. By the time he reached the Culver City lot, the world had the quick, brittle shine of a morning-after. In the wardrobe trailer he became Mercutio—doublet straightened, rapier tested—then drifted to the soundstage where Verona had been built out of timber and light. The scene was the Queen Mab speech, the one that used to unfurl from him like silk. Instead, he took a pull for courage. The words came in bright bursts and then fell away; cues blurred; the camera waited. A second take. A third. Heads turned, voices dropped. The crew learned how to work around his pauses, how to nudge him to the mark without breaking the illusion. He could still flash the old magic—an arched brow, a musical phrase, a laugh that warmed the room—and then the bottle, invisible to the frame, would take the reins back.

MGM had gambled on John Barrymore's Mercutio and tried to control the odds by housing him at Kelley's, but he continued to drink covertly and the shoot bent itself around that fact. Basil Rathbone, who fenced opposite him as Tybalt, would later put it plainly: Barrymore "was drinking and unreliable on the set... It was sad to see him in such a state." The sadness hung between takes like a scrim—everyone could see through it, but no one could tear it down. For a man who had once held Shakespeare like a birthright, the stage directions had become a kind of prayer: hit the mark, find the line, finish the day.

In Hollywood lore, the Barrymores are as renowned for their talent as for a turbulent relationship with alcohol and drugs. That history is not abstract. John Barrymore, the great matinee idol of the 1920s–30s, died in 1942 with cirrhosis and renal failure noted among the causes, a public life shadowed by heavy drinking (Encyclopaedia Britannica, n.d.). His son, John Drew Barrymore, battled alcohol and drugs for decades, a struggle widely reported in obituaries and retrospectives (ABC News, 2004). Into that inheritance was born Drew Barrymore, who reached global fame in childhood and, by her own account, encountered substances almost as early. In her first memoir she wrote that she "had [her] first drink at age nine, began smoking marijuana at ten, and at twelve took up cocaine," followed by treatment at 13 and emancipation as a young teen (Barrymore & Gold, 1990; Hattenstone, 2015; Los Angeles Times, 1990).

None of this happened in a vacuum. Family legacy can act like a script outline, but the performance depends on the stage and the choices. Genetics can raise vulnerability, family norms can normalise risk, availability can remove friction, and early reinforcement can lay down grooves in the brain's motivation circuits—like sled tracks in fresh snow that get deeper with each run. Those tracks are not permanent; with time, support, and sustained change, new routes can be carved.

Drew Barrymore has said that this cycle needed to end with her. Reflecting on her family's past and her own decision to quit alcohol, she put it plainly: "I'm going to be the one to break the link in that chain and maybe my kids and their kids will be better off for it," and "We have to fight genetic follies that our families bring to us" (Naugle, 2024). That language recognises both inheritance and agency. Think of "genetic follies" as a wiring diagram with a few vulnerable switches; environment and behaviour are the hands on those switches. Through therapy, sobriety, and building a different home culture for her children, she chose to flip those switches in the other direction—turning the dimmer down on risk and up on protection.

Her story also highlights a clinical truth: stigma and secrecy make change harder. When families replace shame with support, when clinics meet people with practical help rather than gatekeeping, outcomes improve. Recovery can become a point of pride greater than any marquee role precisely because it rewrites a family narrative. In that sense, Drew Barrymore reclaimed her surname not by repeating its most painful chapters but by editing them—honouring what was beautiful in the legacy and refusing what was harmful.

Coming to America

I arrived in Bethesda in 2003 with battered suitcases, a stack of articles on Hepatitis C and mood disorders, and the stubborn belief that medicine could be both science and sanctuary. The NIH campus felt like a contained city of inquiry—brick and glass, long corridors lined with posters, seminar rooms where acronyms did battle with doubt, and the Clinical Center's echo settling around you like a vow to try again tomorrow.

This was Washington's scientific doorstep, and the era had a particular temperature. Post-9/11 security shaped your day before science did: bollards at the gates, badges checked twice, metal detectors counting the seconds you didn't have. Anthrax had left a cultural residue; public health was now national security, and the word "biodefence" travelled easily through budget meetings. Television screens carried a war starting just down the Metro line; protests and motorcades belonged to the same weather system.

Policy and oversight pressed in close. Research money had swelled in the previous years and was beginning to flatten; every proposal felt a bit more interrogated than the last. Privacy rules had been sharpened, and consent became choreography—more pages, clearer clauses, a new grammar of what you could ask, keep, and share. Ethics committees moved from backdrop to foreground; you learned to design a study as much for its moral geometry as for its statistical power.

Inside psychiatry, the ground shifted under quieter feet. You traced how interferon, meant to fight Hepatitis C, could tilt mood and sleep; immunology and affect began to share a table rather than glare across one. Atypical antipsychotics were ascendant, debate thick in the air; the diagnostic manual felt authoritative and provisional at once. Industry hovered at the periphery with glossy certainties; you learned to separate signal from sponsorship. A presidential commission that year used the word "transformation" about mental health care, and you wondered what that would mean at the level of a single patient and a single morning.

I was a junior physician at the National Institute of Mental Health (NIMH)—part student, part apprentice, part clinician—trying to give the unquiet body a language the data would respect. You felt how a town, a campus, and a cautious decade could shape the questions you chose. I came to NIH to learn; the politics and the place taught me which answers would have to earn their keep.

Dr. Nora Volkow

I had come to the National Institutes of Health to learn, but I did not yet know which questions would claim the rest of my life. I didn't know that the most important lessons that year would arrive not as a graph or a p-value, but as a voice—calm, insistent, and field-tested. The voice belonged to Dr. Nora Volkow.

She had just taken the helm at the National Institute on Drug Abuse (NIDA) in 2003, and you could feel the lens rotate across campus. Leadership can be abstract until it reorients your questions; then it becomes weather. Volkow's presence did that. A physician-scientist trained in Mexico City, she built a pioneering career at Brookhaven National Laboratory, where she used PET imaging to watch the living brain argue with itself in real time. Her work pressed uncomfortable truths into view: chronic drug exposure down-shifts dopamine signalling, blunts motivation, and hijacks attention; the circuitry that helps you pursue meaning can be re-tasked to pursue relief. Those insights echoed outward—into the study of obesity, impulse control, and how environments load risk onto some lives more than others. Her personal history carried its own gravity: great-granddaughter of Leon Trotsky, raised near walls that still remembered violence. That legacy did not harden her; it refined her—toward precision, toward service, toward a stubborn refusal to confuse punishment with care. She built an engine out of questions and declined easy answers.

Hepatitis C patients were teaching me, every clinic day, that a body never suffers alone. A virus could carve pain into the liver while depression carved silence into the mind. Interferon promised viral control and delivered, too often, a winter of mood—sleep unravelled, appetite thin, pleasure out of reach. Substance use arrived in that landscape as both a flawed ally and a merciless thief. Many of my patients tried to self-treat insomnia, memories, loneliness with pills that did not keep their promises. They taught me that addiction lived not only in the brain but in the stories around it—in neighbourhoods where hope felt expensive and police were quicker than social workers; in clinics where labels stuck harder than help; in homes where shame did the talking and love arrived with conditions. You could track lab values all day and still miss the currents moving just under the surface of a life.

Volkow gave me language for what I had sensed but couldn't yet say. In a place where every corridor led to a laboratory, she refused the old indictments. Addiction, she argued, was not a character flaw, not a verdict, not a curse. It was an illness that rewrote circuits of reward, pain, salience, and control—speaking the brain's native syntax to narrow a life to a single loop. She didn't romanticise the problem or scold it. She showed—literally, in images—that substances do not sit on the surface like spilt ink; they infiltrate, bargain with dopamine and memory, redraw the map, and train the brain to walk the same path even when it ends at the same cliff. You could see, slice by colour-coded slice, how desire was being budgeted in the wrong currency.

Under her gaze at NIDA, imaging became evidence and mercy at once. We could see the shadows substances cast on blood flow and receptors. We could see craving as a pattern rather than a mystery. We could see that withdrawal lived not only in shakes and sweats but in the brain's ache for relief. The first time I saw one of her images of a human brain under the influence, it felt like a confession without words. Here was the biology that makes relapse common and willpower fragile. Here was the physiology that can turn a Friday-night experiment into a Tuesday-morning sentence. Here was the reason a mother can love her child and still be unable to stop using; the reason a father can weep in clinic and still meet his dealer a week later. The images did not excuse harm; they explained vulnerability. For a clinician, explanation is a form of compassion because it points toward action. For a system, explanation is a mandate because it clarifies where resources ought to go.

Stigma shrinks under light, and data is one of the brightest lights we have. That is why I began to write and speak more publicly about the people behind the numbers. I wanted to bring the invisible into the room. I wanted to say their names in ways that protected dignity and sharpened resolve. I wanted to turn the phrase brain disease into more than a slogan. I wanted it to become a promise—that we would build clinics, laws, and clinical cultures that treated addiction as a treatable illness rather than a moral indictment. You know how slogans can turn to fog if they are not anchored to practice; I wanted practice.

Those convictions did not arrive fully formed. They were forged in the exchange between my patients' truths and Volkow's clarity. When she wrote about how the words we use can keep people from care, I saw my own language in her mirror and recognised where I needed to do better. When she described how childhood adversity, environment, and genetics braid risk, I saw the faces of my patients who had been children in war zones or in households where love was contingent and safety unreliable. A teenager with a history of neglect does not come to a pill as a toy; he comes to it as a key, because it fits a lock the rest of us cannot see. A woman who has learned to anaesthetise fear does not meet a syringe as a dare; she meets it as an argument she already knows how to win.

Policy, in Volkow's telling, is science brave enough to walk outside. Medication-assisted treatment, harm-reduction strategies, stigma reduction, outcomes over ideology—these were not positions but obligations once you accepted the brain data on its own terms. If imaging shows that craving is a measurable state with predictable triggers, then aftercare is not an optional courtesy; it's part of the treatment. If data show that social stressors amplify risk and fracture recovery, then housing, legal aid, and employment programmes belong in the same breath as buprenorphine or methadone. If the maps show prefrontal control networks going dark under the weight of cue-induced desire, then our clinical algorithms must include more than exhortations to "try harder". The brain was telling us where the doors were. Our job, as she framed it, was to unlock them and keep them unlocked long enough for people to pass through.

Meanwhile, the hepatitis clinics kept teaching me how shame rewires behavior. I watched people skip appointments because they didn't want to be seen; under-dose medications because they didn't want to admit side effects; hide relapses like contraband because they had learned that disclosure triggered exile. In psychiatric wards, I saw labels turn into sentences; "non-compliant" written in notes like a curse that travelled with a person from desk to desk. You can measure viral loads and GAF scores until the forms run out, but if contempt is the first clinician in the room, care begins already injured.

So I started to change the way I spoke and wrote. Case presentations grew a second column, where the social physics of a life were laid next to the neurobiology. Ward rounds included the discipline of asking, "What story does this person have to tell that the chart does not?" Conferences were punctuated by images and names—de-identified but human—because data are more honest when accompanied by a life. I learned to say "people who use drugs" instead of "addicts" and to mean it. I learned to apologise out loud when I failed to do better, because language is a clinical tool and a public signal at once.

The more I understood, the more obvious it became that addiction medicine was where my training and my biography could meet without apology. My own story of displacement and persistence had taught me that the soul can fracture along fault lines no stethoscope can hear. Addiction often begins in those fractures. It promises an end to discomfort and an end to shame, then steals the voice that could have asked for real help. You can call that weakness if you like, but weakness is a poor map; it shows you cliffs and not the stairs carved into them.

In Bethesda, in the shadow of buildings built for discovery, I found the courage to declare that my life's work would be helping people repair those fractures. I would use every tool I had—from neurotransmitter maps to bedside questions to the quiet art of listening. I would practise a medicine that refuses to separate the brain from the person who lives inside it. I would argue, in clinics and committees, for a future where the first response to struggling people is not suspicion but welcome, not punishment but care; where discharge summaries include housing contacts; where research budgets acknowledge that dignity is an outcome; where "follow-up" means we follow, not just that we invite.

Volkow's example kept sharpening the path. She showed how to keep curiosity ethical and compassion organised. She taught, by practice, that the lab and the street are not separate provinces but adjacent rooms in the same house—that a graph that cannot survive a waiting room is unfinished work. When she spoke about how stigma hides in our policies as often as in our attitudes, you could feel the room adjust—because policies are just choices written neatly, and choices can be rewritten.

The first time I presented my work on the intersection of Hepatitis C, mood disorder, and substance use with her sitting in the back row, I felt the moral pressure of being precise. Not precise in a pedant's way, but in a way that honours the stakes. You know that feeling: when accuracy is a form of respect. Afterward, she asked the kind of questions that rearrange your next six months. What happens to adherence when you intervene on sleep first? What if the clinic schedule bent around the hours when craving statistically spikes? Where does trauma education live in your protocol—at consent, at discharge, or in every visit? Simple sentences that made a map.

I started to see the system as a patient with its own diagnosis: a chronic tendency to turn fear into policy and scarcity into rationing. The treatment, I realised, looked like teams and thresholds—teams where infectious disease, psychiatry, and social care planned together; thresholds lowered until entry to care was not a test but an invitation. Imaging helped me argue for that. Pictures have a way of getting past defended minds. A colourful slice of cortex can speak to a legislator in a way a paragraph rarely does.

This is how my field chose me. A campus. A year. A director whose work turned imaging into invitation. A set of patients whose courage taught me that recovery is not the absence of need but the steady practice of asking for help. And a quiet recognition that my purpose was hiding in plain sight, written into those early mornings when you walk past the labs and feel the gravity of a calling you haven't yet named. I walked in a young physician studying Hepatitis C and psychiatric illness. I walked out carrying a vow to spend my life in the country of addiction medicine, where science and mercy share a border and the soul remembers how to come home.

Stigma shrinks under light. Data is a bright light. But data is brightest, I learned from Volkow, when it is angled through a human being and projected onto the wall of the world as policy, clinic hours, medication access, respectful rooms, and staff trained to greet pain without flinching. So I kept writing, kept speaking, kept bringing the invisible into the room, kept turning "brain disease" from a phrase into a promise. Each image I showed, each story I told, was an argument for a particular kind of future—the kind where a teenager with a lock the rest of us cannot see is offered a key that does not poison him; where a mother is not asked to prove she deserves relief before she is allowed to receive it; where a father can come back twice, three times, ten times, and we will still open the door.

In that vow, Nora Volkow's voice still sounds like a compass—not because she told me where to go, but because she showed me how to see. And once you have seen—once you have watched neurons bargain with hunger and hope, once you have watched a brain relearn how to want—you cannot go back to slogans. You build. You measure. You welcome. You keep the light on.

CHAPTER 1

The Silent Intruder

(Genetics - GENES)

> "*Genes are not about inevitabilities; they're about potentials and vulnerabilities.*"
>
> — ROBERT SAPOLSKY, PHD

Understanding Addiction: The Role of Genes and Environment

When people ask, "Is addiction a choice, or are you born with it?", the honest answer is that both forces matter—and they talk to each other constantly. Genes set possibilities; environments decide how loudly those possibilities speak (Volkow, Koob, & McLellan, 2016).

Genes: the blueprint—and what that really means

Think of your genes as a building's blueprint. The blueprint (your DNA) lays out where rooms and wiring *could* go; it doesn't decide the furniture or how the space will be used. Inside that DNA are thousands of genes—small instruction sets—that shape everything from eye colour to how your brain's "reward" system responds to alcohol, nicotine, or opioids (Volkow et al., 2016).

How much risk comes from genes? Twin research gives us a good read. Identical twins share essentially 100% of their DNA; fraternal twins share about 50%. If genes matter, identical twins should "match" for a disorder more often than fraternal twins—and that is exactly what we see. A meta-analysis of twin and adoption studies found substantial heritability for alcohol use disorders (around the 50% range across methods), confirming a strong genetic contribution (Verhulst, Neale, & Kendler, 2015). In the broader addiction literature, authoritative summaries estimate that genes—including environmentally shaped gene expression, or epigenetics—account for roughly 40–60% of a person's overall risk (National Institute on Drug Abuse [NIDA], 2020). Importantly, this kind of estimate describes differences across a population; it never means an individual is "half determined." It means that in a given population, genetic variation explains a sizeable slice of why people differ in risk.

Polymorphisms: tiny spelling changes with real effects

A polymorphism is a small difference in the DNA "text"—like swapping a single letter in a very long book. Most swaps change nothing; some alter how a page is *read*. In biology, certain polymorphisms can make the brain's reward circuit more sensitive to a drug's "sparkle," nudging stronger reinforcement, or change how fast the body metabolises a substance—altering both pleasure and side-effects (Volkow et al., 2016). Picture a car with a slightly different accelerator or brake: small design tweaks that change how the vehicle responds on the same road.

Environment: the performance, not just the sheet music

If genes are the sheet music, your environment is the performance—musicians, acoustics, audience, even the weather outside the hall. Stress, trauma, peer networks, drug availability, family modelling, and community support can amplify or dampen genetic tendencies. Two people can carry similar genetic risks, but very different life experiences will "play" those risks into very different outcomes (NIDA, 2020; Volkow et al., 2016).

As Dr. Gabor Maté puts it, *"Genes do not cause addiction on their own. They can make you vulnerable, but it's your environment—what you experience, feel, and face—that activates those genes."* That perspective reflects his long-standing argument that genes create vulnerability while lived experience decides whether that vulnerability is expressed (Maté, 2014; Maté, n.d.).

Epigenetics: sticky notes and dimmer switches on your DNA

Epigenetics explains how experience can change *which* parts of your genetic blueprint are read—without changing the letters themselves. Think of epigenetics as sticky notes and dimmer switches:

- **DNA methylation** places tiny chemical tags (methyl groups) on DNA like "Do Not Disturb" notes. Heavier tagging on a gene often makes it harder to read—like taping a page partially shut.
- **Histone modification** loosens or tightens how DNA is wrapped around spool-like proteins. Looser wrapping opens the blinds so the page can be read; tighter wrapping pulls the blinds down and the page goes dim.

Stress, trauma, and drug exposure can write and rewrite these sticky notes and dimmer settings in brain regions that govern reward, self-control, mood, and memory—changing craving, tolerance, and relapse risk. Critically, many of these epigenetic marks are reversible—more pencil than tattoo. Safety, therapy, social connection, sleep, exercise, medication-assisted treatment, and time in recovery can help peel off the "Do Not Disturb" notes and reset dimmers toward healthier patterns (Nestler, 2014).

Repeated use: why stopping is so hard

Addictive substances remodel brain circuits that handle motivation, decision-making, and habit. Think of fresh snow on a hill: the first sled run is wobbly; after many runs, deep grooves form and the sled almost *falls* into the same tracks. Brains lay down those grooves too—through learning, dopamine signalling, and habit loops—so "just stop" asks the sled to leap out of a rut while the hill is still icy and steep (Volkow et al., 2016).

Pulling it together—without stigma

Understanding genes, polymorphisms, epigenetics, and environment collapses the false choice between "willpower" and "biology." Addiction is not a moral failing; it is a bio-psycho-social condition. With that lens, calling addiction a "brain disease" becomes more than a slogan—it becomes a promise to build clinics, policies, and everyday practices that treat addiction as a *treatable* illness (Volkow et al., 2016; NIDA, 2020). Most importantly, none of this fixes a single destiny. Genes set a stage; environments and choices (your own and those made by systems around you) determine the script. With the right supports—evidence-based treatment, safe housing, purpose, and people who believe in you—recovery is not only possible; it's expected.

Inherited Risk: Stories of Addiction and Genetics

Addiction can feel like a family story passed down through generations, as if the struggles of parents and grandparents leave echoes in the lives of their children. Inherited risk means that genetics and family history can raise a person's vulnerability, and family environments can either cushion or amplify that risk (National Institute on Drug Abuse [NIDA], 2020). Genes load the possibilities; experience turns the volume up or down.

A family story: two brothers, two paths

Consider one well-known example. Donald Trump has often described his older brother, Fred Trump Jr., who struggled with alcoholism and died at 42 of a heart attack that the family linked to years of alcohol use (Kranish, 2019). He recalls, "I had a brother, Fred... great guy, best personality – much better than mine, but he had a problem. He had a problem with alcohol. And he would tell me: 'Don't drink. Don't drink'." He also says, "I never had a glass of alcohol. Can you imagine if I had, what a mess I'd be?" (DeSantis, 2019; Abramson, 2017). In later reflections he added, "Our family environment, the competitiveness, was a negative for Fred... It wasn't easy for him being cast in a very tough environment, and I think it played havoc on him," and "Perhaps it was my fault and perhaps my father's fault for egging him on... because he didn't like the business" (DeSantis, 2019).

Psychologist Mary L. Trump describes a harsh, status-driven household and characterises the patriarch as a "high-functioning sociopath," arguing that contempt and conditional love damaged multiple siblings, including Fred Jr. (Trump, 2020).

Stories like this do not prove genes at work by themselves; they illustrate how family climate can interact with genetic vulnerability—sometimes pushing one child toward alcohol while another swears it off for life.

Why one brother developed AUD and the other did not

Two brothers may start with similar genetic decks. Exposure is the hinge: AUD cannot develop without alcohol, so lifelong abstinence removes the necessary fuel. Donald Trump's decision not to drink likely closed a door that genetics might otherwise have nudged open (National Institute on Alcohol Abuse and Alcoholism [NIAAA], 2025). For Fred Jr., a mix of genetic vulnerability, high stress, and ready access to alcohol set deep grooves in motivation and habit circuits; once those grooves formed, "just stop" became like asking a sled to jump out of an icy rut. Twin and adoption data support this pattern: inherited risk is real, but environment and behaviour—especially choices about use—determine whether that risk is expressed (Verhulst et al., 2015; Goodwin et al., 1975; Heath et al., 1995; NIDA, 2020).

What this means for families

Knowing your family history is not fatalism; it is planning. If AUD runs in your family, treat alcohol like a high-risk medication: minimise exposure, delay first use, avoid binges, and seek help early if drinking starts to do the job of solving problems (NIAAA, 2025). Genes shape probability, not destiny, and families can write a different next chapter.

What This Means for You

The story of Freddy and Donald Trump is ultimately a story of caution and hope. It shows that even when alcoholism runs in a family, people can make choices that meaningfully alter their outcomes. If you know alcohol use disorder (AUD) appears in your family, it is sensible to approach alcohol with caution. Some choose complete abstinence—AUD cannot develop without alcohol exposure. Others decide to drink moderately but keep a close, honest eye on patterns and set a low threshold for getting help early. A genetic predisposition is like a loaded dice: it nudges probabilities; it does not dictate the throw (NIDA, 2020; NIAAA, 2025; Volkow, Koob, & McLellan, 2016).

If someone in your family is struggling, remember the hard lesson many families learn about shame. Blame and secrecy tend to worsen outcomes; understanding, timely treatment, and practical support help people recover. Stigma is not just an attitude—it is a barrier to care that reduces help-seeking and adherence; changing language, expectations, and clinic routines to be welcoming is part of evidence-based care (National Academies of Sciences, Engineering, and Medicine, 2016; NIAAA, 2025).

Genes matter, but they are not a script carved in stone. Heritability estimates for AUD hover around the halfway mark for population differences, yet outcomes still depend on exposure, stress, co-occurring mental health conditions, and social context. In practical terms, knowledge of family risk is a planning tool: delay first use, avoid heavy drinking, build protective routines (sleep, exercise, purpose), and seek help early if alcohol starts doing the job of coping (Verhulst, Neale, & Kendler, 2015; NIDA, 2020; NIAAA, 2025). The neuroscience is clarifying, not fatalistic: repeated heavy use can etch habits into motivation circuits, but those changes can improve with sustained abstinence and treatment (Volkow et al., 2016; NIAAA, 2025).

Epigenetics adds a hopeful layer. Experiences can act like dimmer switches on gene activity, turning some signals up and others down without changing the DNA letters themselves. Stress and heavy drinking can push dimmers in the wrong direction; safety, treatment, connection, and time in recovery can turn them back. Think of it as removing "do not disturb" sticky notes from pages your brain needs to read again. That plasticity is one reason recovery is possible and why day-to-day lifestyle choices matter (Nestler, 2014; NIDA, 2020; NIAAA, 2025).

You have agency. Donald Trump's lifelong abstinence is one illustration of choosing a high-protection path in the presence of family risk. Not everyone chooses strict abstinence, and many with a family history drink without developing AUD, but everyone can stack the odds in favor of health: set clear limits, avoid binges, keep alcohol out of coping roles, and talk to a clinician early if concerns arise. Families can help by replacing secrecy with support, using person-first language, and making treatment a normal next step rather than a last resort (NIAAA, 2025; National Academies of Sciences, Engineering, and Medicine, 2016; NIDA, 2020).

If you do find yourself struggling with alcohol, reach out. Effective treatments exist, including medication and psychological therapies, and they work best when started sooner rather than later. Recovery is common, especially when shame is reduced and care is continuous. Genetics influences vulnerability; how you live—and the support around you—shapes the destination (NIAAA, 2025; NIDA, 2020; Volkow et al., 2016).

How Addiction Wounds the Soul

Addiction is often introduced to the public through brain scans, lab results, and diagnostic checklists. These are real and they matter. Yet anyone who has lived inside addiction, or loved someone who has, knows there is a deeper injury the scan cannot capture. Something sacred gets dimmed. Something once whole begins to fracture. When addiction takes hold, it disrupts not only the body and the mind; it disturbs the soul. It steals a person's sense of meaning, loosens the ties that make life feel worth living, and replaces wonder with want. This spiritual wounding does not contradict the science; it complements it, because human beings are more than neural tissue alone (Volkow, Koob, & McLellan, 2016; National Institute on Drug Abuse [NIDA], 2020).

At the beginning, the substance or behavior can feel like mercy. It is a warm blanket over a raw nerve; stillness when anxiety rattles the chest; color returning to a gray morning. Over time, the blanket tightens. It becomes a binding. Relief grows shorter while the reach grows longer. The body adapts; tolerance builds; learning pathways deepen. The mind reorganizes to protect the habit. The person who once chose begins to feel chosen by the habit itself. Languages old and new have described addiction with words meaning enslaved or bound—a reminder that the struggle is not only chemical but experiential and existential. It is about what holds you, and what you can no longer hold. In the lab, we see why this happens: repeated exposure reshapes reward, salience, memory, and control networks in the brain, making cue-driven craving more likely and restraint more effortful (NIDA, 2020; Volkow et al., 2016).

When people describe the moral damage of addiction, they rarely mean the person is immoral. They mean the person cannot live in alignment with their own values anymore. A parent who swore never to use again misses a school play. A nurse who loves patients arrives late. A student full of promise avoids friends who still dream. Shame arrives and persuades the person that confession would only make things worse. Secrecy replaces community. Small lies become the ordinary air of the day. The soul is allergic to lying, especially the lies we tell ourselves. Over months and years, the person feels cut off from what once felt pure and true. The soul keeps a quiet ledger. It knows the cost. Clinically, this misalignment maps to neurocognitive changes in prefrontal systems that govern planning, inhibition, and self-monitoring, which helps explain why stopping is not the same as deciding to stop (Volkow et al., 2016; National Institute on Alcohol Abuse and Alcoholism [NIAAA], 2025).

There is a reason many recovery traditions speak in spiritual language. Addiction often functions like misplaced worship. Energy and loyalty move toward the very thing draining life away. Mary Shelley's monster summed this up in the phrase, "Henceforth, evil became my good." This is not choosing a chemical over goodness; it is that the chemical has quietly taken the seat where comfort and meaning are supposed to rest. Some call this a modern form of idolatry, not as condemnation but as description: the drink, the pill, the needle, the online spiral becomes the center of gravity and everything else must orbit around it. Framing the question—brain disorder or spiritual disorder—can be helpful not to pick a winner, but to insist that both dimensions are real and interactive (Holtzhausen, n.d.; Koenig, 2012).

I have treated people who do not use the word soul. They talk about purpose, love, conscience, or the best part of themselves. They say, I cannot find myself anymore. They say, I do not recognize the person in the mirror. They say, I am tired of hiding. The language changes; the feeling is the same. The inner compass is spinning. Night lasts longer than it should. They want to come home to their own life. This language is not naïve. It mirrors what we know about how chronic stress and repeated substance use can narrow attention to relief and erode access to longer-horizon goals and values (NIAAA, 2025).

When a person lives in addiction long enough, night can become a season. Scholars of spirituality have called this the dark night of the soul—not to romanticize suffering but to name the eerie mixture of fear, loneliness, and the sense one is losing their mind. In addiction this dark night is common. People describe bankruptcy inside, a hollowing of the self, a hunger no meal can satisfy, a thirst ordinary water cannot touch. They are not crazy. They are naming a spiritual crisis, and their words tell the truth. Neurobiologically, withdrawal and cue-induced craving engage stress and habit systems while dampening control circuitry, making that "long night" feel inevitable until the cycle is broken (NIDA, 2020; Volkow et al., 2016).

We should say, clearly and without apology, that addiction is also a brain disease. Reward pathways rewire; dopamine signaling tags cues with outsized importance; regions that plan, inhibit, and remember are pulled into the storm. These are not metaphors; this is neuroscience, and it helps explain why good people do things that wound them, why relapse can arrive like weather, and why "white-knuckling" alone rarely suffices (Volkow et al., 2016; NIAAA, 2025). Yet even when the brain is at the center of the map, the map is not the territory. A human is never a brain alone. The full story includes spirit, meaning, and love.

If the injury is both neural and spiritual, the healing must be both. Medical care can steady the body. Therapy can untangle the mind. Community can hold the person in their weakest hours. And there is another layer many overlook: the soul needs restoration too. It needs honesty that cleans the air between people. It needs a return to practices that nourish reverence and hope. It needs a safe place to tell the whole story without being punished for surviving. Treatments that integrate social connection, values clarification, and meaning-making improve engagement and long-term outcomes, in part by reshaping social networks and self-efficacy (Kelly, Hoeppner, Stout, & Pagano, 2012; Kelly, Humphreys, & Ferri, 2020).

This is why connection is not optional. Isolation is oxygen for addiction; connection suffocates it. Recovery communities and twelve-step rooms learned long ago that humility is medicine, surrender is not defeat, and asking for help is wisdom. Social ties are not only comforting; they predict health and survival across conditions, and mechanisms like network change are among the most powerful mediators of sustained abstinence (Holt-Lunstad, Smith, & Layton, 2010; Kelly et al., 2012; Kelly et al., 2020). Spirituality and religious practice are not magic, but for many they are associated with better coping, fewer depressive symptoms, and healthier decisions—especially when coupled with practical supports (Koenig, 2012; Kelly et al., 2012).

To care for the soul in recovery is to reintroduce what addiction edited out of the story. We reintroduce honesty. We reintroduce beauty. We reintroduce service, which turns attention outward and interrupts the spiral of self. We reintroduce compassion for the child inside who learned to hide pain behind a smile. We reintroduce the courage to feel ordinary joy. As people practice these, the body learns to sleep again; the mind learns to focus again; the soul learns to trust again. Helping others, in particular, appears to be more than sentiment—it predicts lower relapse rates and better mood, likely by widening purpose and strengthening recovery identity (Pagano, Friend, Tonigan, & Stout, 2004; Pagano, Zemore, Onder, & Stout, 2011).

Part of soul work is meaning-making. People do not grow by removing symptoms alone; they grow by understanding what those symptoms were trying to say. This is not an excuse for harm; it is a commitment to curiosity. If the bottle was a shield, what was it protecting? If the pills were a bridge, what river were they trying to cross? If the behavior was an escape, what prison did it reveal? When treatment only scrapes away the visible symptom, a new symptom often appears in its place. When treatment asks why the symptom showed up, the person can begin to build a life that does not require it. Practices that cultivate awareness—such as mindfulness and paced breathing—can dampen cue reactivity and support new habits, offering concrete tools for this meaning-making work (Brewer et al., 2011; Brewer, 2012).

For clinicians, a spiritual lens enlarges the questions we ask. We ask about family, trauma, and stress. We ask about biology and coexisting illnesses. We also ask about grief, beauty, conscience, purpose, and belonging. We ask what the person still reveres. We ask what they miss most about who they were before the spiral. We ask where they still feel touches of awe—prayer, mosque, church, mountain, ocean, or the first laugh of a child who does not know their shame. These questions do not replace medical care; they widen it. They invite the person to see themselves as more than a diagnosis and to build a life that is resilient rather than fragile. Guidance from evidence-based resources now emphasizes integrating medical, psychological, social, and spiritual supports in routine care (NIAAA, 2025; Kelly et al., 2020).

There is a common moment in recovery when a person looks back and realizes they have not felt a craving in several days, then several weeks. They begin to trust their own mornings. They tell the truth faster. Their apologies become smaller because their harms become smaller. They stop measuring their worth by the worst thing they have done. They enjoy simple things without needing to be altered to feel them. Humor returns, not as sarcasm but as kindness. Relationships become less about performance and more about presence. These are signs the soul is waking up. Such change is consistent with neural plasticity in recovery—the brain's capacity to rebalance function when exposure stops and supportive routines take hold (NIAAA, 2025; Volkow et al., 2016).

I have watched people make amends no one believed possible. Parents regain the respect of their children. Partners learn to love without rescuing and forgive without pretending. People bring their gifts back to the communities they once harmed. I have also watched relapses that felt like funerals. Recovery does not erase grief; it teaches people to walk with it. It teaches communities to love without enabling. It teaches families to set boundaries that protect dignity on both sides of the door. Longitudinal studies underscore that ongoing help—treatment, mutual-help involvement, pro-recovery networks—reduces relapse risk over years (Moos & Moos, 2006; Kelly et al., 2020).

There are practices that help. Quiet helps. Prayer helps, even when the person does not know who they are speaking to. Mindful breathing helps. Reading that lifts the mind helps. Music helps. Nature helps. Service helps in ways that are hard to measure because it calls us out of ourselves in the most healing way; the soul remembers itself in service (Pagano et al., 2004; Koenig, 2012). Gratitude helps too, not as performance but as a way of claiming the pieces of life that still shine.

Some will fear spiritual language because it has been used to shame people who struggle. That fear is valid. Spiritual care should never be a tool of control or stigma. The point is not to label addiction as sin; the point is to recognize that the hunger that drove the person toward the substance was human hunger for comfort and transcendence. Our task is to offer healthier ways to meet that hunger—and to remove barriers in healthcare and society that keep people from help. Addiction blooms where despair and neglect are allowed to grow. Recovery blooms where compassion and structure share the same room (National Academies of Sciences, Engineering, & Medicine, 2016; NIAAA, 2025).

If addiction can feel like being bound, recovery is learning to loosen the knot. If addiction can feel like misplaced worship, recovery is learning to direct devotion toward what brings life. If addiction can feel like a long night, recovery is learning that morning does arrive. With treatment that respects the body, mind, and soul, people do more than stop using: they learn to hope again, to be trustworthy again, to love without needing anesthesia. The science will continue to advance—we will refine our understanding of circuits and receptors, build better medications, and design safer detox protocols—and we need all of it. At the same time, we cannot neglect the part of healing that has always required presence more than technology. People heal in relationships. They heal where they are seen. They heal where truth is welcomed and shame is refused. They heal where their story can be told without interruption. For a thoughtful perspective on the complementarity of these frames, see "Addiction – a brain disorder or a spiritual disorder" (Holtzhausen, n.d.).

Addiction wounds the soul. Recovery helps the soul remember its strength. The path is not easy and not quick, but it is real. It is open to anyone willing to take the next honest step. It is sustained by practices that keep the heart soft and the mind clear. It is guided by communities that understand accountability and love are not enemies. In this work, we are not only treating a disease; we are honoring a human life.

CHAPTER 2

Under the Influence

(Environment - GENES)

> *"Believe you can, and you're halfway there."*
>
> — THEODORE ROOSEVELT

The Aleppo Appetite

The first lesson arrived from far away. Not a fireball at the door, but a low concussion rolling over rooftops until it reached our street and set the windows trembling in their frames. Spoons rattled against the lips of cups. Somewhere, a siren stitched a thin line through the afternoon. In that small, shaking pause—when the room was the same and not the same—I reached for the only thing that answered back gently: food. Bread if we had it; if not, a chipped glass of sugary tea that steadied my hands by giving them something to hold. I grew up in Aleppo where explosions were not special effects; they were weather. My body learned to translate that distant thunder into a precise instruction: fill the emptiness now, soften the fear for a minute, wait for the window to quiet, then carry on.

I did not have a word for trauma. I had a drill: reach, chew, breathe, watch the glass settle. Repeat when the air wavered again. The ground under our building never tore, but the sound did—threading through my chest, loosening a knot of hunger that was not about food at all.

Years later I crossed oceans and put on a white coat. The blasts followed, changed into hospital noises. The pager's shriek was a siren with good manners. Fluorescent lights buzzed like a far-off engine. I slept in call rooms that felt borrowed and made a pantry out of vending machines. I told patients to breathe, to sleep, to nourish themselves with intention, while I ate like someone on alert: quick, quiet, sugar as triage. When the unit exhaled at sunrise, I rewarded survival with more food. My body learned a second lesson: food is fuel to keep moving—and a friend that never argues.

Bombs stop. Shockwaves linger. They change costumes and enter by other doors. They become deadlines that tick, courtrooms that echo, night shifts that don't end on time. They become the habit of scanning every room for exits—and for something to eat. They become a nervous system that doubts there will be enough: enough time, enough safety, enough belonging. I carried that doubt through every season. Food became my small promise to the body I pushed past its limits: I won't abandon you. Even when I was abandoning myself in every other way, I kept that promise—the window rattling softly somewhere inside me, and my hand, almost without thinking, reaching for something to quiet it.

Trauma Trains Brains

Trauma doesn't retire when the shelling stops. It migrates. It changes costumes. It learns your calendar and hides inside deadlines, courtrooms, and night shifts. It teaches your eyes to sweep every room for exits—and for snacks. It trains a nervous system to live on rations of certainty, to question whether there will be enough. Enough time. Enough safety. Enough belonging. I carried that famine-mind through every season of my life. Food became my small pledge of loyalty to the body I kept drafting into hard duty: I won't abandon you—even as I abandoned it in every other way.

I became a psychiatrist and learned the grammar of the brain. I learned how cortisol primes the body for threat, how dopamine threads a bright wire through reward, how ghrelin and leptin whisper hunger and fullness like out-of-sync air-traffic controllers. I learned how "hyperpalatable" foods—salt, sugar, fat in concert—are engineered to strike the reward circuits like a perfect chord. I learned how stress chemistry widens appetite and how sleep loss saws through restraint. The science didn't absolve me; it annotated me. It explained why my internal brakes failed precisely when I needed them most, why a 2 a.m. craving could outvote a 2 p.m. conviction. Knowledge gave me language and compassion. It didn't give me immunity.

My weight turned into a biography you could read without opening a book. At first, a little above average. Then a lot. I climbed to a number on the chart that scared my physicians and my family. I descended. I rose again. I rode the cruel elevator of loss and regain, each floor labeled with a year and a reason: grief, depositions, twelve-hour clinics, public attacks, private ache. Every story ended at the same pantry door, late, when the house was quiet and willpower was out on the tarmac asking for clearance. I ate to muffle the noise. I ate to reward endurance. I ate to feel human when life tried to turn me into a headline instead of a person.

Some hear "addiction" and picture needles or bottles. I hear "addiction" and see a kitchen light at midnight and a refrigerator humming like a promise. I see my own hands fixing a plate while my heart won't slow down. I hear myself say this is the last time, and I know it isn't. Food addiction doesn't flatten lives with the spectacle of heroin or whiskey. It erodes them—tablespoon by tablespoon, year by year—with the patience of water and the memory of a fault line. It steals confidence. It steals sleep. It steals the simple freedom to live in your own skin without armor. And it does it quietly, so the world can applaud your discipline at noon and never hear the cupboard open at night.

Neglecting Ourselves

Neglect feeds addiction. Not only the kind stamped into childhood—though that scar never entirely fades—but the quieter neglect that blooms when you succeed on the outside and forget yourself on the inside. The neglect of putting everyone else first until your own name falls off the list. The neglect of movement, of sleep, of water and simple meals. I did that to myself during the most productive and most punishing years of my life. I poured attention into patients, projects, and long fights with institutions. I tried to wrestle justice out of a world that didn't always care. I left my body to fend for itself, then scolded it for scavenging comfort wherever it could find it. That is how neglect works: you starve the parts that keep you human and then blame them when they beg.

There is an environmental truth we have to say out loud. Many communities are food deserts bordered by stress swamps. The cheapest calories are engineered to hit the brain like fireworks. Our streets and schedules make movement inconvenient and isolation effortless. Screens keep us sitting and keep our minds humming long past midnight. Urgency gets rewarded; patience gets punished. In that landscape, a gallon of ice cream is not just dessert—it's anesthesia with no paperwork, a dimmer switch for a nervous system that was never given permission to rest. And when the world is built to keep you buzzing, silence feels like withdrawal. So you dose the noise, and the noise learns your name.

SHAME!

Shame loves addiction. It shows up before the craving and after the slip, polishing the mirror and asking if I care enough to be better by morning. It tells me discipline would fix this if I had any. It tells me to keep this private because no one wants to hear about my weakness. It keeps a finger to its lips and turns the lock from the inside. Shame convinced me for years that I had to master this alone. I was a physician. I knew the guidelines. I wrote them on discharge summaries and whispered them to patients at 3 a.m. I should be able to follow them.

What shame ignored was the other truth: I am also a human being whose early life taught survival through immediate relief. That wiring doesn't vanish because you memorize a protocol. Willpower can steer a straight line at noon and skid on black ice at midnight. Shame pretends not to notice the weather. It runs a private courtroom in my head where I am always both defendant and prosecutor. It calls secrecy a virtue and hides the evidence—the wrappers, the late-night orders, the hollow vows that start with "never again."

You do not unlearn that by force. Muscle only makes the mask tighter. You unlearn it by gentleness, by interrupting the trial, by telling the truth to someone who knows how to hold it. You unlearn it by practicing the kind of courage that doesn't look brave on camera: texting a friend before the urge crests, eating a real meal before the hunger turns feral, saying "I need help" while your pride hisses "don't." Shame starves in daylight. Recovery begins the moment you open the blinds.

Progress, Not Perfection

My turning points were never grand. They did not come with headlines or speeches. They came on quiet mornings when the air was cool enough to make my breath visible and the city hadn't decided what kind of day it would be. I would walk before the noise started, shoes whispering on pavement, and notice the simple fact that I was still here. One lap around the block became two. Two became a route I could trace with my eyes closed. On those dawns I didn't try to conquer anything; I tried to keep company with myself.

Other turning points were domestic and almost ceremonial. I chose to cook a simple meal and eat it at an actual table. No phone near me. No screen offering distraction disguised as rest. Knife, board, pan. Heat, salt, and patience. I would plate the food as if someone I loved was coming over, and then remember: someone was. I drank water before coffee and noticed the way that one small kindness softened the speed of the day. I paused before seconds long enough to ask whether I was still hungry for food or hungry for comfort. Sometimes I ate more. Sometimes I didn't. The ritual mattered more than the result. It was a way of saying to my nervous system: you are safe enough to choose.

Therapy was another pivot, and not the kind where I sit in the expert chair offering language for other people's storms. I went as a man who carries his own weather. I learned to answer questions with fewer footnotes and more truth. I said out loud what the body keeps trying to say through habits: I am tired; I am scared; I am trying. I practiced not performing competence. There is a unique kind of relief that comes when you stop auditioning for your own life.

I built rituals that didn't glorify willpower because I had worshiped willpower long enough to know it wouldn't save me. I made a short checklist taped inside a cupboard: water before coffee; plan the first meal; step outside once before noon; a five-minute pause when urges spike; text someone if it doesn't pass. I kept a grocery list that looked like respect: protein I would actually cook, fruit I actually like, vegetables that don't turn into compost by Friday. I had honest conversations with family about the nights that tempt me and the days that feel like a slide. We talked about what help sounds like and what it doesn't. We made small contingency plans—a walk after dinner; tea instead of silence; going to bed earlier, not as surrender but as strategy. None of this was magic. It was connection and repetition and an ordinary reverence for how hard it is to be alive and not use food for every emotion.

There were relapses. There are still relapses. Anyone who promises you a straight line has never sat through a craving that sounds like thunder and feels like it brings its own weather. The change for me was not that storms stopped; it was that the seasons shortened. I learned to make the interval between the slip and the repair smaller. I learned to end the shame cycle before it could extend its lease. After a binge, I stopped writing essays about my worth and made breakfast. I didn't wait for Monday. I didn't wait for the first of the month. I restarted with the next meal—plain food, water, a short walk, a text to say "rough night, trying again." I learned the muscle memory of repair.

Curiosity helped. I made space between the urge and the response to ask simple questions: What set this off? A headline? A memory? Fatigue dressed up as hunger? Did I skip lunch and expect discipline to fix biology? Did something good happen and I didn't let myself feel it? The answers didn't need to be profound; they needed to be honest. Over time, patterns emerged. I started to treat those patterns the way a pilot treats crosswinds: not as moral failings, but as conditions to account for.

I also learned to name hunger with precision. Not all hunger is a mouth problem. Sometimes I am hungry for food. Sometimes I am hungry for relief—ten minutes without a task attaching itself to my name. Sometimes I am hungry for sleep because my brain is trying to keep me upright on fumes. Sometimes I am hungry for contact with someone who won't judge me, the kind of conversation that doesn't fix anything but makes the room feel less narrow. Sometimes I am hungry for meaning, because stress without purpose eats the soul in a way no snack can satisfy.

When I can name the hunger, I can choose the treatment. A walk doesn't fix grief, but it lets grief move through the body instead of stagnating. A call to a friend doesn't change a legal battle, but it reminds me I am not defined by the ugliest thing someone said about me this week. Prayer doesn't burn calories, but it burns off the despair that makes calories feel like medicine.

I started keeping small substitutions ready like tools on a pegboard: a shower when my skin feels like it doesn't fit; three songs loud enough to drown out rumination; a ten-minute tidy to give my hands something to do that isn't feeding a feeling; stretching on the floor with the lights low; stepping outside and naming five things I can see, four I can touch, three I can hear, two I can smell, one I can taste. These are not tricks; they are ways to tell the animal body that the threat has passed.

As a psychiatrist, I see the same map in many lives. Early adversity that taught immediate relief; chronic stress that never gives the nervous system a clean landing; cheap, hyperpalatable food within arm's reach; cues to consume hitting us from waking to sleep; very little time to recover. The system profits while people blame themselves. We tell individuals to steer better without acknowledging the crosswinds we engineered into the runway. Healing starts when we rewrite the story. Not a tale of moral failure, but of adaptation that outlived its usefulness. The child who reached for food to calm fear was intelligent and resourceful. The adult has to honor that intelligence and then teach the body a new sequence: pause, name, choose. The sirens may be gone, but the body still listens for them. Our work is to convince it—with practice, not speeches—that morning is here.

That shift is not easy. It is possible. It happens in the scale of minutes, not years. It looks like leaving two bites on the plate because you caught the moment satiety whispered. It looks like closing the laptop at 10 p.m. because tomorrow deserves a rested mind. It looks like adding one vegetable because "healthy" is a direction, not a personality. It looks like failing on Wednesday and trying again at Wednesday lunch. It looks like telling someone you trust the truth before shame can edit it. Over time, these small edits become authorship. You don't control the weather, but you learn the routes that keep you out of it longer. You don't silence every craving, but you stop treating each one as a sovereign command.

My turning points were never grand. They were the kind of choices that would embarrass a motivational poster. But they built a life I could live inside without bracing. They stitched a new reflex into my days: care first, decide second. They taught me that change is not a performance; it is a practice. And a practice, if you keep showing up to it, becomes a way of being that can hold you when the old storms rumble and the windows rattle and the night does what nights do. You don't have to be heroic. You have to be present, again and again, until presence becomes home.

Maintain and Sustain

I won't pretend I've solved this. My weight still keeps a calendar. There are seasons when I am steady and strong, and weeks when old echoes and new pressures take the controls. What holds me is not a breakthrough but a daily practice of honesty and compassion. I track what I eat without turning the ledger into a weapon. I choose whole foods because they make my thinking cleaner. I plan for celebrations because joy deserves a place at the table. When I drift, I ask for help. I say out loud that stress makes me reach for comfort eating. Speaking it breaks the spell; secrecy loses its leverage the moment air hits it.

There's another truth: purpose is a kind of nutrition. When I write, when I sit with patients, when I teach about trauma, I feel fed in a way no meal can imitate. Purpose doesn't replace food; it restores proportion so food can be food again. Inside purpose I remember why health matters to me—not to fit an image, but to stay present for my family, to keep doing the work, to bear witness for people harmed by systems and by silence. I want to show that survival can grow up into healing.

If you hear your own story in mine, know this: you are not weak because you eat to soothe. You were resourceful enough to find relief when relief was scarce. Now you deserve better tools. Begin with kindness toward your body. Build simple routines that can survive a bad day. Seek therapy that understands trauma's fingerprints. Gather a circle that can hold you accountable without cruelty. Move your body to shift both mood and metabolism. Sleep, because nothing repairs decision-making like rest. Drink water, because thirst loves to dress up as hunger. Forgive yourself faster than you used to. Keep going.

My history with food is the most human thing about me. It records the battles I fought and the love I needed. It's how a child in a city at war learned to feel safe—and how an adult learned to rewrite that lesson. I am still writing. Some days the sentences are steady. Some days the pen slips. I accept both and continue. I hope this story helps you treat your own body with more respect and less judgment. I hope it helps you see addiction not as a character flaw, but as a response to pain and a request for comfort. When we honor the pain and offer real comfort, eating can become nourishment again rather than numbing.

I am a physician who has lived this. I am a patient who is still learning. I am a person who believes healing is possible even when history is heavy. Trauma carved its initials in my nervous system, but it does not own my future. I own my choices—imperfect and real. I choose connection over secrecy. I choose planning over chaos. I choose compassion over shame. I choose to tell this truth so someone else can set the fork down, take a breath, and feel, for the first time in a long time, that they are not alone.

Rusted Iron - Robert Downey Jr.

It's past midnight in Malibu, 1996. A woman walks down the hall to check on her 11-year-old and freezes—the bed is already occupied, not by her son, but by a stranger in his underwear, folded clothes on the chair like a guest who forgot to leave. The police will learn the stranger is Robert Downey Jr., hours earlier charged with possession of heroin, cocaine, and an unloaded .357 Magnum. By morning he'll be under arrest again, the incident tabbed forever as the "Goldilocks" episode—rock bottom rendered as a nursery image gone wrong. (Los Angeles Times, 1996a; Helfand & Brennan, 1996)

"Remember just because you hit bottom doesn't mean you have to stay there," Downey is widely quoted as saying—a line that only lands because of how far he fell.

Sometimes the influence of family on addiction is a twisted braid of genes and upbringing. Few stories show this more starkly than Downey's. His father, filmmaker Robert Downey Sr., struggled with his own addictions and—by the son's account—introduced him to drugs shockingly early. *"When my dad and I would do drugs together, it was like him trying to express his love for me in the only way he knew how,"* Downey once said, describing a childhood where *"there was always a lot of pot and coke around."* That entanglement of love and dysfunction handed him both a loaded genetic deck and direct exposure. Unsurprisingly, he spiraled—cocaine and heroin, arrests and rehabs, probation violations, even prison time. (Moyer, 2014; Garbarino, 2000)

As an adult and father, Downey feared he had passed this vulnerability to his own children, especially his eldest, Indio—whose 2014 arrest for cocaine possession made the family pattern feel painfully literal. Science doesn't excuse the behavior, but it explains the risk: genetics account for roughly 40–60% of susceptibility to addiction, with the rest shaped by environment and experience. In alcohol research specifically, studies have long observed that sons of alcoholic fathers can face dramatically higher odds—up to nine times the usual risk—underscoring how heritable liability and home environment can reinforce each other. In the Downey family, it's impossible to parse exactly how much was DNA and how much was a permissive, chaotic milieu. Realistically, it was both—nature and nurture weaving a pattern that was hard to escape. (D'Zurilla, 2014; National Institute on Drug Abuse [NIDA], 2020; Windle, 1997)

But here's the hopeful part: the pattern was escaped. Downey got clean, rebuilt trust, and helped his son seek treatment. The man who partly fell under a father's influence decided to be a different kind of father himself. And the broader evidence is encouraging for any family carrying similar worries. Inherited risk is real; destiny is not. As contemporary genetics reminds us, vulnerability isn't a verdict—especially when people have access to support, treatment, and an environment that lowers triggers. (NIDA, 2023)

Downey's arc—darkness to discipline, secrecy to accountability—offers a practical lesson rather than a fairy tale. Knowing your history can be a lever, not a label: a reason to seek help early, to change routines and rooms, to build guardrails that make the next right choice easier than the next wrong one. The same public that watched him fall then watched him stand—proof that "bottom" can be a place you pass through, not a place you live.

Healing Through Understanding

Both the Barrymore and Downey family stories carry a clear message: knowing your inherited risk can be a source of strength, not a sentence. If addiction has loomed large in your family, fear or guilt can feel like a curse hanging over your shoulder. But a predisposition is not predestination. You are more than your genes. Recognizing a family pattern can be the first act of healing—an invitation to make different choices, to stay alert to the environments and stressors that trip your switches, and to reach for support sooner rather than later. In families marked by addiction, open conversation is not optional; it's protective. What used to be taboo—an uncle's drinking, a parent's overdose—can become shared knowledge that dissolves shame and points toward care. These stories don't indict character; they illuminate a disease shaped by biology and upbringing, one that deserves treatment, not secrecy.

Reading multigenerational struggles like Drew Barrymore's or Robert Downey Jr.'s can stir complicated feelings: relief that you're not alone, grief for what was inherited, and hope for what can change. Their arcs remind us that many parents and grandparents were not villains; they were often victims of a condition poorly understood and poorly treated in their time. Compassion widens the frame. Their story is part of yours, but it does not define your destination. With clarity about where you come from and resolve about where you're going, you can choose wiser rooms, safer routines, and kinder self-talk. Vigilance becomes a skill, not a burden; asking for help becomes strategy, not shame. And when setbacks come—as they sometimes will—you can view them as information rather than condemnation, a signal to adjust stress, sleep, support, or surroundings.

Turning awareness into action is where families change course. Share a simple "family risk briefing" with those you trust: what tends to trigger you, what helps, what language to use in hard moments. Agree on early warning signs—missed meals, insomnia, secretive drinking, isolating—and on early responses that are compassionate but firm. Build protective routines that make the next right choice easier than the next wrong one: keep alcohol out of the house if that's your risk, schedule meals and sleep like appointments, swap high-risk social settings for ones that don't revolve around substances, and practice "first call" plans (who you contact before a lapse becomes a spiral). Education helps too: learn how stress, deprivation, and cues amplify vulnerability, and teach the same to teens so they can recognise risk without shame.

It also helps to reframe identity. If your family history has been a story of chaos, write a counter-story of boundaries and care. Treat your predisposition as you would a family history of diabetes or heart disease: a reason to screen earlier, plan smarter, and intervene faster—not a reason to hide. Small, steady investments add up: therapy that understands trauma, peer support that normalises struggle, exercise that stabilises mood, hobbies that create flow and meaning, friendships that don't require you to numb yourself to belong. Recovery capital—skills, supports, and structure—can outgrow risk over time. Think of inheritance as a map, not a GPS: it shows the terrain, but you still choose the route, the pace, and the companions.

In the end, inherited risk is a chapter, not the whole book. Some of us start on a rough road with baggage we never asked to carry. Yet, like Drew Barrymore ending a hedonistic family tradition or Robert Downey Jr. refusing to lose another generation, you can draft a different ending. Learn from your family's missteps, interrupt your own risk patterns, and build a support system that makes change sustainable: sleep that protects judgment, food that steadies energy, stress practices that defuse cravings, honest check-ins that keep secrets from growing teeth. Let your history explain your past without dictating your future. The pen is in your hands now. With understanding, community, and self-compassion, you can write a new story—one of resilience, recovery, and hope—and pass down not a curse but a set of tools: language for hard feelings, plans for hard days, and proof that cycles can be broken.

CHAPTER 3

Chemical Messengers Gone Rogue

(Neurotransmitters - DANCES)

> "*Strength does not come from physical capacity. It comes from an indomitable will.*"
>
> — MAHATMA GHANDI

Key neurotransmitters significantly affected by drugs:

DANCES

D - **Dopamine** *(pleasure, reward, motivation)*
A - **Adrenaline** *(alertness, stress response)*
N - **Noradrenaline** *(attention, focus, arousal)*
C - **Cortisol** *(stress hormone, anxiety)*
E - **Endorphins** *(pain relief, euphoria)*
S - **Serotonin** *(mood, appetite, sleep)*

Dancing with the Devil

The studio lights had gone cold. The loudest thing in the room wasn't a voice or a melody, but the throb of a nervous system that had been sprinting for years. On a July night in 2018, Demi Lovato felt the gap between the person the world saw and the person trying to hold herself together. Some nights, pain won't be bargained into the next hour. On this one, she didn't reach for a single escape; she reached for many. Later, she would put it plainly: "I crossed a line that I had never crossed... I snapped. (Nakamura, 2021)"

A month earlier, she had warned the world in a song. "Sober" landed June 21, 2018—three minutes of confession and apology: "Mama, I'm so sorry I'm not sober anymore... To the ones who never left me... I'm so sorry, I'm not sober anymore." It wasn't a headline; it was a flare (Wikipedia Contributors, 2025).

On July 24, paramedics were called to her home. She was transported to Cedars-Sinai in Los Angeles, treated for a suspected overdose, and stabilized. First responders administered naloxone (Narcan), the opioid antidote that can yank a dying brain back from the edge—a literal "Lazarus" turnaround. Some reports later suggested counterfeit oxycodone pills laced with fentanyl were involved, though the exact combination of substances was not confirmed publicly (Taylor, 2018).

The medical reality was stark. "I had three strokes. I had a heart attack. My doctors said that I had five to 10 more minutes," she would say in 2021. She also described lasting brain damage and blind spots in her vision—reminders that oxygen lost in minutes can change years. "I'm on my ninth life," she said (Cohen, 2021).

Her first public words after the crisis were as steady as she could make them: "I have always been transparent about my journey with addiction... What I've learned is that this illness is not something that disappears or fades with time... I will keep fighting." The statement read like a vow made from a hospital bed (Eyewitness News, 2018).

In her docuseries, Lovato let the curtain drop on both stages of the story—the visible one with sirens and IV lines, and the silent one inside the skull where chemistry decides whether a cue becomes a craving and a craving becomes a cliff. "I crossed a line that I had never crossed," she repeats, naming the moment the brain's safety rails gave way and the switches flipped from caution to compulsion. The quotes aren't drama; they're data—evidence from the person who survived the night (Bricker, 2025).

What followed wasn't a movie montage; it was rehabilitation and relearning: vision therapy for blind spots, stepwise rebuilding of memory and trust, and the daily work of recovery in public. The same voice that once sang "Sober" now carried a different message—that relapse isn't a verdict, and survival can grow into healing if the right people, medicines, and habits meet you where you are (Russo, 2021).

We will come back to the drugs that Demi danced with that night later in this chapter to look at just how they affect users.

The Memphis Years and the Chemistry of Addiction

Bethesda was polished corridors and card readers, journals stacked like skyline, mornings that turned glass to gold. Memphis was porch light and neon, blues rolling out of doorways on Beale, barbecue smoke drifting across the river. In Bethesda, questions wore badges and moved between seminar rooms; in Memphis, they rode the heat and sat down next to you at midnight in a lab that never fully slept. The federal campus felt like a city engineered for curiosity. Memphis felt like a city that sang its pain and made something living out of it. I needed both: the marble logic of Bethesda and the cracked, honest music of Memphis.

I arrived in Memphis with a carry-on bag, a notebook, and a restless curiosity that did not sleep. The University of Tennessee lab smelled faintly of ethanol, warm plastic, and paraformaldehyde. Freezers thumped, water baths whispered, and the centrifuge announced each run like a train departing. That hum became the soundtrack of my summers, then the rhythm of two full years funded by the National Institutes of Health. I had come to study the chemistry of craving and the biology of will—why some minds are captured by a substance while others can walk away; how the brain choreographs its own messengers and sometimes forgets how to call the dance off.

Very early on I found a language that let me teach the story to myself: DANCES.

- **D is for dopamine**—the bright arrow of wanting, the circuitry that tags a cue as important and makes the future feel near.
- **A is for adrenaline**—the body's surge, the quick flood that prepares muscles and memory to move.
- **N is for noradrenaline**—focus and arousal, the pencil that underlines what the moment demands.

- **C is for cortisol**—stress logic that begins as protection and, when over-learned, hardens into anxiety.
- **E is for endorphins**—endogenous relief, the hush after hurt that can masquerade as euphoria.
- **S is for serotonin**—mood, appetite, sleep; the quiet gardener of equilibrium.

DANCES became a compass. Every protocol had to point somewhere on that dial. If a slice of ventral striatum lit under the microscope, I asked what step of the dance it belonged to. High-performance liquid chromatography peaks weren't just peaks; they were a sketch of desire over time. A blot wasn't a band; it was a memory trace of stress, promising to return unless interrupted. When a graph didn't fit the acronym, I kept asking why—was our dose wrong, the timing off, or was the brain telling us there was a seventh step we hadn't named yet?

Memphis taught me that chemistry is never just chemistry; it is biography written in molecules. Street sirens outside could raise a lab tech's noradrenaline the same way a conditioned cue can in a clinic waiting room. A long call shift could nudge cortisol up and serotonin down before a single choice was made. In that heat, with those instruments, I learned to watch the brain's dance without flattery or blame: how wanting can outrun liking, how stress can turn a shortcut into a rut, how relief can be mistaken for love. And once you can name the steps, you can begin—slowly, stubbornly—to change the music.

Come up to the Lab...

Dr. Kafait U. Malik, a Professor of Pharmacology and Addictions, welcomed me with the calm of a teacher who prized both precision and patience. He demanded clean lines, clear controls, and intellectual courage. He trained me to think on two planes at once: technique and meaning:

1. Are the data real (valid, reliable, reproducible)?
2. Are they important (clinically or mechanistically consequential)? He never let me forget those are different questions.

We began with animals, because a living brain keeps secrets that only reveal themselves in motion. I learned to handle mice with a firm, gentle grip. I learned the ritual of the tail-cuff—an external sleeve that senses pulsations at the tail to estimate blood pressure without surgery; it's noninvasive but exquisitely sensitive to stress, so technique and acclimation matter (Krege et al., 1995; Harrison, 2023).

Then radiotelemetry: we implanted a tiny pressure transducer connected to an antenna so freely moving mice could stream blood pressure and heart rate in real time—physiology without restraints or anesthesia (Mills et al., 2000; Kramer et al., 2000; Alam et al., 2016).

I learned to place micro-osmotic pumps—matchstick-sized devices that deliver a compound at a constant, zero-order rate for days to weeks—so a drug enters the system with the regular pulse of a metronome. The pumps were tiny; the implications were large. The brain listens to time as intently as it listens to dose.

Afternoons belonged to the stereotaxic frame. Imagine a jeweler's vice, but built for the brain: it fixes the head in three-dimensional space so a needle can be guided to a precise set of coordinates, almost like following a map. With it, I could deliver tiny amounts of liquid into different parts of the brain. Sometimes that meant injections into the clear fluid that bathes the brain and spinal cord, spreading substances broadly. Other times it meant aiming at specific neighborhoods—like the nucleus accumbens, a hub for weighing reward and risk, or the medial preoptic area, which helps regulate motivation, balance, and social or sexual drives.

Into these regions we introduced testosterone and its relatives—dihydrotestosterone (DHT) and estradiol, which the body can make from testosterone. The question was simple: how do these "male hormones" change the way the brain makes decisions about risk and reward? The answers were not so simple. Testosterone can work slowly, by changing which genes inside cells are switched on or off, or quickly, by altering how signals move across the surface of brain cells (Dominguez & Hull, 2005; Nelson, 2011).

To see this clearly, we sometimes performed orchidectomy—surgically removing the testes to silence the body's natural testosterone. Then we could add the hormone back in carefully measured amounts and watch which behaviors and brain functions returned. It was delicate work. The brain is no place for clumsy hands.

At the bench, the focus shifted from behavior to chemistry. We measured catecholamines—adrenaline, noradrenaline, and dopamine—the body's fast messengers for "fight or flight." These chemicals, made from the amino acid tyrosine, are the ones that make your heart race, your blood pressure rise, your senses sharpen. Their levels in blood and urine act like fingerprints of the sympathetic nervous system, as long as the samples are collected with care (Paravati & Pepe, 2022).

That's harder than it sounds. To draw blood at the right moments, we worked with clock-like choreography, because if the animals sensed our tension, they would become stressed themselves. Then the experiment would stop being about catecholamines and instead become a study of cortisol, the body's main stress hormone. In rodents this is corticosterone, and while it's vital for mobilizing sugar and adjusting the immune system, too much for too long reshapes brain circuits and harms organs (Herman et al., 2016; McEwen, 2007). Good technique, we learned, is the art of measuring only what you meant to measure.

Nights, at last, were for methods and manuscripts. Western blotting was one of the first skills I learned. Imagine sorting a crowd of people by height, pressing them onto paper, then shining a spotlight that illuminates only one face. That is Western blotting: proteins are separated by size, transferred to a membrane, and antibodies reveal the one you care about (Mahmood & Yang, 2012).

Real-time PCR came next. Here, messenger RNA—the instructions cells use to make proteins—is copied into DNA and amplified in cycles. Each cycle makes a fluorescent glow burn a little brighter, like a lantern gradually flaring. By watching when the glow passes a certain threshold, you can count how much of the original message was there with surprising accuracy (Bustin et al., 2009).

There were other tools too: ELISA, which works like an antibody sandwich to catch and measure soluble proteins; immunoprecipitation, where antibodies reach into a molecular soup to pull out just one protein or complex; and gel electrophoresis, where DNA, RNA, or proteins march across a gel, lining up by size or charge.

Science rarely rewards you with a perfect picture. Many blots yield nothing but blank silence. Many gels demand you start again. Slowly you learn to see the failures as lessons, and to celebrate not just the rare beautiful results but also the stubborn patience that makes them possible.

In the brainstem lies the locus coeruleus, a small blue-stained cluster of neurons that floods the system with noradrenaline. It tunes attention, heightens arousal, and helps us learn under uncertainty (Sara, 2009). The same sympathetic traffic that sharpens awareness also squeezes the kidney's tiny arterioles, pushes renin release, and shifts how sodium is handled—all of which drives blood pressure up and burdens the kidneys (DiBona, 2002; Sata et al., 2018).

Bridges between brain and body don't stop at nerves. Stress kindles the immune system too. In the brain, microglia—the resident immune cells—wake up, while astrocytes, the star-shaped support cells, become reactive. Together they reshape how synapses in places like the amygdala and striatum function. The same inflammatory cascades, when they spill into the kidney, lay down scar tissue, a fibrosis that stiffens and chokes the organ (Sofroniew & Vinters, 2010; Calcia et al., 2016; Frank et al., 2019; Liu, 2011).

To study this, we cut across disciplines as easily as we cut tissue. We dissected brain and kidney, froze them, sliced them thin, and stained for the markers of glial activation in the brain and for inflammation and fibrosis in the kidney—collagen I and III, α-SMA. Under the microscope the stains glittered like constellations, each point a star in a story written by stress.

The patterns told us something simple but profound: addiction is not only in the head. It leaves fingerprints in the heart, the kidneys, even the gut. The chemistry of craving shares a border with the chemistry of blood pressure. What we think and feel is braided tightly to how we pump and filter (Volkow & Morales, 2015; Volkow, Koob, & McLellan, 2016).

The Dance Partners

Dopamine was our most familiar dancer—the one who steps onto the floor, throws a spotlight across the room, and makes everything feel urgent and near. When we raised dopamine tone in the nucleus accumbens, the mice learned with startling speed which chamber had been paired with that feeling. Conditioned place preference looks like a simple two-room rehearsal, but it's also a mirror: the animal votes with its feet for the stage where desire last took a bow. We measured that vote, then followed the music upstream, hunting for the signals that kept the melody alive.

Dopamine rarely danced alone. When it surged, noradrenaline often rose alongside it—two partners turning plain wakefulness into appetite, sharpening attention, and pinning meaning to the moment. Together they didn't just wake the body; they wrote notes into memory, tagging the scene as valuable. That's the first step of reinforcement: the choreography that makes the next entrance smoother than the last.

Then the pit orchestra joined. Adrenaline from the adrenal medulla spilled into the bloodstream like drums rolling from the wings—heart rate lifting, vessels changing tone, muscles priming to move. Repeat that cue often enough and the cardiovascular system begins to rehearse it. Baselines shift; peaks sharpen. On telemetry, you can see the body start the dance before the music starts. Anticipation becomes physiology, and physiology tilts behavior toward the next dose. It's one of the oldest patterns in addiction: expectation setting tempo.

Cortisol wrote a darker counterpoint. The hypothalamic–pituitary–adrenal axis answers threat with precision, but it taxes the future to pay for the present. When we introduced stressors on a schedule, cortisol didn't merely raise anxiety; it widened the river mouth that empties into self-medication. Reward cues grew louder; the choreography of relief learned its marks faster. Mice living inside repeated stress chased calming rewards more quickly—and people do, too. If you ignore trauma and hardship, you're not treating the brain that actually shows up; you're critiquing a dancer while refusing to fix the stage.

Endorphins remained the tender poets of the company. Turn up endogenous opioid tone and pain steps back; a soft euphoria takes your hand and says, "Rest here awhile." Turn it down and both pain and preference shift in the other direction. The lesson isn't new, but it lands personally: when relief is scarce, pleasure becomes medicine; when pleasure is the only medicine available, dependence slips in through the side door, nodding like an old friend.

Serotonin threaded through everything like a quiet choreographer's assistant—setting tempo, smoothing transitions, keeping meals, sleep, and mood in time with the music. Sometimes when we raised serotonin, the bright, brassy notes of a stimulant's reward dimmed; sometimes it simply steadied the oscillation between craving and satiety so the ensemble could hold its line. Serotonin is neither hero nor villain; it's the metronome that keeps the dance from tearing itself apart.

Dopamine, Adrenaline, Noradrenaline, Cortisol, Endorphins, Serotonin—DANCES—kept our minds organized while our hands moved through protocols. But as the Memphis work deepened, a harder question kept tapping its foot: why do some brains learn this choreography so quickly while others miss the beat? I found a doorway in sex differences and steroid biology. And there, backstage, were the enzymes and receptors most clinicians never name—the costume designers and lighting crew—quietly altering fabrics and colors, changing how each dancer catches the light. The show out front looked the same—urge, cue, relief—but the understory had shifted. To change the dance, we would have to step behind the curtain and work where the steps are made

Doing the Science

We set out to understand why stress and reward can affect males and females differently. A big part of the answer lives in our hormones and how our bodies process them. Hormones like estrogen and testosterone don't just flip one big switch in the body. They act in two main ways:

1. The classic route: they enter a cell and bind to "nuclear receptors," which then turn certain genes on or off.

2. The fast route: they get broken down by enzymes into new substances that send their own messages.

Think of enzymes as tiny machines on a factory line. One of these machines, called CYP1B1, takes estrogen and turns it into "catechol estrogens." These new versions of estrogen can do things the original hormone didn't. Some make nerve cells (neurons) fire more easily—like turning up the volume on a speaker. Some wake up microglia, the brain's cleanup and defense cells, so they react faster. Others push the body toward inflammation, the immune system's "red alert." All of this can change how dopamine neurons fire (dopamine helps tag things as important and motivates us to act) and how the prefrontal cortex (the brain's planner and impulse-controller) puts on the brakes. In some animals, these hormone breakdown products made reward cues feel louder; in others, they made stress feel bigger—so that chasing relief felt more necessary. What can look like "personality" may actually be chemistry working behind the scenes.

To follow these chemical messages, we focused on an enzyme called cytosolic phospholipase A2 (cPLA2). Think of it as a molecular pair of scissors. When cPLA2 switches on, it snips a fatty acid called arachidonic acid out of the cell's outer membrane. Arachidonic acid then sits at a crossroads, with several possible routes it can take.

- **Cyclooxygenase (COX)** converts it into prostaglandins. These molecules act like local messengers: in blood vessels they control how much the vessels squeeze or relax, and in the brain they adjust how strongly neurons communicate across synapses.
- **12/15-lipoxygenase (LOX)** steers it into making leukotrienes and related compounds. These are the body's "rallying signals," calling immune cells to the scene and triggering inflammation.
- **CYP4A enzymes** turn it into 20-HETE (20-hydroxyeicosatetraenoic acid). This signal tells the smallest blood vessels to tighten, which raises resistance to blood flow—like narrowing the pipes in a plumbing system, increasing the pressure inside.

In this way, a single fatty acid released from the cell's surface can launch very different responses: fine-tuning brain signals, summoning immune defenses, or squeezing blood vessels tighter. Which path is chosen depends on which enzymes are active in that moment.

Most people never use these names, but their bodies use the signals every day. They help decide how firmly a blood vessel muscle cell squeezes, how far a microglial branch reaches toward a synapse, and how a neuron adjusts its firing rate when stress chemistry washes over it.

In one set of experiments, we worked with three groups of animals. The first were normal adult males. The second had undergone orchidectomy—the removal of the testes, which shuts down the body's natural supply of testosterone. The third had testosterone carefully added back.

Even before the statistics, the microscope showed a difference. Microglia, the brain's watchful immune cells, wore a different look. Their markers had shifted, as if they were on new duty. The chemical conversations between cells—the cytokines that carry immune signals—spoke in a different dialect.

The dopamine system moved too. The changes were small but real: a tweak in how much dopamine was made, and in how sensitive the brain seemed to it. When testosterone was restored, some brain regions slid back toward their original state, while others shifted further away.

The point was clear. Hormones don't act like a simple switch, pushing everything in one direction. They redraw the map. Which way the journey bends depends on the neighborhood of the brain you're standing in, and on the toll booths along the road—the enzymes that decide which routes can be taken.

We saw the same patterns outside the brain, especially in the kidney. The very hormone byproducts that nudged neurons were also changing how the kidney handled inflammation and blood pressure. One signal in particular, 20-HETE from the CYP4A pathway, told the kidney's tiniest vessels to clamp down, raising the baseline pressure in the system. At the same time, the sympathetic nervous system—the body's quick "go" wiring—carried the brain's stress message straight to those vessels. The kidney did not stay silent.

In some animals, the combination of steady sympathetic drive and altered eicosanoid signaling—the whole family of signals spun from arachidonic acid, like prostaglandins and 20-HETE—left visible marks. Under the microscope, the kidney's filters and the spaces between them showed tiny scars, exactly the kind a renal pathologist would stop at and point to. The message was unmistakable: brain and kidney were reading from the same script.

Here's what that really means in plain terms:

- Hormones are not single notes; they are chords. Just as a single piano key sounds different from a chord of three, testosterone and its byproducts carry overlapping but distinct effects. One may fuel drive, another may fan inflammation, and together they make a more complex "song."
- Enzymes like CYP1B1 and CYP4A are the arrangers. Think of them as remix artists who take a familiar tune and spin it into something new. The original hormone is the melody, but once enzymes get involved, the beat changes—and so does the message the body hears.
- Microglia are the brain's groundskeepers and guards. When they are primed, they are like security staff on high alert. They rush to every alarm—helpful if there's real danger, but exhausting and damaging if the alarms never stop.
- Dopamine is the brain's marker for what is worth chasing. It's the highlighter ink in your notebook, making certain cues—food, sex, drugs, even social approval—stand out in neon. When hormones tune dopamine circuits higher, the highlight pen grows thicker and brighter, making temptations harder to ignore.
- The prefrontal cortex is like an internal coach. On a good day, it calls the plays, keeps you disciplined, reminds you to think twice. But under constant chemical stress, that coach loses their voice. The brakes fail, and impulses run wild.

- cPLA2 is the gatekeeper that opens a whole traffic system of signals. Once opened, it unleashes a convoy of messengers—prostaglandins, leukotrienes, 20-HETE—each like vehicles headed to different neighborhoods, carrying orders that affect blood flow, inflammation, and brain activity all at once.
- The kidney is not just a filter. It is more like a pressure valve in a plumbing system, tuned by the brain's stress wiring. Push it too hard for too long, and the valve begins to scar and leak. Those changes in turn send signals back upstream, reinforcing the stress loop between kidney and brain.

Why should this matter to anyone outside a lab? Because it helps explain why stress, sex, and biology can make the same situation feel completely different depending on the person. Two people can face the same challenge—an exam, a breakup, a craving, a sleepless night—and walk away with very different outcomes. For one, the stress becomes fuel. For another, it tips into exhaustion or relapse. The difference isn't always "character" or "willpower." Often, it's chemistry.

What looks like sheer determination—someone gritting their teeth and pushing through—may actually be the way their hormones and brain circuits happen to align in that moment. What looks like "just anxiety" might be a genuine biological shift: blood vessels narrowing, microglia in the brain sounding alarms, dopamine circuits turning the brightness knob on temptations until they are hard to ignore. These aren't imaginary states; they are physical signals running through nerves, enzymes, and immune cells.

This matters in everyday life. Think of the person who says they'll quit smoking "cold turkey" and succeeds, versus the one who collapses back into the habit within days. Or the person who handles heartbreak with resilience, compared to another who spirals into depression. Biology doesn't excuse choices, but it does set the stage. A brain more sensitive to dopamine cues, or a body under constant sympathetic pressure, will find certain battles harder to fight.

The better we understand these pathways, the more precisely we can support recovery, healing, and resilience. Sometimes the right move is to ease the stress itself—helping the body switch off its constant alarms. Sometimes it's adjusting hormones, or blocking enzymes that keep inflammation smoldering. And often, the best results come not from a single big intervention but from many small ones layered together: better sleep, steadier routines, the right therapy, medication if needed. Like tuning an orchestra, each small adjustment helps the whole system play in harmony again.

Lessons Learned

From the outside, our results can look like an eclectic walk through pathways. From the inside, they read like a single score. Addiction is not only a drug meeting a receptor. It is a biography written in enzymes. It is a stage set by stress hormones, a tempo conducted by catecholamines, and a quiet retuning of instruments by steroid metabolites. Ignore sex differences and you miss half the orchestra. Ignore inflammation and you mishear the melody as only a rhythm problem when timbre—the color of the sound—is changing, too. How a note sounds matters as much as when it arrives.

There were days of triumph. A Western blot that settled an argument the way a clean chord resolves a song. A telemetry trace that matched the model we sketched on a napkin, as if the data had been waiting to be asked the right question. A field of astrocytes blooming around a lesion, suddenly explaining the one odd behavior that had bothered me all week. And there were many days of frustration. A microinjection that missed by a millimeter might as well have missed by a mile; the animal doesn't care what the atlas promised. A pump that clogged mid-experiment taught humility faster than any lecture. Dr. Malik had a way of turning those failures into questions instead of verdicts. What did the fault reveal about the system? What did it reveal about us?

Writing became its own apprenticeship. I learned to turn raw notes into a road a reviewer could follow. Argue for the importance of a small observation without pretending it's a revolution. The best scientific writing is honest and brave: it admits limits and insists on consequences. Dr. Malik edited with a pencil that left gentle but unmistakable marks. Choose the one figure that matters most, he'd say, and build the story around it. A good paper is a map: clear landmarks, true scale, and a route others can follow to the same mountain—and climb it again.

What did Memphis do to my thinking about addiction? It cured me of simple answers. It made me comfortable with a model that runs from molecules to cells to circuits—and onward to organs outside the skull. It made me respect the body's memory. Give a system the same experience again and again, and it will build a scaffold to carry it. In the brain, that scaffold looks like receptors trafficking at a synapse or microglia primed in a fear nucleus. In the body, it can look like structural change in a kidney living too long under sympathetic overdrive. Once the scaffold exists, behavior tends to follow its rails.

Memphis also taught me to keep asking about sex differences. Too much addiction research treats male data as universal. That isn't just lazy; it's wrong. Estrogen and testosterone don't make people different only in the obvious ways. Their metabolites rename the rules of plasticity and stress response. They change how pain is felt and how relief is pursued. They alter the speed at which a reinforcement loop closes. If you want medicine that is precise and humane, you must hear these parts of the score and plan the treatment with the whole orchestra in mind.

Theory into Practice

The DANCES framework still guides my clinical work. When a patient sits down with a story of craving and relapse, I listen for those six letters as if I'm tuning an orchestra. Is dopamine playing too loud, tagging every cue as important? Is adrenaline pushing everything into a sprint? Is noradrenaline turning ordinary life into an exam that never ends? Is cortisol grinding down the thinking brain and handing the keys to reflex? Is endorphin tone so low that pain drowns out every other signal? Is serotonin struggling to steady sleep, appetite, and mood so the rhythm keeps breaking? Once I hear which instruments are off the staff, I can choose a plan that respects the music instead of fighting it.

The research on steroid metabolites and arachidonic-acid pathways found a home in my clinic, too. Hypertension is common in people living with addiction and chronic stress. Chronic kidney disease changes how the brain feels and thinks. So when I treat substance use, I also watch the sympathetic system, the blood pressure that drifts upward with life's storms, and the inflammatory "noise" that makes the brain impatient. Sometimes the best relapse prevention is not another speech about willpower—it's a plan that lowers the background volume of stress in vessels and in glial cells. That plan might include psychotherapy and social support. It might include sleep repair and nutrition that stabilizes energy. It might include a beta blocker to soften adrenaline's spikes while we teach the brain new routes to calm. It might include a medication that steadies serotonin so mood and appetite don't drag the mind toward the quickest comfort. The science doesn't replace the art; it fertilizes it.

I think often about one experiment that never made it into a paper. On the surface, it was designed as a *negative control*. In lab science, a negative control is the part of an experiment where you deliberately set conditions that should produce no effect. It's a way to make sure that when you do see a result, it isn't just noise or coincidence. In this case, we combined a mild stressor with a very low dose of stimulant—well below the level that normally produces any measurable behavioral effect. The expectation was simple: nothing much should happen.

But the animals told us otherwise. Using telemetry—tiny implanted sensors that continuously track blood pressure and heart rate—we noticed something subtle. In a subset of animals, the baseline blood pressure crept upward, just a little, and then stayed there for days. Not the kind of dramatic surge you'd show in a figure. But real, persistent, undeniable.

Later, when we examined the brain tissues, the same animals showed another quiet change. In a stress-sensitive brain region we hadn't even targeted, the microglia—the brain's resident immune cells—looked activated. Normally, microglia sit in a "resting" state, gently surveying the environment. When they sense trouble, they shift shape and chemistry, ready to mount a defense. Here, they weren't in full battle mode, but they were clearly more alert than usual, as if standing guard at the city gates.

The lesson was sharp. What looks clinically invisible—too small for a doctor to spot in a quick exam—can still be biologically important. Low-grade changes accumulate. A little extra vessel tightening here, a small increase in immune vigilance there, and over time the whole system resets itself.

It's like living in a house where the foundation tilts by a millimeter each week. No one notices at first. But after months or years, the walls lean, the doors don't shut right, and the floor feels crooked. By the time people sense something is off, the structure has already rebuilt itself around a new, unhealthy normal.

That experiment, meant to prove "nothing," instead reminded me that the body whispers long before it screams.

Memphis taught me to respect the quiet beginnings. It taught me to look for the link between a hard week and a blood pressure that won't come down. To look for the link between a trauma history and a dopamine system greedy for relief. To look for the link between sex hormones and a brain that reacts differently to the same dose of stress. Those links aren't theories. They're rooms I've stood in, slides I've stained, numbers I've plotted.

Later, standing with patients who felt trapped in cycles of use and shame, I remembered the animals who learned to expect their next dose like weather. A brain that anticipates is not a bad brain—it's a smart brain badly taught by circumstances. The task is to teach it again. You can teach it with structure and support. You can teach it by lowering pressure in the system so stress isn't screaming at every synapse. You can teach it with noninvasive neuromodulation that nudges the prefrontal cortex back into leadership. You can teach it by repairing sleep so serotonin isn't fighting a losing war. You can teach it by treating pain honestly so endorphins aren't the only exit from a hard day. The research gives us a map for these teaching routes.

I don't romanticize the lab. It's a place where living animals become data. That demands gratitude and responsibility—and that we use the lessons well. When I imagine the future of addiction care, I see DANCES linked to personalized profiles of steroid metabolism and inflammatory tone. I see a clinic that measures not only craving, but also the enzymes that helped write it. I see sex-specific prevention strategies that start before the first use. I see treatments aimed at both brain and kidney, at both microglia and vessel smooth muscle, at both stress and reward. I see medicine that refuses to choose between biology and biography—because the person in front of us is both.

On the last day of one early summer, I stood alone at the microscope and looked again at a field of astrocytes I'd stained the day before. The image wasn't special. It was mine. It carried the memory of careful hands, repeated steps, and a mentor's voice reminding me to ask better questions. DANCES floated back into my mind as if the cells were whispering the letters. What began as a mnemonic had become a way of seeing. The brain dances with its messengers. The body listens and answers. Addiction enters when the choreography gets hijacked by stress, opportunity, and chemistry. Recovery begins when we learn the steps again—with patience, kindness, and the right music.

The Memphis years gave me that music. They gave me a respect for detail and a wide lens for meaning. They gave me the courage to say addiction is not a moral failure—it's a biological and biographical event that can be understood and changed. They gave me a story I could share with patients who needed science that honored their suffering, a language that can stand in a courtroom, in a clinic, and in a quiet office at the end of a long day. Working with Dr. Malik did more than produce data. It produced a way of thinking I carry into every hard conversation.

When I teach young clinicians now, I tell them about the pumps and the tail-cuff, the telemetry and the blots, the stains and the long nights. I tell them about Dr. Malik's pencil and his unhurried questions. I show them how DANCES can shape a care plan that actually works. How steroid metabolites and eicosanoids matter in the life of a person trying to stop using. How kidneys and brains talk in the shared language of stress and blood flow. Most of all, I show them that science is a kind of love: you pay attention, you tell the truth, and you use what you learned to help someone walk free.

That's what we were doing in Memphis—listening for truth in small signals, drawing a map for a problem that touches every family, preparing to meet patients with more than sympathy. The lab door closes with a soft click on many evenings. The work doesn't end there. It flows forward into clinics and communities, where the dance continues—and where, with the right music, people can learn new steps.

The Night of Many Dancers

On nights like Demi Lovato's in July 2018, the floor doesn't fill all at once—it fills in sequence. One substance enters, then another, until the brain is flooded with signals it cannot coordinate. Lovato later named them: "I went on a shopping spree... I tried meth. I mixed it with molly, with coke, weed, alcohol, oxycontin. And that alone should've killed me." She added, "I crossed a line that I had never crossed." The aftermath was devastating: "I had three strokes. I had a heart attack. My doctors said that I had five to 10 more minutes" (Cohen, 2021a).

First onto the stage was methamphetamine—the sprinter. Meth acts directly on monoamine systems. It enters dopamine and norepinephrine terminals, interferes with the vesicular monoamine transporter (VMAT2), alkalizes vesicles, and forces dopamine out of storage into the synapse. At the same time, it reverses the dopamine transporter (DAT), ejecting dopamine into the cleft in a surge (Sulzer, 2011). Dopamine encodes reward value—"remember this, do it again"—while norepinephrine sharpens attention and primes the body for action. Flood both systems and the night feels laser-focused, purposeful, and nearly invincible. The subjective rush matches the mechanism: a sudden, forced release of monoamines into circuits never designed for that load.

Then came MDMA—the empath. MDMA primarily targets the serotonin transporter (SERT), flipping it into reverse and expelling serotonin into the synapse (Green et al., 2003). Serotonin regulates mood and social perception, so its surge shifts emotional tone: warmth increases, edges soften, belonging feels closer. At higher doses MDMA also releases dopamine and norepinephrine through DAT and NET, layering stimulation on top of the serotonin "glow." Its prosocial, empathogenic effects depend on serotonergic outflow through SERT, which is the core mechanism behind its reputation as the "love drug."

Cocaine joined—the echo artist. Unlike meth, cocaine does not force release. Instead, it blocks the reuptake pumps—DAT, NET, and SERT—that normally vacuum neurotransmitters back inside the cell (Ritz et al., 1987). The synapse fills with leftover dopamine, norepinephrine, and serotonin, prolonging their signals. With crack (smoked cocaine), brain entry is almost instantaneous, and speed of delivery magnifies reinforcement. The same molecule, arriving faster, becomes far more addictive because learning circuits weight rapid signals more heavily.

Opioids followed—the lullaby. Oxycodone and heroin bind to mu-opioid receptors (MORs), disinhibiting dopamine neurons and spreading a powerful sense of relief (Volkow et al., 2018). Pain diminishes, vigilance fades, fear softens. But those same MORs are present in the brainstem—particularly in the preBötzinger complex and parabrachial/Kölliker–Fuse nuclei—that control breathing rhythms. Suppress them too far and the chest simply fails to rise. In a market where fentanyl, 50–100 times more potent than morphine, contaminates supplies, what once looked like a "standard" dose can become lethal. Combined with alcohol or benzodiazepines, the risk of respiratory depression is not just additive but multiplicative, because all three act on overlapping inhibitory circuits.

Alcohol drifted in with its familiar mask of relaxation and sociability. Beneath that mask it enhances GABAergic transmission and suppresses glutamatergic drive, especially at NMDA receptors, while still tickling dopamine release in reward hubs (Lovinger & Roberto, 2013). The result is paradoxical: judgment blunted, caution muted, yet approach behaviour enhanced. A balm and a lure at once, alcohol is why so many "ordinary nights" tilt toward disaster.

Cannabis softened the edges. Acting mainly through CB1 receptors, the endocannabinoid system sits upstream of dopamine circuits and can adjust their gain (Volkow et al., 2014). Depending on context, it can blunt the binge or smooth the path to the next "yes." In a mix already overloaded with stimulants and depressants, cannabis is one more lever in the same control room.

Put together, Lovato's account maps onto known pharmacology. Meth and MDMA forced monoamine release. Cocaine jammed reuptake, trapping neurotransmitters in the synapse. Opioids removed the brakes while endangering breath.

Alcohol multiplied inhibition while rewarding continued intake. Cannabis adjusted the volume of reward pathways. This was not chaos—it was chemistry, choreographed by the way drugs interact.

The second act played out in the hospital. She was found unconscious; machines kept her alive while clinicians worked. Later she counted the toll: three strokes, a heart attack, and a brush with death measured in minutes (Cohen, 2021a; CBS News, 2018). Even years later she described blind spots and brain fog, the price of oxygen lost echoing across time. Her candour turned a private collapse into public instruction: polydrug nights are lethal not just because of what is taken, but in what order, in what doses, and at what speed. A stimulant first stamps value onto everything that follows. Serotonin floods promise connection. Cocaine ensures the signals linger. A depressant removes hesitation. An opioid crowns it all with hush that feels like safety—until breath stops.

Lovato told the story so others could map their own nights before they fill with dancers they cannot dismiss. She named the sequence, the stakes, and the survival. That honesty matters, because it lets us discuss the chemistry without losing the person who lived it—and nearly didn't.

The Lesson of "Many Dancers"

Demi Lovato's near-fatal overdose in 2018 is more than a celebrity story; it is a vivid case study in how human brain chemistry responds when several drugs collide at once. When people hear the word "overdose," they often imagine a single powerful drug overwhelming the system. What makes Lovato's story different—and so useful for understanding—is that she mixed multiple substances in a sequence that shows exactly how fragile and powerful the brain can be.

In neuroscience, we often talk about brain chemicals as if they were simple caricatures: dopamine the villain, serotonin the "happiness molecule," GABA and glutamate as eternal enemies, opioids as the dark force behind addiction. But the truth is more complex.

Dopamine is not bad, nor is it pleasure in pure form. It is a teacher. Dopamine's role is to assign value to experiences: to stamp them with a tag that says "remember this; repeat it" and to adjust expectations when something unexpected occurs (Schultz, 2016; Volkow & Morales, 2015). That is why winning a prize, eating a favourite food, or falling in love can feel unforgettable—and why methamphetamine, which floods dopamine circuits, feels compelling in ways ordinary life cannot match.

Serotonin is also misunderstood. It is not bottled happiness. Instead, serotonin acts as a regulator, smoothing sensory experiences, stabilising mood, and moderating social interactions so they remain tolerable (Cools et al., 2008). When MDMA, often called ecstasy, pushes serotonin systems into overdrive, it produces feelings of warmth and empathy that can make a crowded dance floor feel like family.

GABA and glutamate are often described as opposites, but they are better understood as collaborators. Glutamate excites neurons, turning up signals like raising the volume on a speaker. GABA dampens activity, balancing the signal so it does not become overwhelming (Isaacson & Scanziani, 2011). Together they create messages that are both strong and intelligible. Without this balance, the brain's messages would either vanish into silence or dissolve into noise.

Opioid receptors, too, are unfairly demonised. They are not simply "addiction switches." In evolutionary terms, they are survival tools. They reduce pain, soften fear, and reinforce social bonding. A child feeling safe in a parent's arms or a runner experiencing a natural high is experiencing the opioid system at work (Fields, 2007). Drugs like oxycodone or heroin exploit these receptors, not by creating new feelings, but by pushing the system beyond safe limits.

Drugs of misuse are powerful because they hijack ordinary systems and push them into extremes. They do not invent new kinds of reward or relief; they borrow the machinery of the brain and turn up the volume to unsafe levels (Koob & Le Moal, 2008; Volkow, Koob, & McLellan, 2016). Lovato's "night of many dancers" was an example of every dial being turned at once—each system pushed beyond its natural range until the brain could no longer keep balance.

Why Mixing Drugs Is So Risky

Clinicians say that polydrug use—taking several substances together—is one of the most dangerous patterns they encounter. This is not because of stigma but because of biology and arithmetic. One depressant drug, such as an opioid, already slows breathing by acting on brainstem circuits that control the rise and fall of the chest. Add alcohol, and the effect multiplies. Introduce benzodiazepines, and the reflex to breathe may stop entirely (FDA, 2016; Tori et al., 2020; CDC, 2024).

The language used to describe this risk changes depending on context. In public health, the phrase is "increased mortality risk." At a kitchen table, the truth is said more plainly: "she did not wake up." In the emergency department, it becomes a blunt fact: "the chest won't rise." If luck and speed are on the patient's side, naloxone may be given in time to displace opioids from their receptors and restart breathing (NIDA, 2024). But even successful rescues can leave behind strokes, brain injury, or other permanent consequences.

This is why doctors, nurses, and addiction specialists are so alarmed by polydrug use. It is not simply "more drugs" but a combination effect that pushes the brain's safety systems past their breaking point.

The Hopeful Side: Brains Learn

There is another truth that matters just as much: brains are not only fragile, they are also adaptable. Just as the brain can learn to crave a certain song, place, or ritual because of its association with drug use, it can also be retrained to form new associations. This process is called extinction learning. When old triggers are no longer reinforced, their power fades. A song once tied to cocaine use can, with repetition, become tied to a new and safer activity. A neighbourhood that once held dangerous memories can be walked in daylight with a friend until it carries new meaning. This reshaping of memory and association is the foundation of recovery (Bouton, 2004; Nader & Hardt, 2009).

Recovery is built on steady, unglamorous practices: getting regular sleep, maintaining consistent meals, moving the body, attending therapy, and taking medications when appropriate. Perhaps most importantly, it is built on honest human connection. Over time, these practices retrain the brain. Dopamine comes to value different rewards, serotonin comes to signal safety in new places, and the opioid system comes to recognise healthier forms of relief (Volkow & Morales, 2015; NICE, 2022). The work is slow, but it is how the brain learns new meanings for reward, safety, and comfort.

Teaching Through Story

When explaining these concepts, Lovato's story makes the science clear. Each drug she used maps onto a specific brain system. Methamphetamine hijacks dopamine, forcing the brain to label the experience as vitally important. MDMA floods serotonin pathways, making connection feel guaranteed. Cocaine blocks reuptake pumps, leaving dopamine, serotonin, and norepinephrine stuck in the synapse like a song that cannot end. Alcohol suppresses excitatory circuits while rewarding the choice to keep drinking. Opioids silence the circuits that regulate breathing while offering profound relief. Cannabis can sometimes soften cravings or, depending on dose and timing, remove inhibitions that guard against further use.

This sequence shows that overdose was not about weakness or failure of willpower. It was about biology. The human brain is both immensely powerful—capable of love, art, and memory—and deeply fragile, vulnerable to molecules that mimic natural signals and override natural safeguards.

Why Honesty Matters

Lovato has described her scars without self-pity, which makes her account not just powerful but instructive. Her honesty allows families and clinicians to look at addiction without judgement, to move past myths and towards treatment plans that combine biology and biography (Koob & Le Moal, 2008; NICE, 2022). It also helps people struggling with substance use see themselves in her story, and begin the process of naming their own without shame.

What to Do If Someone You Love Is Using

For families, the science translates into practical actions that can save lives and reduce harm:

- Remove cues where possible. Objects, songs, or places associated with drug use can trigger cravings. Changing the environment helps weaken old associations.
- Reduce access to drugs. This may mean securing medications, limiting cash, or ensuring that substances like alcohol are less available in the home.
- Help build daily structure. Predictable routines—regular meals, bedtimes, appointments—help stabilise the nervous system and reduce chaotic patterns that fuel use.
- Encourage alternative rituals. Replace old habits with new ones: a walk at the time cravings usually strike, a call to a friend, or a different activity in a familiar setting.
- Keep naloxone nearby. This medication can reverse opioid overdoses if used quickly. Family members should know how to use it and stay with the person until help arrives (NIDA, 2024).
- Encourage safe connection. Addiction thrives in isolation. Honest conversations, support groups, and friendships create protective bonds.
- Model calm and patience. Recovery does not happen overnight. Families who remain present and steady send powerful signals of safety.
- Support the basics. Adequate sleep, nutrition, and physical activity make brains less vulnerable to relapse.
- Work with professionals. Therapy, medical treatment, and evidence-based interventions strengthen the brain's ability to re-learn healthier patterns.

Most importantly, remind the person—and their nervous system—that comfort can be found in safer, longer-lasting ways. Every repeated act of safety and support helps the brain build new maps of relief and meaning.

Respect, Not Fear

This story is not a call to fear drugs or to condemn people who use them. It is a call to respect the biology of the human brain. Drugs are dangerous because they exploit the very systems that make us human: learning, bonding, rewarding, protecting. Respect means listening when someone like Lovato describes the reality of overdose. Respect means valuing recovery not as a single dramatic decision, but as thousands of small choices that gradually retrain what the brain calls valuable, safe, and relieving.

Lovato described her "night of many dancers" so others could recognise their own. Science does not diminish her courage; it gives it language. And language is one of the few tools that can reach both stages at once: the public stage where stories are shared, and the private stage inside the brain where new choices wait to be rehearsed.

CHAPTER 4

The Hidden Players

(External Forces - GENES)

> *"That which does not kill us makes us stronger."*
>
> — FRIEDRICH NIETZSCHE

Bedside Manor

Labs—MyFuture?

I remember the stale coffee, the worn fabric of the waiting chair, the chill of air conditioning that never matched the season. It was 1998, and I was shuttling through interviews—moving like fingers following beads on a rosary from one conversation to the next—asked to compress years of training and weeks of thought into a handful of minutes. I'd spent my summers, and then two full years, inside the machinery of the brain, learning the language of neurotransmitters and the stubborn poetry of synapses. I handled mice with the care of a pianist's hands. I implanted micro-osmotic pumps that whispered medicine into tissue. I aimed needles through a stereotaxic frame as if pointing a telescope at a star. I watched numbers crawl across monitors and learned to read their verdicts at 2 a.m.

The science had its own music. It always does. D—Dopamine, the bright trumpet that teaches value: remember this; do it again. A—Adrenaline, the drumline that launches the body forward. N—Noradrenaline, the highlighter that sharpens focus and keeps the eyes on the ball. C—Cortisol, the conductor of stress, brilliant in emergencies and costly in overtime. E—Endorphins, the strings that soften pain and let the system exhale. S—Serotonin, the metronome that steadies mood, appetite, and sleep so the rest of the orchestra can play in time. I learned how each note can climb, how each can crash, how the chords bend when a drug drops into the synaptic cleft and demands the stage. It felt like decoding a private alphabet. It felt like standing outside a cathedral and finally understanding why the bells ring when they do.

Then came an invitation that should make any young scientist say yes on the spot. Dr. Alfred Gilman wanted me to join him. Only a few years earlier, he had won the Nobel Prize in Physiology or Medicine for his work on G proteins—the tiny molecular couriers that sit between a signal outside the cell and a decision inside it.

He showed the world how a touch at a receptor becomes a sentence a cell can read, a sentence that can change the life of a neuron and sometimes the life of a person. Before his work, the chain of events linking hormones, neurotransmitters, and drugs at the cell surface to the sweeping changes inside was mostly a black box. Gilman's discovery opened the box and revealed the translators inside.

A G protein works a bit like a messenger waiting by the phone. Most of the time it sits quietly, switched off, doing nothing. But when a signal arrives—a hormone, a nerve chemical, or even a drug—the signal touches the cell's outer receptor like a call coming in. That touch flips the switch, and the G protein "wakes up."

Once awake, the messenger splits into two helpers that rush off in different directions inside the cell. One might speed up energy use, another might open gates that let important ions flow, another might release calcium, and yet another might influence which genes are turned on or off.

In this way, a single knock at the cell's door turns into a flurry of instructions that ripple through the whole cell—a cascade of signals that can change what the cell does next.

It is both elegant and universal. In neurons, these cascades decide how excitable a cell is, or whether it strengthens the connections that encode memory. In the heart, they set the tempo and force of each beat. In the immune system, they tell white blood cells which direction to crawl in pursuit of bacteria. This is why

Gilman's discovery was so powerful: it was not just a detail of cell biology, but a universal key to communication across tissues and organs.

The impact on medicine is enormous. Roughly a third of all prescription drugs work through G protein–coupled receptors. The inhaler that opens an airway in asthma, the beta blocker that steadies a racing heart, the antidepressant that eases mood—all of them speak the same language, using receptors and G proteins to change what a cell does next.

For a young scientist, to be invited into Gilman's lab was not just a career step. It was a chance to stand at the nerve center of a revolution. He had shown that biology's most mysterious questions—how the outside world talks to the inside of a cell—could be answered with precision. A receptor's touch could be read as a sentence, and that sentence could shape the biology of a cell, the behavior of a brain, and in some cases, the course of a human life.

We met in a room without ceremony. He spoke with the calm cadence of someone who knows the difference between noise and signal. Kind. Curious. Clear questions, room for honest answers. He sketched a program that would let me untangle how neurochemicals talk to one another in the strict light of the lab. Pathways became roads; receptors, doorways; second messengers, couriers. He made the invisible visible. He had earned the right to invite people into that world, and I could feel the pull.

There are moments when life forks and the air goes still. I sat in that quiet knowing the opportunity was real and the consequences were real. I had spent years building the muscles of a laboratory scientist. I could have kept going—tracing signaling arcs with finer pens, asking better questions about the molecules that make a mind possible. All of that was inside me.

Something else lived there too. I had seen what trauma can do to a person—how violence and neglect sink roots into a nervous system and grow vines that pull a life toward the ground. I had seen addiction from the wrong end of a hospital bed, where pupils sometimes tell you more than words. I had held the callused hands of someone who swore they would stop using and meant it with every cell they could still command. I had watched shame silence the room and pain bargain for one more hour of relief. In that stillness between two paths, I heard the DANCES again—dopamine, adrenaline, noradrenaline, cortisol, endorphins, serotonin—and realized I didn't want only to map their steps in a dish. I wanted to help people learn the choreography again in the middle of their lives.

The Joy of Healing

The lab taught me to respect the truth. Patients taught me to love it.

I thanked Dr. Gilman for the invitation—and did the thing that still surprises me when I say it aloud. I turned him down. I chose the bedside: emergency rooms, clinics, and jails, places where biology and biography collide. That wasn't a rejection of science; it was using science for what it's meant to do—help people.

At the time I couldn't explain the choice this clearly. I just felt a pull: you've spent years with microscopes; now go where the heat is. Go where people bleed, shake, lie, hope—and ask you to hold the truth of their body and the truth of their story at the same time.

I went.

In those early years we used what we had:

- Methadone for opioid use disorder.Methadone is a long-acting opioid medicine given at special clinics called OTPs (opioid treatment programs). "Long-acting" means it stays in the body for a long time, so people don't ride the rollercoaster of withdrawal and craving all day. It keeps the opioid receptors—tiny "docking stations" in the brain—from screaming for the next dose, so people can work, parent, and live. The tradeoff: daily clinic visits at first, which can be hard without transportation or childcare.
- Clonidine and "comfort meds" during detox. Detox means medically supervised withdrawal—the days when a person stops using and the body protests. Clonidine calms the automatic "fight-or-flight" symptoms like sweating, chills, and a racing heart. "Comfort meds" are the helpers: anti-

nausea pills, ibuprofen for aches, loperamide for diarrhea, and sometimes a short-acting sleep aid. Detox is a bridge, not a cure. It gets you to the starting line.

- Counseling when we could get it, and creativity when we couldn't. CBT (cognitive behavioral therapy) — learning skills to catch triggers, challenge runaway thoughts, and choose different actions.
- Contingency management — small rewards (like vouchers) for clean tests and kept appointments—the same way you train for a sport with milestones.
- Trauma-informed therapy — care that assumes many people were hurt before they ever used drugs, and makes safety and trust the first step.

We fought stigma constantly. Some pharmacies wouldn't fill prescriptions "because of the patient." We called, explained, called again.

Then the world changed.

Congress passed the Drug Addiction Treatment Act of 2000 (DATA 2000). In effect regular medical offices—not just methadone clinics—could treat opioid addiction. Care moved closer to real life. The message was simple: addiction belongs in health care.

Two years later the FDA approved buprenorphine (brands like Subutex and Suboxone) for opioid dependence. For us, that was relief plus responsibility.

What buprenorphine is, in plain English:

A partial agonist at the mu opioid receptor—Imagine the opioid receptor as a dimmer switch for opioid effects. A drug like heroin or fentanyl slams the switch all the way up—maximum brightness, maximum effect. That can relieve pain or create euphoria, but it can also dangerously suppress breathing. Buprenorphine, by contrast, turns the light on only partway. It gives just enough brightness to ease cravings and stop withdrawal, but not enough to push the system into the danger zone of full respiratory shutdown in most cases. This "ceiling effect" makes it much safer.

High affinity and slow dissociation—Buprenorphine is like a strong hand holding onto a doorknob: once it grabs the receptor, it holds on tightly and does not let go quickly. This means that even if someone uses heroin or fentanyl while on buprenorphine, the dangerous drugs have trouble finding space to act. Buprenorphine is already sitting in the chair, blocking many of the harmful effects. This "receptor occupancy" is one of the key reasons it protects against overdose.

Suboxone combines buprenorphine with naloxone—Suboxone is a brand that includes both buprenorphine and naloxone in one strip or tablet. Taken as prescribed, under the tongue, the naloxone is inactive—it just passes through without doing anything. But if someone tries to misuse the medication by injecting it, the naloxone wakes up. It blocks the opioid receptors and prevents the rush the person is seeking. In other words, it is built with a tamper-resistant safety lock.

Blocks kappa receptors a little—Beyond its main action, buprenorphine also nudges another type of receptor, called the kappa receptor. These receptors are often linked with feelings of despair, stress, and hopelessness. By dampening kappa activity, buprenorphine can lighten some of the emotional weight that drives relapse. Patients sometimes describe it not just as taking away withdrawal, but as lifting a fog.

How we start it (an "induction"), and why timing matters. We ask people to come in with some withdrawal already underway. Why? If buprenorphine arrives too early, it can shove a stronger opioid off the receptor all at once and cause a sudden crash called precipitated withdrawal. We avoid that by waiting for moderate withdrawal (we use a simple checklist called the COWS score) and by dosing slowly, watching pupils, blood pressure, and symptoms. Within hours many people say, "I feel normal." Normal is a miracle when you haven't felt it since high school.

A note about fentanyl

Fentanyl is an extremely strong opioid. It can "hang out" in fatty tissues and cling to receptors. That makes timing tricky. When fentanyl is likely, we often use a micro-induction (also called the Bernese method): tiny doses of buprenorphine, several times a day, while the person tapers other opioids. Think of it as easing two trains onto the same track so they don't crash.

Other tools

- Naloxone (Narcan): the overdose "antidote" you spray into a person's nose. It knocks opioids off their receptors so breathing can restart. Families, friends, and bystanders can use it.
- Sleep and food plans: steady sleep and regular meals lower cravings because a tired, hungry brain grabs for quick relief.
- Social support: a few reliable contacts who answer the phone at 10 p.m. can be lifesaving.
- Practical help: ID cards, transportation, clinic hours that match real work schedules.

Making progress

The science was in the room with us. Partial agonist. Ceiling effect on breathing. High affinity. Those aren't trivia; they're why a person can live long enough to rebuild. Buprenorphine made space for therapy to work. Methadone gave structure where chaos ruled. Naloxone turned a fatal mistake into a second chance.

Most important, the medicine created space for life. When your day isn't ruled by withdrawal and chasing relief, you can talk about grief, about the night your parent didn't come home, about the first pill that made silence feel safe, about the partner who loved you until they loved the drug more. You can talk about work without the constant fear of being found out. You can choose new friends who don't need you to be in crisis to feel close.

I watched people rebuild with quiet wins that never make headlines: fixing teeth, calling a sibling, buying a used car and making every payment, sleeping through the night, learning that "boring" is another word for "stable."

Not everyone cheered. Some called it "enabling." Some pharmacies refused to stock the meds. Some health systems made it hard to get authorized to prescribe, as if treating addiction were a risk instead of a skill. We argued in exam rooms and boardrooms: addiction medicine is medicine. People who use drugs are people. Our job is to protect life and dignity.

Policy moved again in 2023: the federal X-waiver (an extra permit to prescribe buprenorphine) was eliminated. That means more regular doctors and nurse practitioners can prescribe it without jumping through extra hoops. It didn't fix everything, but it widened the doorway.

That's the arc the lab prepared me for: respect the truth, then use it. Treatments aren't magic wands; they're tools. Methadone steadies the ground. Clonidine eases the storm. Detox gets you to the starting line. Counseling rewires habits and meaning. Buprenorphine creates the quiet where life can be rebuilt. Naloxone keeps a mistake from becoming a memorial. And patients—more than any protocol—teach us how to put the pieces together, one clear, ordinary, lifesaving day at a time.

Success Stories

I keep circling back to that quiet room in 1998 and the choice I made. Sometimes I imagine mailing a letter through time to the younger me: the lab will miss you and you will miss the lab, but the people you meet will prove, day after day, that you chose well. Dr. Gilman's discoveries will still light your path in every clinic you enter—G-proteins (the tiny "go-betweens" that carry a message from a receptor on the cell's surface to actions inside the cell) will keep translating biology into behavior. The pharmacology you loved will become the grammar you use to write new stories with patients—stories where despair is not the last chapter.

People call the treatment of addiction a war. I never liked that. Wars have winners and losers; wars leave ruins that become monuments. Good addiction care feels more like irrigation. You learn where the roots are thirsty. You clear the channels trauma has filled with silt. You stake young shoots before the storm. You measure success in harvests—in the ordinary grace of a Tuesday that used to be impossible.

When buprenorphine arrived, people asked what changed. The honest answer: everything, because possibilities changed. Someone who couldn't get through a day without using could now meet you halfway. A person who had cycled in and out of jail could sit still with their own mind. Parents stepped back into lives where children had learned not to expect them. Grandmothers cried in clinic waiting rooms when grandsons walked out with a plan—and a first dose under their tongue. Employers who had seen only risk began to see reliability. Congregations found a new way to practice mercy. The language shifted—from "failure" to "treatment and response."

I think of a woman whose memories had gravel in them—years of heroin, years of loss. She arrived shaking, tired of hearing herself promise. We started buprenorphine. We lined up therapy that didn't scold. We found a group that told the truth without romance or judgment. Her primary care doctor treated the blood pressure she'd been ignoring. We called a dentist. We helped with a job application she no longer had to lie on. She relapsed once when a cousin came home from prison with a bag and a story. She returned the next day and told me before shame could gag her. We adjusted the plan. Two years later she brought a photo: her and her daughter in front of a small apartment that smelled like new paint. No caption needed.

I think of a man who sold oxycodone to pay for oxycodone, a ledger where his heart should have been. He believed any medicine that touched an opioid receptor could only harm. We sat a long time. We talked about what "partial" really means, about "high affinity" (a tight grip on the receptor) and why that grip protects a life from fentanyl (too potent for willpower to outmuscle at the receptor). He asked hard questions. Then he said yes. Months later he called from his car after work. “I forgot to think about pills today,” he said. “Not once.” He laughed, then went quiet. “I didn’t know a brain could be this quiet without dying.” “That feeling,” I said, “is what many people call peace.” He said the word softly, as if it might break.

Addiction writes itself into circuits for reward, stress, and attachment. It’s a biography written in chemistry and experience. That’s why care has to speak both languages. Medication calms the hijacked biology. Therapy, community, and purpose revise the biography so the old chapter stops dictating the ending. This isn’t “swapping one drug for another.” It’s building a life sturdy enough that drugs become unnecessary—a life whose gravity keeps you grounded when the wind picks up.

Stigma is its own toxin. Some still declare that suffering is the “right” way to get sober. Some systems make it harder to get the medicine that helps than the drug that kills. Some whisper that the “consequences” should be allowed to fall. The heart of medicine rejects that. Our work is to see clearly, to name a disease without naming a person as the disease, and to use every safe tool we have to move a life from threat to dignity.

Medicine and Psychiatry gave me a home for this work; the lab gave me a way to explain it—to my patients, to myself in 1998, and to you now. When someone sits in my office with pupils a little too wide and hands a little too still and says they’re tired of the life drugs have built around them, I think about receptors and signals—and I think about their mother’s voice, their first panic attack, the afternoon oxycodone made silence feel bearable. I think about how trauma trains a nervous system to expect pain, and how drugs whisper that pain can stop. It is hard to say no to a whisper you learned to trust more than any person.

Then we build a plan:

- Medication to quiet the receptor-level chaos (buprenorphine or methadone to stabilize; naltrexone when appropriate to block).
- Therapy to give words to old wounds (CBT for triggers; trauma-informed care for what happened before the drugs).

- Sleep that isn't hostage to withdrawal (a regular schedule; brief sleep aids when needed).
- Food as fuel, not a bribe (regular meals to keep cravings down).
- Walks that are proof of life (movement that steadies mood and sleep).
- Work that rebuilds agency.
- People—friends who answer at 10 p.m., groups where honesty is normal, faith communities or meetings where you don't have to lie.
- Practical safety: naloxone for the house and the glove box (an overdose antidote anyone can spray into a nose); simpler refills; clinic hours that match real jobs.

Buprenorphine isn't the whole plan—but it lets the plan happen. It's the oxygen mask you put on before asking someone to help others. It's a bridge with guardrails. It's science with a heartbeat.

I still think of the lab sometimes—the hush of a building at night when experiments keep their own calendar; the moment a graph shows you something no one has seen; the satisfaction of adding a plank to the raft of human knowledge. I miss it the way you miss a place you once lived and loved. But the letter I'd send backward ends the same way every time: the lab taught you to respect the truth; your patients will teach you to love it. And that love—steady, ordinary, stubborn—is what turns treatment into recovery, and recovery into a life.

Final Words

When I look back over the decades—the mornings someone walked in shaking and walked out steady; the afternoons a patient slid a new apartment key across my desk; the nights when a family's number on my phone meant joy instead of catastrophe—I know the choice I made in 1998 was right for me. Dr. Gilman's work showed how a knock at a receptor becomes a decision inside a cell. My work has been to watch how a knock at a life becomes a decision inside a person. Those are not rival projects; they're neighboring rooms in the same house. The G-proteins he taught us to honor still carry the signal, and that signal is the doorway through which therapy, hope, and community step. The bedside is where those messages are translated into lives that can be lived.

When I tell patients I've been here since the beginning of the buprenorphine era, it isn't to boast. It's to steady the ground under their feet. I've seen what happens when medication is respected and used well. I've seen what happens when people are treated as people, not as problems. I've seen clinics and courts move—slowly, then faster—toward the truth that addiction is a chronic medical condition worthy of the same seriousness we give diabetes or heart disease. The law has moved. Clinics have moved. The culture is following—not fast enough, but faster than before.

This chapter isn't a defense of a career choice; it's a field report from the border between pharmacology and mercy. It's a reminder that a molecule can be the difference between a funeral and a future; that a law passed a thousand miles away can open a door on a block where hope once refused to knock; that a quiet conversation in a clinic can rewire a brain and nudge a life onto steadier ground—no headlines required.

If you're reading this because addiction has taken something from you, the story is not over. The same machinery that kept you trapped can be turned in your favor. The receptors that learned craving can learn calm when the right medicine occupies them with a steady hand. The brain that learned to expect pain can learn to expect peace. The road won't be smooth. There will be days when your body remembers a drug with an ache that embarrasses you; nights when old friends call; mornings when you barely recognize the person you're trying to become. Keep going. Ask your clinician about medication for opioid use disorder (MOUD) and how it works. Bring someone you trust to appointments. Ask questions until the answers fit in your mouth. Carry naloxone. Demand respect. Accept help. Practice honesty like a skill—because it is one—and watch how many other skills become possible once that one takes root.

If you're a clinician who's hesitant to treat addiction, remember why you came to medicine. You came to preserve life, to use science to move people from danger to safety, and to feel that quiet relief when a patient gets better. There is relief here. There is beauty, too—the everyday kind that doesn't trend on social media. The frustrations are real, but they are the honest friction of meaningful work. The legal barriers are lower than they were. Your colleagues will help. Your patients will teach you how to persevere.

If you're a policymaker, visit a clinic that pairs medication with counseling. Sit in the waiting room and watch the traffic of small miracles. Talk to pharmacists who wrestle supply, stigma, and prior authorizations; to judges learning that punishment is not treatment; to employers who took a chance on someone stable on buprenorphine and discovered a reliable worker; to nurses who have made a humane induction into an art. The spreadsheets will tell one story; the faces will tell another. Believe both—and fund accordingly. Make lifesaving medications easy to start and simple to keep. Remove hurdles that reward relapse and punish adherence.

I chose the bedside because the bedside is where science learns its manners—where numbers become names and names become futures; where a Nobel insight can become a parent's second chance. I honor the lab every time I explain to a patient how their receptors are learning a new rhythm; every time I argue in a hearing that laws should make survival easier, not harder; every time a clinic day ends with tired gratitude because people arrived in distress and left with a plan.

Addiction is not a sentence. It's a condition that responds to care. In 1998 I chose to sit with people in that condition and do the work. We have more tools now. Better laws. Better data. More clinicians willing to say yes. The work continues, and I'm still here—on the clinic side of the doorway—ready to welcome the next person brave enough to walk through.

CHAPTER 5

The Pressure Cooker

(Society - GENES)

> *"Character cannot be developed in ease and quiet. Only through experience of trial and suffering can the soul be strengthened, ambition inspired, and success achieved."*
>
> — HELEN KELLER

The Mighty Fall Too

The glass on the sideboard caught the light like a dare. He had learned to leave it there—untouched, a prop that reminded him who was in charge tonight. The hotel room hummed with the dull electricity of bad headlines, the way a television hums after you switch it off. Staffers' voices floated through the door: clipped, polite, contagious with worry.

It was October, Cambridge already wearing its early dark. He would speak at Harvard in an hour, and everyone knew why the room would fill. Not for policy. For penance.

He straightened his tie with hands that had done this a thousand times. The mirror gave him the usual face, but the eyes were new: a man who had been forced—again—to see himself as strangers saw him. He could hear the phrases the papers liked: club, night out, a family name pronounced like a verdict. He had made it worse with small, ordinary decisions, the kind that don't look historic at the time: one more round, one more laugh, one more hour he should have given to silence.

A knuckle tapped the door. "Senator? Five minutes."

"Thank you," he said, the old Irish warmth still there, the practiced courtesy. It had gotten him through funerals and fundraisers; it would get him to the stage.

He sat on the edge of the bed and let the flood of years come and go—the brothers, the long corridors of Massachusetts politics, the roar of a crowd when he still believed the crowd could save him. He thought about the private cost: a first marriage that had drowned in public water, children who had learned too early what a headline could do to a breakfast table, the family pact of unspoken concern every time he slipped out at night.

Alcohol did not announce itself as an enemy. It arrived as a balm: a way to quiet the room inside your chest, to blunt the sharp news of living. It liked company; it liked the easy brilliance of a bar where everyone knew your name and no one asked for anything you could not give. It also liked consequences. It left little notes on the desk of your life: missed calls, late mornings, staffers with tight smiles. And, when you were a Kennedy, it left notes for the whole country to read.

He stood. The sideboard glass caught the light again. He moved past it.

The ride to the hall was short, the kind that tempts a man to look out the window and rehearse the story he wishes he had lived. He chose not to. The car stopped. A door opened. The night air had that university smell of old brick and warmed books.

Backstage, a student volunteer clipped on the microphone with hands that trembled more than his. He thanked her, meaning it. He had learned that gratitude lowers the temperature in a room where judgment hangs like fog.

When he stepped out, the applause was careful. Not entirely kind. It wasn't meant to be. He began with the words that always came easy—policy, committee work, the mechanics of law. Then he turned the ship. The hall leaned forward.

"I have made mistakes," he said, and the sentence hovered longer than it looked on the page. He spoke about responsibility in a voice that still held a baritone of hope. He did not bargain with the past; he did not drink from the chalice of explanation. He acknowledged, and for once the acknowledgment felt like the whole point. The words didn't absolve; they arranged. They gave his staffers something to say on the phone besides "no comment." They gave his children a line to circle in the paper and say, "He said it." They gave him a path that looked, for the first time in months, like something other than a loop.

Afterward, in the green room, the untouched glass was waiting again, because somebody always thought hospitality meant the same thing to everyone. He asked for tea. The staffer blinked, then moved. Small miracles rarely make the news.

On the ride back, the city slid by in flats of light. He thought about the work that begins where speeches end: how you make different choices when the barstools are full of friends who still love the older version of you; how you learn to leave five minutes earlier than temptation; how you carry regret like a stone in your pocket instead of a crown on your head. He thought about the men in his family who had found the dark too easy. He thought about being, finally, the age at which you learn that a life is not a single story but a series of edits, some of them public, all of them costly.

The hotel room was as he had left it: the sideboard glass, the hum behind the walls, the stack of messages arranged by urgency. He loosened his tie and sat. He could still hear the hall—its coughs and shuffles and, at the end, that brief, undecided applause. The moment didn't transform him. Moments rarely do. But it placed a stone on the other side of the scale.

The phone rang. His sister's voice, soft and simple: "You did well."

"Thank you," he said, and this time the words landed differently. The room did not spin. The night did not beckon. He poured the tea and let it steam. For once, the quiet felt like company.

The Senator

A Cold March Morning

I remember the cold of that March more than the exact date. Washington still had winter in its bones. The jetway at Reagan National smelled metallic—the smell you catch right before stepping into a plane, a small sealed world where strangers share the same air for a few hours. I was traveling to Boston as an NIH employee, buried in notes and deadlines, thinking about patients and unfinished work. Then I looked up and saw him in the boarding area. Senator Edward Kennedy. Not shielded by security or tucked into a private cabin. Just there, among the rest of us.

He moved like someone who had learned to treat crowds as weather: let them flow, nod, smile, drift. No hard edges. On the US Airways flight to Boston, he did something I had only read about—he took a coach seat. A leather folder. A pen. Ordinary props that made a life look smaller than it was. I found my seat a few rows back and watched an entire lifetime of public service settle into the fabric of a narrow chair.

Airplanes as Temporary Democracies

There's a social contract on airplanes. For a while, the world shrinks to a tin cylinder crossing a continent of cloud, and strangers build a temporary neighborhood. No one owns more space than the armrest allows. Power becomes a folded pair of knees. In that small democracy, I watched a man who had spent his life in a larger one behave like a decent neighbor. He greeted flight attendants. Helped a woman lift her bag. Asked a young man in a Bruins cap whether he thought this would be the year. It wasn't political theater. It was unforced. The public man was also the private man—someone who had learned not to make others carry his fame for him.

Somewhere over the gray stretch of coast, I passed him in the aisle. We exchanged the kind of short words people use in tight places. He asked what I did. I told him I worked at the National Institutes of Health. He smiled in that way people do when a symbol meets a system that still promises more good than harm. He said something kind about research and service. I went back to my seat feeling both the lightness of that moment and the weight it carried.

Trauma as Invisible Cargo

No one escapes the mathematics of their own life. Every kindness answers a previous wound. Every habit has a backstory. I knew even then that the Senator carried a history that would have broken many of us—two brothers taken by bullets, a family expectation that turned grief into public performance, the glare of cameras that can make a person confuse numbing with coping.

Trauma leaves fingerprints on the nervous system. It rewires sleep, appetite, anger, memory. It trains the body to scan for danger, to brace, to soothe. Sometimes the soothing comes in a bottle. Sometimes in work. Sometimes it doesn't come at all.

I have never drunk—not out of purity or vows but out of knowing what my mind can do when it seeks escape. War doesn't end when the shooting stops. It lingers in the child who learned that doors can open to shouting and that quiet can be a trap. Years later, in labs and conference rooms, I still startled at slamming sounds. Scanned faces for threat. Slept lightly as if rest were a trick. That is how post-traumatic stress disorder behaves: it colonizes time, taking your past and playing it on repeat until the future sounds like the same song.

Recognition Without Judgment

On that flight I looked at a man who had also been trained by loss—not in the same way, not in the same rooms, but trained all the same. His struggle with alcohol was no secret to anyone who read the news. What I felt in the presence of the man in seat 15C was not judgment. It was recognition.

Addiction is not a failure of character. It is a set of learned answers to pain. The brain keeps doing what works until the cost becomes unbearable. Alcohol is simple and fast: it turns down the noise in the amygdala, greases the locks on memory, warms a body gone cold from vigilance. It teaches the system that relief lives a few sips away and then recalibrates the entire day around getting there. To the outside world it looks like weakness. To the nervous system it feels like survival. The first time is a choice. The hundredth is not.

In my own case the anesthetic took different shapes—food, work, achievement. Nothing illegal. Nothing you couldn't dress in respectability. White coats make good armor. Schedules can become substances. And yet the body keeps score. Weight builds. Sleep thins. Patience frays. The same circuits that alcohol quiets can be flooded by cortisol, adrenaline, or the reward loop of constant doing.

The Unfairness of Blame

Sitting a few rows behind a man who had weathered storms far more public than mine, I thought about how unfairly we assign blame. We praise resilience when it looks clean. We punish it when it looks messy. We expect a person who has been shattered to heal on a timeline convenient to our attention span. We forget that grief has no calendar. That healing is not an elevator with buttons for faster service.

If the body remembers, the country remembers too. The assassinations that took his brothers were not just family events—they were collective scars. Some pay that bill privately. Some publicly. Some in both currencies.

Why People Drink and How to Help

I do not romanticize alcohol. I have seen it destroy careers, marriages, and bodies. But I also refuse to lie about why people drink. People drink because pain is impatient. Because the nervous system is persuasive. Because the first relief becomes proof that relief is possible, and after that the brain will do almost anything to find it again.

If you want to help someone stop, you cannot begin with shame. You begin with the story. You begin with the day the noise got loud. You begin with the moment their life asked for more anesthesia than their soul could afford.

Leadership, Humanity, and the Descent into Boston

The Senator in that seat had been honest enough, often enough, to name his struggle and keep working. That is not nothing. Public atonement is a rough medicine. It humbles. It does not erase. Yet he kept showing up. He was complicated and human—fit for representing complicated, human people. Leadership is not the absence of injury. It is the ability to carry injury without passing it on.

As the plane began its descent into Boston, the light through the oval window turned the clouds into layered glass. The cabin took on that patient silence of landing. The Senator folded his newspaper. Stood slowly. Let others move before him. On the jetway he paused to talk to a mother with two children holding tin-foil gladiator helmets. He laughed at their seriousness. He thanked the crew. He disappeared into baggage and arrivals and the next thing.

Lessons I Carried Off the Plane

I walked out behind him thinking about how easily we judge the way others survive. Perhaps my not drinking was luck, culture, or a different set of rituals. Perhaps it was early witness to what alcohol had done to people I loved. I will not claim virtue. Only that I know where my mind goes when threatened, and I have tried to train it toward building rather than eroding.

Post-traumatic stress does not care if you have a title. It only cares that your nervous system learned a language of alarm, and it keeps speaking it—wake up, check the door, scan the room. You look fine. You work. You achieve. You hide in plain sight. That is what trauma looks like after the headlines are gone.

Working with patients who name their pain forces me to name mine. It keeps me honest about the stories I tell myself. That day on the plane I promised again to keep my judgments close and my curiosity open. To see the person before the diagnosis.

The Broader Principle: Compassion Scales

In the years since, I have told this story not to claim proximity to a famous man but to show how proximity to anyone can remind us of a principle. Compassion scales. If you can extend it to one complicated person, you can extend it to a city. Policy matters. Programs matter. Money matters. But none of it lands without the simple habit of seeing the person entire—a history, a set of injuries, a set of attempts to heal, a new plan.

Trauma sits at the root of so many addictions. Sometimes it is dramatic. Sometimes it is the chronic abrasion of poverty, racism, humiliation, or isolation. Sometimes it is the one betrayal that taught a nervous system that no one will come. Alcohol, opioids, or a life without rest all answer these with speed and force. My work has taught me to subtract shame and add structure, care, and patience. You cannot scold a body out of its survival skill. You can only teach it another, better way and practice until the neurons believe you.

The Final Descent

When I think back to that day, I think about endings. The Senator would die five years later. My life would take turns I did not foresee. Healing is iterative. It likes small rooms where trust can grow. It respects honesty more than victory. On that plane we were two passengers among many, both carrying invisible weight. Same sky. Same metal tube. Two nervous systems trying to stay in the present without being pulled backward by ghosts. That is the work. Not winning every day. Not pretending the past is gone. Just staying. Breathing. Choosing the next right thing and then the next.

When we reduce addiction to a headline, we erase the architecture of pain that supports it. When we reduce trauma to a diagnosis code, we miss the way it changes the climate inside a person. Compassion is not a luxury. It is clinical skill. It is policy choice. It is how a city treats the parts of itself that are not pretty.

The plane touched down. A cheer went up near the back. We stood. We filed out. The Senator and I went our separate ways. The airport swallowed us both. Yet I walked toward the exit with a clearer sense of what it means to be human in public and private. We are all experiments, some more visible than others. We are all asked to metabolize the impossible and keep walking. If we can build systems that make it easier for others to do the same, then the worst days did not win. They tried to hijack our minds. They did not keep the plane.

What We Learn From Each Other's Eyes

We do not choose the era we are born into. We do not choose the playground rules of our culture, the scripts our media airs on repeat, or the unspoken laws our friends enforce with a shrug and a smile. Yet these forces seep in early. They shape how we see ourselves, how we see each other, and how we come to see addiction. They also shape how addiction looks back at us.

Social norms whisper the invitation to take the first sip. Stigma clamps down on the first plea for help. Media sells a glamorous beginning and a tragic end, skipping the middle where real people live their lives. Peer pressure does the rest—sometimes as a subtle nudge, sometimes as a hard shove. Together, these forces create a pressure field that bends lives in predictable ways. This chapter is about that field, how it distorts choices, and how we can learn to walk through it without breaking.

I have spent a lifetime at the bedside and at the front lines of recovery. In that time, I've learned that one person's story often reflects another's, like mirrors facing each other in a long hallway. No life is identical, but patterns emerge. A teenager in Boston echoes the words of a patient in rural Kentucky. A mother's struggle with prescription painkillers resonates with the grief of a father lost to alcohol halfway across the world. Addiction wears many faces, but beneath the details runs the same current.

Before we talk about how society and culture shape this current, we need a clean picture of the disease itself. Addiction has a trajectory. It is not a moral failure or a single bad decision frozen in time. It is a process—a story that unfolds in steps, each one understandable if we are willing to look closely. When we strip away shame and superstition, the pattern becomes visible. And once the pattern is visible, it becomes something we can name, explain, and treat.

The Trajectory of Addiction

Addiction rarely begins by announcing itself. It creeps in quietly. At first, there is use—social, medical, or recreational. Then misuse. The body adapts. Tolerance builds. Dependence follows. Over time, use becomes compulsive, meeting criteria for a substance use disorder.

Many people cycle through abstinence and relapse not because they are weak, but because addiction is chronic. Like diabetes or heart disease, it relapses when it is not actively managed. And unlike those conditions, the world around a person with addiction is full of cues—smells, songs, bottles, rituals—that trigger craving in the nervous system. That is not a metaphor. It is biology.

The trajectory can unfold in weeks or stretch over years. A doctor's prescription given in good faith can be the first step. A beer at a party can be the first step. So can loneliness. So can untreated trauma. Family history, permissive environments, and depression tilt the slope further. None of these factors guarantee fate, but together they stack the deck. Even relapse, so often misunderstood, is not proof of failure. It is part of the natural course of the illness—and it calls for adjusted care, not shame.

Keep this arc in mind as we look at the forces that accelerate it.

Social Norms: The Water We Swim In

Social norms are invisible water. We move through them without noticing—until we try to swim against the current. In some communities, heavy drinking is a rite of passage, expected at weddings, holidays, and after hard days. In others, pill sharing is treated as casually as swapping recipes.

I meet people who have never seen a holiday table without bottles lined up like trophies. I meet high achievers who learned to mask exhaustion with stimulants because their workplaces reward stamina over sleep. The brain remembers the relief, not the cost. Society claps for productivity and sociability, and the nervous system learns those lessons too well.

Norms also shape what we consider dangerous. Ask a teenager what drug scares them most and they will often name something exotic—cocaine, methamphetamine—while overlooking the pills in the cabinet or the beer in the fridge. Legality and familiarity create an illusion of safety. But legal does not mean harmless. Common does not mean safe. And combining "ordinary" substances—like alcohol and prescription sedatives—multiplies risk.

How we push back against norms:

- Redefine celebration. Build gatherings around food, music, or shared activity instead of alcohol. A karaoke machine or a firepit can create more connection than a row of bottles.
- Model alternatives. Offer sparkling water or mocktails with the same flourish you'd give champagne. Making choice visible normalizes health.
- Name the invisible current. Talk with young people about how "everyone does it" is rarely true, and give them simple language for "Not tonight."

Stigma: The Second Disease

Stigma is the disease layered on top of the disease. It silences pain. It delays care. It convinces people to hide what could be treated.

I have watched patients wait until withdrawal became unbearable before seeking help. I have seen them skip follow-up appointments because they feared judgment. I have heard them lie to clinicians, not because they wanted to deceive, but because honesty had been punished before. Stigma does not just slow recovery; it reroutes it entirely.

Even in recovery, stigma lingers. Job applications still carry questions that make a person's hardest season stick to them like glue. Families swing between support and silence, between love and fear. Shame becomes a permanent tag, altering how people see themselves. When society ties shame to a disease, shame itself becomes part of the disease. It is that simple—and that cruel.

How we push back against stigma:

- Use medical language. Say "substance use disorder" instead of "addict" or "junkie." Words frame a disease as treatable instead of damning.
- Reward honesty. When someone shares, meet it with thanks, not judgment: "I appreciate you telling me." That keeps doors open.
- Separate person from problem. "You're a good person facing a hard illness" lands differently than "You're broken."

Media Influences: Frames That Hold a Life

The media tends to use two lenses for addiction: glitter and catastrophe. First comes the glamour—the wild parties, the fast rise, the rebellious edge. Then the crash: the arrest, the overdose, the mugshot.

What gets erased are the middle years—the long, unglamorous work of recovery. The small victories. The honest routines. The rebuilding of trust. The quiet persistence of making it through a Tuesday without relapse. Those stories rarely make headlines, but they are the heart of recovery.

When public figures share their struggles, the effect can cut both ways. It can reduce stigma and save lives. But it can also invite commentary that reduces a disease to entertainment. We need to receive these stories as instruction, not spectacle—to listen for wisdom rather than consume someone's pain as a cautionary poster.

How we push back against media frames:

- Amplify the middle story. Share accounts of recovery that highlight therapy, setbacks, and rebuilding—the real work people live.
- Question the script. When media glamorizes or catastrophizes, talk about what's missing: What about the years between the party and the mugshot?
- Celebrate public honesty. When a public figure tells the truth, treat it as a gift of instruction, not gossip.

Peer Pressure: The Soft Hand on the Back

Peer pressure rarely looks like a movie cliché—a dare in a dark parking lot. More often it looks like the raised eyebrow when you decline a drink. The coworker who says, "You'll be fine if you take what I take." The friend group that treats bingeing as bonding.

The brain is wired for belonging. Isolation feels like danger. The nervous system will trade almost anything to avoid exile. That is why choosing health inside a group where use equals inclusion feels unbearable.

How we push back against peer pressure:

- Create safe circles. Join or host spaces where sobriety is normal—book clubs, hiking groups, game nights.
- Be the buffer. If someone refuses a drink and another presses, step in: "I'll grab them a soda." Deflecting pressure protects.
- Make belonging the prize. Groups that celebrate the choice to stay sober send a message louder than those that tease it.

A Life in Public: Matthew Perry as a Mirror

Matthew Perry's story resonated so widely because it carried two truths at once: he made millions laugh, and he showed what pain looks like when the cameras are off. His journey into addiction began young. He started drinking in his teens, long before fame, at a time when many young people test limits and lean into social norms. Later, in his mid-twenties, a jet ski accident introduced prescription painkillers into his life. The combination of alcohol, opioids, and the relentless pressure of celebrity became the tinderbox for a struggle that would last decades.

By his own account, Perry was taking as many as 55 Vicodin pills a day at the height of his use, a level that left him dangerously thin and often barely functioning. He moved in and out of treatment repeatedly—more than a dozen rehab stays in total. At one point, he described spending $9 million over his lifetime on recovery efforts. The revolving door of detox, treatment, relapse, and return to work was familiar to clinicians, but shocking to fans who mostly knew him as Chandler Bing, the witty voice of Friends. He later said that during entire seasons of the show he had no memory of filming, the result of cycles of intoxication and withdrawal robbing him of time (Hunt, 2023; Chang, 2021)

The costs were not only emotional or professional. Perry endured severe medical consequences from years of use. In 2018, his colon ruptured due to opioid-induced gastrointestinal damage, an emergency that left him in a coma for two weeks, on life support for months, and recovering from more than a dozen surgeries. He joked later with characteristic dark humor that doctors gave him only a two percent chance of survival. His survival, however, came with scars that were both visible and hidden, and he carried them into the later years of his life.

When he died at 54, early reports focused more on what was not found in toxicology than on what was. Over time, official findings clarified that ketamine toxicity was central to his death. Investigators traced back supply lines and eventually charged several people in connection with the substances involved. To the public, the story arrived in fragments, as it often does when media covers the loss of a beloved figure. To families who have lived through similar tragedies, the headlines carried an echo of the familiar: a story that begins in medical care, strays into misuse, and without careful guardrails, ends in preventable loss (Sherer, 2023).

From his story we can learn at least three things.

First, Perry's trajectory follows the clinical arc of addiction. Early use, often in adolescence. A new drug introduced by accident or injury that provides dramatic relief. Tolerance that creeps upward. Dependence that locks in. Function maintained on the surface—work, friendships, reputation—until cracks spread. Treatment helps, but often requires multiple rounds. Relapse is common, sometimes many times over. None of this means a person is beyond hope. It means they are living with a chronic disease that demands sustained care.

Second, fame changes nothing about the biology of addiction. The brain adapts to substances in the same way whether the person is a Hollywood actor, a teacher, or a construction worker. But fame changes everything about how society responds. The spotlight amplifies stigma, simplifies complex struggles into neat arcs of success or failure, and leaves little room for the middle ground of daily maintenance and partial victories. People without fame experience the same forces, only in quieter forms shaped by neighborhood, workplace, and family culture.

Third, honest storytelling matters. Perry spent much of his later life speaking openly about his illness, writing about it in his memoir, and framing his story as service to others. He often said he wanted to be remembered less for Friends and more for helping people find recovery. For many patients, hearing a familiar face talk about their illness reduced the loneliness that addiction so often brings.

Some have said that his candor gave them the courage to pick up the phone and ask for help. That is the quiet power of vulnerability when it is carried with honesty and generosity.

Lessons From Matthew Perry's Life

- **Addiction has no respect for talent, wealth, or status**—Perry was one of the most recognisable actors of his generation, living a life many would envy. Yet the same brain biology that drives dependence in a teenager experimenting in secret applied to him as well. Addiction is an equal-opportunity illness. Recognising this removes the illusion that some people are "immune" because of success or privilege.
- **Early use and medical exposure are real risks**—His drinking began in adolescence, a time when the brain is still wiring reward and impulse systems. Later, a doctor's prescription for painkillers after a jet ski accident became the doorway to opioids. For families and clinicians, his story underlines how seemingly ordinary starting points—a party drink, a post-injury prescription—can tilt into dependence when risk factors are present.
- **Tolerance and dependence creep in silently**—Perry himself described how his doses climbed to shocking levels—up to 55 pills a day. That escalation is biology, not choice. The body adapts, demands more, and slowly steals the ability to feel normal without the drug. Recognising this helps shift the lens from blame to treatment.
- **Relapse is part of the chronic course**—He went to rehab over a dozen times. Each round was not a failure; it was another attempt in the context of a long illness. Families and patients alike need to see relapse not as shame but as data—signals that treatment needs adjusting, support needs strengthening, or triggers need to be better addressed.
- **The medical consequences are real and severe**—His colon rupture and near-death experience illustrate what long-term use can do to the body. These were not abstract "risks" but lived realities: coma, surgeries,

pain. Addiction is not only about behaviour—it is about organs, nerves, and tissues reshaped by chemistry.

- **Fame magnifies stigma**—The world saw his weight change, his absences, his struggles in headlines. But many patients experience a quieter version of the same stigma in workplaces, families, or communities. The lesson is that society's gaze—whether from a tabloid or a neighbour—can hinder recovery when it shames instead of supports.
- **Honest storytelling reduces isolation**—Perry said he hoped to be remembered for helping people find recovery, not just for making them laugh. Patients have reported that hearing him speak candidly gave them permission to ask for help. This is the gift of vulnerability: one person's truth can open a door for thousands.
- **Guardrails matter**—His death, linked to ketamine toxicity, is another reminder that substances which begin in medicine can become lethal outside of proper oversight. Families and policymakers can take from this the urgency of better safeguards around prescribing, monitoring, and access.
- **Legacy is more than fame**—Perry left behind not only a body of work but a model of candour. His willingness to say aloud what many hide is itself a kind of public health intervention. We can carry that forward by making recovery talkable at kitchen tables, clinics, and classrooms.

How Social Norms Push the Arc

Think again about the stages of addiction. At every stage, social norms are there, nudging the arc forward.

Initial use often happens in groups. A college freshman is told that blackout drinking is a tradition. A new employee learns that the "real meeting" happens after hours over cocktails. A teenager with a sports injury hears teammates praise pain pills as though relief and euphoria were the same word. In these moments, the first use is not always reckless—it can be obedient, or even strategic. The goal is belonging, fitting in, or finding relief. The risk feels invisible because the group frames it as normal.

Misuse grows faster in cultures that prize short-term performance over long-term health. If grinding through pain, fatigue, or anxiety earns social status, then substances that mute pain, blunt fear, or boost stamina can be seen as tools, not risks. People don't call it "misuse" in these settings—they call it coping, or meeting expectations.

Tolerance and dependence accelerate when environments are saturated with triggers. If every celebration ends with alcohol, if every stressor is answered with a pill, the brain stops separating the ritual from the substance. The ritual becomes a script, and the script becomes a reflex.

Addiction takes root most deeply when a person's world offers fewer alternatives for belonging and relief. The disease lives in the brain and body, but the soil that feeds it is often social. That is why peer groups that normalize recovery are so powerful: they change the soil, offering new rituals and new scripts.

Relapse becomes more likely when a person leaves treatment and returns to the same environment that shaped their misuse. If every friend still drinks every weekend, or every family ritual still revolves around pills or alcohol, the return to health is not a choice—it feels like a wall. And no one should have to climb that wall alone.

Stigma as Fuel for the Cycle

Stigma threads through every stage and makes each one heavier. It turns early warning signs into secrets. It makes treatment the last resort instead of the first. It transforms relapse into exile. Even healthcare can become a barrier when patients feel judged by the very professionals meant to help them.

If we want fewer relapses, we must give people fewer reasons to hide. If we want earlier treatment, we need policies that protect jobs and families when someone seeks care. If we want survival, we must stop treating overdose as scandal and start treating it as the medical emergency it is—one that deserves compassion and science.

The Media's Role in Either Direction

The media can shift social norms in either direction. When stories are told with honesty and context, people see the stages of addiction clearly and understand that recovery is real, if often uneven. When stories are told as punchlines or spectacles, the lesson absorbed is that addiction is either glamorous or shameful. Neither is true, and neither helps a family deciding at three in the morning whether to call for help.

Responsible storytelling shows that addiction is treatable. It makes clear that relapse is not failure but part of chronic illness. It highlights the middle years—the daily work of therapy, medication, and honest routine. It treats people as full human beings, not as headlines or cautionary tales.

Peer Pressure Across a Lifetime

Peer pressure is not confined to high school dare culture. It evolves with us. Teenagers face initiation rituals and social risks. College students face binge traditions tied to group identity. Adults are expected to network at events that revolve around alcohol. Parents may slip into nightly "relief rituals" once the children are in bed. Retirees face loneliness, and alcohol or pills can slide into that space too.

At every age, the antidote is the same: belonging in a group that protects health. Building rituals that give comfort without destruction. Recovery is easier when someone offers you a chair at a table where you do not have to drink to be welcome.

What Matthew Perry's Story Teaches Households Across America

When Matthew Perry spoke about his addiction, many people saw their own lives reflected. Early drinking. Injury leading to pills. A period of high-functioning success that masked struggle. Friends who noticed what you couldn't see. Hospitals. Treatment. Recovery that held for a time. Relapse that startled even him. A public that misunderstood relapse as weakness instead of part of the illness. A desire to help others born from his own pain.

He admitted to losing whole years of memory to substance use. He acknowledged the steady presence of friends who couldn't fix him but refused to abandon him. He tried to transform his experience into service, creating sober living spaces and advocating for recovery. Even the circumstances of his death echoed a broader national pattern—where treatment collides with misuse, and supply chains drift from clinics to the street.

For families across America, Perry's story was not just about Hollywood. It was about them. About how quickly a prescription can become a prison. About how fragile recovery can feel. About how survival often depends less on willpower than on the scaffolding of peers, family, and systems willing to support change.

If you are reading this and thinking about your own life, remember this: the brain learns, but it also relearns. The same plasticity that helped a substance take hold can be redirected toward healing. That effort is easier in a world without shame. It is easier in a family that listens without panic. It is easier in a circle of peers who protect your decision to stay alive.

How to Change the Water Around You

We cannot rewrite the culture overnight. We cannot remove every billboard, cancel every tradition, or reprogram every workplace. But we can change our corner of it.

It begins at home. A household can decide that alcohol is not the only way to celebrate or relax. A loved one who chooses not to drink should be handed something non-alcoholic without commentary, as casually as if they had asked for water. Prescriptions should be handled with the same seriousness as firearms—clear questions about dose, duration, and alternatives; locked cabinets; leftovers disposed of, not saved "just in case."

Language is another tool. A handful of simple sentences—No thank you. I am not drinking tonight. I am in recovery. I am tired and going home early—can protect health and set boundaries. They need practice. Say them aloud until they feel natural. Teach them to your children. Praise them when they use them. Belong to circles where those sentences are respected, not ridiculed.

Recovery itself requires structure. A person in recovery can design a schedule that places support where vulnerability lives. If Friday evenings have always been dangerous, put a meeting there. If holidays have been landmines, plan them with people who understand. If medication for opioid use disorder is part of your care, treat it as what it is: lifesaving therapy. If counseling is needed, frame it not as punishment for the past, but as practice for building a new nervous system.

Changing the water is not grand. It is ordinary. It is a steady layering of small decisions that, together, make health feel possible.

Practical Ways to Change the Water Around You

- **At Home**
  - Keep non-alcoholic options at every gathering and serve them without commentary.
  - Treat prescription drugs with the same seriousness as dangerous tools—lock them, track them, and dispose of leftovers.
  - Model rituals for stress relief that do not rely on substances—walks, cooking, music, conversation.
- **With Words**
  - Practice protective sentences until they come easily: "No thank you." "I'm not drinking tonight."
  - Teach children to say no without apology, and affirm them when they do.
  - Challenge jokes or peer pressure that frame refusal as weakness.
- **In Recovery**
  - Place support where vulnerability lives: meetings before risky times, safe people on speed dial.
  - Plan holidays with those who understand recovery, not with those who jeopardize it.
  - Treat medication for opioid use disorder as essential care, not as a crutch.
  - See therapy as training for the brain, like physical therapy is for the body.

- **In Community**
    - Create gatherings where sobriety is assumed to be normal.
    - Offer protection when someone declines a drink by casually redirecting the conversation.
    - Build peer groups where health is the ticket to belonging.

A Word to Clinicians and Leaders

If you lead a workplace, you are shaping norms whether you intend to or not. The policies you create, the celebrations you design, the way you respond to absence or struggle—all of these teach people what is acceptable. You can normalize wellness days that are truly about rest rather than code for drinking. You can design company gatherings that do not revolve around alcohol, so that belonging is not tied to a glass in someone's hand. You can make it safe for employees to seek help without fear of losing their job or their standing. You can ensure that insurance or benefit plans cover evidence-based treatments, including medications for substance use disorder, without extra hurdles that send a message of mistrust.

If you are a clinician, you carry just as much influence in how a person feels about their illness as in how you treat it. You can take the lead in removing shame from the exam room. Ask about alcohol or drug use with the same calm tone you use when asking about blood pressure. Treat relapse as a stage of care, not a personal failing. Offer treatment pathways that reflect the chronic nature of the illness, not a one-time crisis intervention. Build warm handoffs to support services rather than sending a patient out the door with a phone number on a slip of paper. Teach families how to support without controlling, how to listen without panic.

Your posture matters as much as your prescription. A kind word spoken without judgment can be as therapeutic as the medication you prescribe. A workplace policy that values health over performance-at-any-cost can protect lives as much as any clinic protocol. Leadership—whether in an office, a hospital, or a household—sets the water others must swim in. Changing that water is one of the most powerful interventions we have.

When the Story Is Yours

Maybe your story echoes Matthew Perry's—public, dramatic, punctuated by visible struggles. Or maybe it is quieter, hidden behind the walls of your home, invisible to your neighbours and colleagues. Either way, you are not a headline. You are not your worst day. You are not the entertainment of others. You are a person with a treatable illness living in a culture that sends mixed messages about pleasure, pain, and performance. You deserve care. You deserve dignity. You deserve a circle that keeps you alive and helps you find joy again.

If you feel alone, hold to this truth: humans heal in connection. Begin with one trusted person. Tell them your truth. Then tell another. Each conversation becomes a thread, and threads become a net strong enough to hold you when you feel like falling. Stand in a room where people nod because they know exactly what you mean. Sit with a clinician who speaks to you as a partner, not a problem. Choose peers who defend your health rather than lure you back to a life that almost killed you.

The disease will whisper that you are beyond help. It will use shame as its amplifier. Do not let stigma be its microphone. Lower the volume by remembering that relapse is not proof of failure, but evidence that the illness is still present. Give your brain the time it needs to relearn. Give your nervous system the practice it needs to calm. Give your spirit the space it needs to return.

You do not need to be perfect. You need to stay. To keep breathing. To accept help even when it feels undeserved. Recovery is not about erasing the past; it is about building a present that is wide enough to hold both your wounds and your hopes. The story is yours, and it is still being written.

Closing the Loop

Addiction follows a trajectory. It does not appear suddenly or move randomly; it has stages we can see and name. Social norms can either accelerate that arc or slow it down. Stigma makes each step heavier. Media can mislead with glitter or catastrophe, or it can enlighten with truth and context. Peer pressure can be a trap that pulls someone under, or it can be a lifeline depending on which peers you choose.

Matthew Perry's life put all of this on display. Early use, prescription exposure, cycles of relapse and recovery, health consequences, and finally a death that reminded the public of how fragile and pervasive this illness is. But Perry was not only a celebrity; he was a mirror. His story echoed what millions of families face outside of the spotlight, often without the resources, visibility, or compassion that should be standard. What we owe him—and all those who fight this illness quietly—is a culture that reduces shame, increases support, and treats addiction with the seriousness and compassion it demands.

Takeaways to Carry Forward

- **Addiction has a path.** Knowing the stages makes them easier to interrupt.
- **Culture shapes risk.** Change your corner of the water and you change lives.
- **Stigma is not medicine.** Replace shame with compassion, always.
- **Words matter.** How we talk changes how the brain and body respond.
- **Connection heals.** No one climbs the wall of recovery alone.
- **Relapse is not failure.** It is a stage that calls for more care, not less hope.
- **Media frames matter.** Look for stories of recovery, not just glitter and collapse.
- **Peers are powerful.** Choose circles that protect your health.
- **Every person is more than their worst day.** Dignity belongs in every care plan.
- **The current can shift.** Together we can change the water toward survival and joy.

Conclusion

In this chapter, we have traced the arc of addiction from its earliest steps through the forces that shape it. We have seen how culture creates currents, how stigma multiplies pain, how media frames influence perception, how peer groups set the stage for either relapse or recovery. We have looked at Matthew Perry not as a cautionary tale but as a fellow traveller whose honesty gave others permission to seek help.

Carry this with you: the way we treat each other changes the course of an illness. The words we use can quiet stigma or amplify it. The rituals we build at home, at work, and in our communities decide whether recovery feels possible or impossible. Humans heal in connection, and cultures heal when enough people decide to make survival easier.

The chapters ahead will keep building the practical side of that culture. For now, remember this simple truth: we cannot change the fact that water surrounds us, but we can change the current. Together, we can shift it toward life.

PART ONE

A Tour of the Hijacked Brain (BRAINS)

CHAPTER 6

Reward Central

(Basal Ganglia)

> "*Fall seven times, stand up eight.*"
>
> — JAPANESE PROVERB

Reward Central: When the Loop Takes Over

Samuel L. Jackson did not look like a man circling the edge of collapse. On set, he moved with the precision of someone who understood the rules of professionalism: turn up, know the lines, hit the marks, keep the machine running. Colleagues saw reliability, not ruin. If anything, he appeared calmer than most—focused, contained, the kind of actor directors trust because nothing rattles him. And then the working day ended. He went home, closed the door, and stepped into a different life entirely. The world shrank to a pipe and a flame, to chemical clarity and then chemical erasure, to a cycle that promised escape and delivered a smaller cage each time. Freebasing cocaine was not a rebellion or a thrill; it was a ritual that hollowed out the hours (Vanity Fair, n.d.).

This double life continued for years—quietly, efficiently, almost invisibly—until the night it couldn't. His wife and young daughter found him unconscious on the kitchen floor, surrounded by the detritus of a life collapsing inward: burnt foil, glass, crumbs of the substance that had consumed more than money. He woke not at home but in rehab, dazed and alive, his body cooperating even when everything else had stopped listening. That could have been the ending: a cautionary tale sealed off by a period. A private tragedy, a fading obituary. Instead, it became the hinge on which an entirely different life swung open (Vanity Fair, n.d.).

He left treatment and walked almost immediately into Spike Lee's *Jungle Fever*, taking on the role of Gator—a character so close to the bone that people on set said it felt less like performance and more like exposure. Jackson didn't imitate addiction; he inhabited it with the precision of someone who knew its architecture from the inside. The scenes were electric, uncomfortable, unforgettable. The portrayal was so devastatingly true that the Cannes Film Festival created a special award just to honour it—an honour that exists because one man came back from the brink with his craft sharpened by survival rather than destroyed by it (Vanity Fair, n.d.).

From the outside, the story reads like a cinematic plotline: overdose, rehab, improbable resurrection, artistic triumph, career ignition. The kind of narrative that makes recovery look swift, clean, even glamorous—three acts, satisfying arc, credits roll. But beneath the headline moments was something slower and far less theatrical: deep neural machinery grinding, resetting, resisting and relearning. Jackson has said in interviews that addiction isn't what most people imagine. It isn't a wild, rebellious adventure. It isn't a morality play about weak will or bad decisions. It is repetition. It is narrowing. It is a loop that becomes so familiar the rest of life begins to fade around it. And climbing out is not a single decision; it is thousands of tiny ones made long after the applause, long after anyone is watching (Vanity Fair, n.d.).

This chapter is about those loops and the machinery that powers them. It is about the brain's Reward Central: the basal ganglia—a cluster of deep structures that sit like a silent operations unit beneath conscious thought. These circuits decide what matters enough to pursue, what gets stored as routine, and what eventually becomes automatic. They are the quiet architects of both self-destruction and self-discipline. The same system that once pulled Jackson back toward the pipe with the force of gravity later helped him construct a life defined by consistency, precision, and craft. Habits do not disappear; they are redirected. And your loops—however entrenched, however unhelpful—are not fixed tracks. They can be rewritten, repurposed, and trained toward something that builds rather than breaks. The tools that dug the hole can also be the ones that lift you out.

BRAINS: A Map of the Hijacked System

To keep things grounded, we use one simple acronym throughout this book: **BRAINS**. It is not perfect neuroscience, and it is not meant to replace the complexity of real neural circuitry. Instead, it is a teaching map—a shorthand for remembering the major systems that drugs lean on, distort, and, in recovery, can slowly be brought back online. Think of it as a compass rather than a satellite image: not every detail, but enough to keep you oriented when the terrain feels overwhelming.

BRAINS

B – Basal Ganglia: reward pathways, habit formation, craving, and the shift from intentional action to automatic repetition

R – Reward Chemicals: dopamine, endorphins, and other "pay attention" messengers that tag experiences as worth chasing

A – Amygdala: emotional memory, fear, threat detection, anxiety, and the alarm system that sometimes never switches off

I – Impulse Control: prefrontal cortex, planning, decision-making, future thinking, the mental brakes that make restraint possible

N – Neuroplasticity: the brain's capacity to adapt, prune, strengthen, and rewire—not just in youth but across the lifespan

S – Stress Circuit: the HPA axis, cortisol, and chronic stress responses that can push behaviour from coping into compulsion

In this chapter, we sit with the **B: the basal ganglia**. This is the territory where *liking* and *wanting* start to pull apart, where what once felt pleasurable becomes something simply necessary, and where repetition moves from choice to reflex. It is where patterns become grooves, and grooves become tracks the brain follows without asking for permission.

This is also the region where cue-driven urges can feel as pushy and insistent as Samuel L. Jackson walking back into his old apartment after a day on set—long before he chose rehab over the next hit. The basal ganglia does not care about intention or personal narrative; it cares about what has been repeated, rewarded, and burned in through practice. In recovery, this same system doesn't disappear—it becomes the foundation for new habits, new automatisms, and eventually a new normal.

Reward Central: The Basal Ganglia

Think of the basal ganglia as your brain's reward hub and habit engine. These deep structures help you learn what feels good, repeat it, and eventually run it on autopilot so your conscious mind can focus on other things. In a healthy system, this handover is efficient: you don't relearn how to walk every morning, or reconsider brushing your teeth. The basal ganglia streamline behaviour so the thinking brain can spend its energy on planning, problem-solving, and staying alive in a complicated world.

Anatomically, the basal ganglia include:

The striatum

Think of this as the brain's behavioural sorting office.

Ventral striatum (including the nucleus accumbens): the *"reward gatekeeper"*—it decides what feels worth pursuing, like the internal thumbs-up button that says *yes, do that again*.

Dorsal striatum (caudate and putamen): the *habit autopilot*—it turns repeated actions into routines, the reason you can tie your shoes while thinking about something else.

The globus pallidus

The traffic controller.

It helps regulate movement and behaviour by deciding which signals get a green light and which get held at red—preventing the system from becoming jumpy, frozen, or chaotic.

The subthalamic nucleus

The emergency brake and fine-tuner.

It steps in when actions need quick correction—like stopping yourself mid-sentence or swerving when someone steps in front of you.

The substantia nigra

The dopamine power station.

Located in the midbrain, it supplies the dopamine needed for smooth movement, motivation, and learning—like the battery pack that keeps the circuits running. When these cells fail, as in Parkinson's disease, the system loses power and movement becomes stiff and slow.

These regions talk constantly to one another and to the cortex and thalamus in looping circuits. One loop tracks reward and motivation. Another shapes habits. Others support movement and various forms of learning. They all share players, and they all rely on timing and balance. When these loops are well-tuned, behaviour feels smooth and instinctive; when they fall out of sync, actions can become rigid, impulsive, or hard to stop once started (Nature, 2020; PMC, 2019).

When the system is healthy, you learn to chase what helps and skip what harms. You try something, evaluate the outcome, and adjust without having to think about it every time. But when drugs enter the picture, the signal gets hijacked. The same machinery designed to automate helpful patterns starts automating destructive ones, and the brain gives them priority simply because they have been strongly stamped in.

Dopamine: Not "Pleasure Juice" but a Teacher

In everyday conversation, dopamine is often called the "pleasure chemical," but that misses its real job. In the basal ganglia, dopamine is more like a highlighter pen or a teacher's red ink. When it surges at the right moment, it marks an event as important:

This mattered. Remember it. Do it again.

Neuroscience calls this reward prediction error signalling. If the outcome is better than expected, dopamine bursts. If it is worse, the signal dips. Those changes teach the striatum which actions are worth repeating and which are not. This process happens constantly and mostly outside awareness—every time you choose a route home, pick a favourite snack, or stop bothering with something that never pays off (Nature, 2020; PMC, 2019).

Addictive drugs flood this system. Cocaine blocks the pumps that clear dopamine. Amphetamines push dopamine out of storage. Opioids disinhibit dopamine cells so they fire more. Nicotine excites them directly. Alcohol, cannabis, and sedatives work more indirectly—but they still end up boosting dopamine in the nucleus accumbens, the ventral striatal "gate" for reward learning. The brain reads these chemical surges as evidence that something astonishingly good just happened, even if the body is collapsing in the background. Different doors, same hallway, same loud message: this is a win, do it again (Nature, 2020; PMC, 2019).

Over time, the brain adapts. The drug itself produces less obvious joy. The cues that predict the drug produce more pull. The "like" fades; the "want" persists. That shift—wanting without liking—lives in the basal ganglia (Nature, 2020; PMC, 2019).

You see it in Jackson's story: eventually he was not chasing euphoria; he was chasing normal. The body leaned forward before he did. The loop kept firing even when the reward disappeared, because once the basal ganglia are trained, they do not ask for permission—they simply repeat what has been rehearsed.

How Cues Take Control

Here is where the trap tightens. Early on, dopamine spikes mostly when the drug arrives—when the substance hits the system and the brain registers something unusually rewarding. But as learning deepens, the spike moves backward in time. The brain starts predicting rather than reacting. The lighter, the room, the street, the friend's voice, the smell of a hallway, the clock on the wall—these become predictive cues. The basal ganglia begin to fire at the cue, not just the chemical, treating anticipation as if it were the reward itself (PMC, 2019; Vanity Fair, n.d.).

This shift is subtle at first. You walk past an old bar. Your stomach flips. Your chest tightens. Your breathing changes before you've even had a thought about drinking. You have not ordered a drink, but your body is already preparing—blood pressure rising, attention narrowing, muscles bracing. That urge—the shove from the inside—is your basal ganglia playing back a rule it learned very well: *when I see this, do that.* No conscious choice required.

Over time, cues multiply. The brain begins responding not only to obvious triggers but to the background scenery of a life: a certain time of day, the end of a shift, payday, loneliness, celebration, boredom. You can be blindsided by a craving while washing dishes or hearing a song you forgot you remembered. The loop doesn't ask whether the outcome still makes sense—it simply runs the script it was trained to run (PMC, 2019; Vanity Fair, n.d.).

This is exactly what makes "just stop" such thin advice. You are not fighting a single decision; you are interrupting a well-rehearsed loop. A cue-driven craving is not a thought to be argued with—it is a neurological reflex, rehearsed hundreds or thousands of times. Samuel L. Jackson described years of going to work by day and using by night. The gig, the wrap, the drive home, the silence in the apartment—those became part of his cue structure. By the time he collapsed, the loop was running faster than his intentions could catch it (PMC, 2019; Vanity Fair, n.d.).

The good news is that what was learned can be unlearned—or overwritten. New cues can be built, old ones weakened, and the basal ganglia can be trained to fire in response to different routines. But that process takes time, repetition, and patience. Recovery isn't about erasing a craving; it's about teaching the brain a new ending to an old story.

This cue-shift has a long scientific lineage. Pavlov's famous dogs learned to salivate when a bell predicted food, proving that the brain can transfer a physical response from the reward itself to the signal that comes before it. Addiction follows the same rule—just with higher stakes and deeper wiring. Over repeated pairings, the bar doorway, the lighter click, or the end of a workday become conditioned cues, triggering craving before the drug appears. Modern neuroscience has shown that this isn't just a behavioural trick but a change in the basal ganglia's learning circuits: cues gain motivational power, and the anticipation becomes the driving force rather than the reward itself (Robinson & Berridge, 2008; Everitt & Robbins, 2016).

From Choice to Habit

At first, drug use feels chosen and deliberate. You weigh pros and cons (even if the weighing takes seconds and the scale is biased). The ventral striatum—especially the nucleus accumbens—is active here: it evaluates value, links outcomes to actions, and broadcasts the internal headline *"this was worth it."* In the early phase, behaviour still feels linked to intention, and stopping still feels possible with enough determination (Nature, 2020; PubMed, 2018).

But with repetition, control shifts. Behaviour migrates from the ventral striatum to more dorsal regions that specialise in routine and automaticity. The dorsal striatum is where sequences live—reach, click, buy, use—chained together like a familiar dance. Once encoded, the sequence can run with minimal debate, much like typing your PIN without consciously recalling each number. The brain isn't asking *"should I?"* anymore; it is simply executing a well-rehearsed programme (Nature, 2020; PubMed, 2018).

In lab animals, you can watch this shift on recordings: early in learning, reward-responsive cells fire in ventral regions; as the behaviour becomes habitual, dorsal neurons take the lead. Experiments show that when the dorsal striatum is disrupted, well-established habits fall apart, but early, reward-driven actions remain intact. Human imaging finds a similar pattern—ventral activity during early reward-driven use, dorsal activity during engrained, near-automatic routines. The brain literally transfers the steering wheel from decision-making circuits to habit circuits (Nature, 2020; PubMed, 2018).

In real life, it looks like this:

1. you intend to drive straight home
2. you find yourself parked outside the old dealer's street or bar
3. your mind catches up after your body has already arrived
4. the urge feels less like a choice and more like momentum you didn't notice building

A useful analogy is learning to type versus compulsive scrolling. At first, typing requires effort—locating each key, thinking through every movement. Over time, it becomes automatic, freeing your mind to focus on the content instead of the mechanics. Compulsive scrolling works the same way, but with a different outcome: your thumb moves before you realise you've unlocked your phone. Addiction follows this automatic pathway—the behaviour runs ahead of intention because the brain has practised it into reflex (Nature, 2020; PubMed, 2018).

The basal ganglia are not malicious here; they are efficient. They are doing what they do for every practised skill, from tying shoelaces to driving a car: automating to save effort and free up mental space. In addiction, the problem is not that you have a habit system—it is that the wrong behaviours got the VIP pass, bypassing intention and slipping into the category of *automatic*. And once a behaviour becomes automatic, reversing it is less about willpower and more about rewiring circuits that were only ever trying to help you survive with less thinking (Nature, 2020; PubMed, 2018).

Adolescence: When the System Is Extra Teachable

The basal ganglia—deep brain structures that act like the body's habit and reward engine—continue to mature during the teen years, and they do not do so quietly. Levels of tissue iron (a mineral that helps brain cells use dopamine efficiently, like oil keeping an engine running smoothly) rise in dopamine-rich striatal regions, the parts of the brain involved in motivation and learning through rewards (PubMed, 2019; Nature, 2020). At the same time, the prefrontal cortex—the brain's planning and self-control centre located just behind the forehead—is still wiring itself up. The accelerator shows up before the steering wheel.

This is not a "broken" teenage brain—it is an exquisitely sensitive learning system. Rewards land harder. Habits take root faster. Novelty flashes brighter. And in emotionally charged or peer-heavy moments, risk evaluation can be temporarily turned down, because the reward system reacts faster than the thinking system can respond (PubMed, 2019; Nature, 2020). What adults dismiss as forgettable can strike a teenager like a signature moment—etched, not just noticed.

In the right environment, this sensitivity is a superpower. Teens can absorb skills, languages, music, movement, and social values with astonishing speed—turning repetition into fluency while adults are still warming up. But in a landscape saturated with drugs, high stress, or low support, that same plasticity—the brain's ability to change and strengthen pathways—can carve deep ruts. What starts as curiosity can become choreography, and choreography becomes a path the brain follows without asking.

If you picture Samuel L. Jackson when he first began using, the loops were still soft—wet clay that could still be reshaped. Years later, when his family found him unconscious, those loops had hardened into grooves that ran ahead of intention. The same is true for many who start using in adolescence: the brain is learning at full volume and remembers with fierce loyalty (PubMed, 2019; Nature, 2020).

Circuits You Should Know

Two pathways matter most.

First, the mesolimbic route:

This pathway begins in the ventral tegmental area (VTA)—a cluster of dopamine-producing neurons in the midbrain, like a motivational power station—and sends signals to the nucleus accumbens, the part of the brain that tags experiences as rewarding or worth repeating. This is the classic reward highway—the fast lane where motivation accelerates and the world gains meaning. Most addictive substances dramatically increase dopamine along this path, which tells the brain not just that something felt good, but that it was *important* (PubMed, 2019; Nature, 2020).

Second, the cortico–basal ganglia–thalamic loops:

This is a communication circuit linking three major hubs:

- the cortex — the "thinking brain," responsible for decisions, planning, and conscious control
- the basal ganglia — the habit and action-selection system, weighing past rewards and repeated behaviours
- the thalamus — the relay station that sends the final signal back to the cortex, saying "do this now"

You can think of it like a railway network: the cortex is the control room choosing destinations, the basal ganglia the signal box switching tracks based on past journeys, and the thalamus the dispatcher sending the train back out. In healthy learning, routes change as life changes. In addiction, the same train keeps being routed down the same track—even when the destination is disaster—because the switch has been practised too many times to question.

In a well-supported life, this loop helps you choose actions that match your values and surroundings—study over distraction, rest over risk. In addiction, it keeps selecting the same behaviour long after the pleasure fades and harm takes centre stage. The system isn't stubborn—it's efficient. It repeats the script it was trained to run (PubMed, 2019; Nature, 2020).

And here's the hope: the same teenage-style plasticity that once carved automatic loops can—slowly, with repetition and support—be recruited in recovery to build new pathways that eventually run just as effortlessly in another direction.

What Drugs Do to Reward Central

Most addictive drugs share a final common pathway: they sharply boost dopamine—a chemical messenger involved in motivation, learning, and "pay attention to this" signalling—in the nucleus accumbens, the reward gateway inside the ventral striatum (the part of the basal ganglia that helps the brain decide what is worth repeating). These increases are far stronger and more reliable than almost any natural reward the brain evolved to handle, such as food, laughter, achievement, or connection (Nature, 2020; PubMed, 2018).

- Stimulants like cocaine and methamphetamine flood the system quickly, creating a rapid spike in dopamine—like turning the volume from zero to maximum in a single second.
- Opioids, benzodiazepines, nicotine, alcohol, and cannabis take different biochemical routes: some reduce the brain's internal braking system, others excite reward cells more gently, but they all converge on the same circuitry and send the same loud message—*this is important; remember it* (Nature, 2020; PubMed, 2018).
- Even when they act slowly, the result is the same: the brain tags the experience as unusually meaningful, not just pleasurable.

With repeated use, the baseline settings of the dopamine system begin to shift. The brain tries to protect itself from overstimulation by reducing its own dopamine production and lowering the sensitivity of its receptors—like turning down the brightness because the light has been too intense for too long. This process is called downregulation, and it's the brain's attempt to maintain balance (Nature, 2020; PubMed, 2018).

Everyday rewards—food, friendship, music, nature—start to feel muted or strangely distant. The world becomes flatter, not because anything is wrong with life, but because the reward system has recalibrated to expect bigger signals. Meanwhile, the drug and its cues still cut through easily, not because they are morally special or glamorous, but because they have been paired with large dopamine spikes and strong learning signals, known in neuroscience as *prediction errors*—moments when the brain says, *this was better than expected, stamp it in* (Nature, 2020; PubMed, 2018).

People often say, "I don't get high anymore. I just feel normal." That is the basal ganglia—the brain's habit and reward machinery—trying to preserve a familiar pattern with a tool that no longer delivers the same effect. The system is not chasing pleasure; it is chasing equilibrium. Over time, the drug stops creating *liking* and only maintains *not feeling awful*, which is a very different form of motivation.

The tragedy—and the hope—is that the same brain that adapted *toward* the drug can, slowly and with support, adapt *away* from it. The circuitry that once narrowed can widen again, allowing ordinary rewards to regain colour, meaning, and weight.

Why Stress and Mood Matter

The basal ganglia do not work alone. They are part of a wider conversation across the brain. The amygdala, which is an almond-shaped region involved in detecting emotional significance and possible threat, feeds information into these loops. The body's stress system, known as the HPA axis (a chain of communication from the hypothalamus to the pituitary gland to the adrenal glands), also sends signals that influence how decisions are made. When the HPA axis is activated, the body releases stress hormones like cortisol, preparing you for action but narrowing focus at the same time (Nature, 2020; PubMed, 2018).

Under stress—sleep-deprived, hungry, frightened, ashamed, overwhelmed—the brain shifts its priorities. It becomes less interested in long-term planning and more interested in fast relief. The prefrontal cortex, the part of the brain behind the forehead that helps with self-control and weighing consequences, becomes less effective when stress is high. Delay-of-gratification becomes harder. Risk calculation gets noisy. In that state, the brain leans toward anything that promises quick comfort, even if the comfort is temporary or harmful (Nature, 2020; PubMed, 2018).

When stress is high and the prefrontal brakes are thin, cue–habit circuits have the advantage. The basal ganglia fall back on what they already know: automatic, well-rehearsed patterns. This is why cravings can feel stronger during exhaustion, conflict, or loneliness, and why old behaviours can resurface even after long periods of progress. It is not moral failure; it is the brain conserving energy and choosing the fastest route it remembers (Nature, 2020; PubMed, 2018).

This is also why basics like sleep, regular meals, hydration, movement, and predictable routines are not "soft" extras in recovery. They are direct interventions in the brain's decision-making environment. When stress circuits quiet down, the prefrontal cortex can come back online, and Reward Central—the basal ganglia—can start learning again. Routines lower the background noise so the brain has space to form new patterns instead of replaying old ones (Nature, 2020; PubMed, 2018).

Samuel L. Jackson's turning point was not only detox and a new role; it was also structure. Rehab routines, honest conversations, and dependable support gave his brain new data to work with. The predictability lowered stress, the relationships provided safety, and the repetition created different associations. His recovery was not just willpower—it was a change in conditions that allowed his basal ganglia to build a new loop instead of following the old one.

Learning Theory, Without the Jargon

You can describe addiction as learning that has been supercharged and pushed in the wrong direction. Each time a person uses a drug, several things happen at once, and the brain treats those events as a package deal (Nature, 2020; PubMed, 2018).

- The drug acts as a powerful reward, releasing a surge of dopamine—the chemical that helps the brain decide what is important and worth repeating.
- Cues around the drug—the time of day, the people nearby, the street you walked down, or internal states like boredom or excitement—get linked to that reward. The brain learns not just from the substance, but from the setting.
- The basal ganglia, the brain's habit-forming and pattern-selecting structures, update their internal rulebook: when you encounter this cue, take this action.

At first, this process feels like choice. You notice the decision, think about it, and act. But with repetition, that rule solidifies into a habit. The cue begins to activate the loop almost automatically, before conscious thought has time to weigh in. The brain is no longer asking, "Do I want this?"—it is simply following a well-rehearsed instruction (Nature, 2020; PubMed, 2018).

You can see the same mechanism in everyday life, just on a smaller scale. If you walk past a bakery every morning and sometimes buy a pastry, the smell and the sight of the shop eventually trigger a craving—not because you chose to want it, but because your brain linked the cue with the reward. If you stop buying pastries, the craving fades fairly quickly. With smoking, the structure is the same but the learning is far more intense. The lighter, the break at work, or the first sip of coffee become cues the basal ganglia have rehearsed thousands of times. The urge arrives before the thought, and ignoring it requires planning rather than preference (Nature, 2020; PubMed, 2018).

This is the same system that allows you to learn ordinary skills. It is how you can drive home without remembering each turn or reach for your phone without intending to. The brain automates whatever has been repeated so that the conscious thinking systems can focus on something else. In addiction, the machinery is the same; the outcome is different. The habit forms around a behaviour that carries harm rather than benefit.

You can override the loop, but it is not a matter of willpower alone—you need a plan. Interrupting an automatic pattern means creating a gap between the cue and the action: changing routines, avoiding certain triggers when possible, and practising alternative responses until the brain begins to learn a different rule. Over time, new associations can form and old ones can weaken, but the process is gradual rather than instant (Nature, 2020; PubMed, 2018).

A simple, biology-informed plan looks like this:

- Reduce cue exposure where you can. This means changing the situations that trigger the automatic loop in the first place: taking a different route home, altering the time you pass a familiar shop, removing objects linked to using, or spending less time with people who still use. The goal isn't perfection—it is reducing how often the basal ganglia receive the old signal, giving the brain space to learn something new (Nature, 2020; PubMed, 2018).

- Add friction between the cue and the act. The basal ganglia operate quickly and automatically, while the cortex—the planning and decision-making part of the brain—needs a few extra seconds to come online. Even small interruptions like delaying for two minutes, changing rooms, stepping outside, drinking water, texting someone, or slowing your breath can create a pause long enough for the thinking system to participate. Cravings often rise and fall like a wave rather than increasing endlessly (Nature, 2020; PubMed, 2018).
- Swap rewards. The brain learns by replacement, not just removal. Putting something genuinely rewarding—like a call with a friend, music that shifts your mood, stepping into fresh air, exercise, or a small treat—where the old cue usually lands gives the basal ganglia a different association to rehearse. The aim is not to match the intensity of the drug, but to offer the brain another source of relief or comfort that is safe and repeatable (Nature, 2020; PubMed, 2018).
- Rehearse scripts. Simple phrases like "not today," "I'm stepping away," or "I've got other plans" may sound small, but they matter. Language activates the cortex and provides a ready-made response when the automatic loop starts. Without a script, the brain reaches for whatever is most familiar; with a script, the cortex has something to hold onto when clarity shrinks (Nature, 2020; PubMed, 2018).

Every time you interrupt the loop, the basal ganglia take note. These structures update their patterns through repetition, just like learning a physical skill. The first interruption may feel impossible, the fifth slightly awkward, and the twentieth surprisingly ordinary. Over many repetitions, the groove changes—not all at once, but gradually—until the new response becomes the easier one to follow (Nature, 2020; PubMed, 2018).

A simple example shows how this works in daily life. Someone who usually smokes after lunch takes a different route back to work on the first day and delays for two minutes. The next day, they step outside for fresh air and call a friend instead. A week later, the craving still appears, but it feels thinner and passes more quickly. Nothing dramatic happens in the moment, but the brain is collecting data. The basal ganglia begin to learn that the cue no longer leads to the old behaviour, and the new response slowly becomes the one that feels more natural (Nature, 2020; PubMed, 2018).

Small interruptions repeated often can reshape the brain more effectively than one big burst of willpower (Nature, 2020; PubMed, 2018).

For anyone wanting a simple structure to follow, the same idea can be framed as steps that support the brain while it relearns:

1. Notice the cue: where you are, what time it is, and how you feel.
2. Reduce exposure when possible: change routes, routines, or environments.
3. Add delay: pause for two minutes before doing anything.
4. Move your body: change rooms, step outside, shift posture.
5. Slow your breathing or ground yourself: feet on the floor, long exhale.
6. Contact someone: a quick text or call.
7. Swap the reward: choose something that soothes or lifts your mood.
8. Use a rehearsed phrase like "not today."
9. Repeat the new response whenever the cue appears.
10. Track progress weekly rather than daily—the brain changes over time.

Adolescents, Equity, and Design

If teenage brains are especially good at learning from reward, then policy and prevention need to meet biology halfway. During adolescence, the reward system is highly sensitive—dopamine signals are louder, and the basal ganglia, which help form habits and routines, learn quickly from whatever is repeated. At the same time, the prefrontal cortex, the part of the brain that supports planning and long-term thinking, is still maturing. This makes teenagers both more open to positive learning and more vulnerable to rapid habit formation (PubMed, 2019; Nature, 2020).

That means environments matter as much as messages. Practical design looks like:

- high access to healthy rewards—sports, arts, peer groups, paid work, and volunteering—activities that give teenagers dopamine from achievement, connection, and purpose rather than from substances
- low access to drugs in places where teens naturally gather, not just through rules, but through thoughtful design: well-supervised spaces, transportation options, and safe evening activities
- simple, honest education about how cues and habits work, without shame, explaining that the brain is doing what it was built to do—learn quickly—rather than failing morally (PubMed, 2019; Nature, 2020)

Teaching young people that their brains are powerful learning systems, and showing them how addiction takes advantage of that strength, is more respectful and more effective than waving posters that say "this will ruin your life." When teens understand that their sensitivity to reward is normal—and temporary—they are more able to notice cues, anticipate pressure, and ask for support without feeling defective. Helping them feel capable rather than frightened changes the entire frame: from threat to skill-building.

Equity also matters here. Not all teenagers grow up with equal access to healthy rewards. Some communities have abundant sports teams, arts programmes, safe parks, and affordable activities. Others have few structured options and higher exposure to stress, instability, or drug availability. When the environment offers mainly negative cues and few positive ones, the brain learns from what is there. Supporting adolescent health is therefore not only about individual choice—it is about designing surroundings that make the healthy loop the easiest one to learn (PubMed, 2019; Nature, 2020).

Imaging, Physiology, and What They Show

Modern brain imaging helps confirm what many people in recovery have described for decades. When someone with addiction sees drug-related cues—such as a lighter, a neighbourhood, or even a memory—the nucleus accumbens, which is part of the ventral striatum and acts as the brain's reward gateway, shows strong activation. This region helps signal motivation and "pay attention" learning. In contrast, during well-established routines, it is the dorsal striatum, the part of the basal ganglia involved in habits and automatic sequences, that becomes more active. This shift matches what people report: early use feels like a choice, but later behaviour feels more like momentum than decision-making (Nature, 2020; PubMed, 2018).

With sustained recovery—especially when supported by medication, therapy, social stability, and predictable routines—these activation patterns can change. Brain responses to drug cues gradually decrease, a sign that the cue no longer carries the same motivational pull. At the same time, other networks strengthen, including those involving the prefrontal cortex, the region behind the forehead that helps with planning and self-control. This does not happen overnight, but imaging studies show that the brain remains capable of reorganising, even after years of use (Nature, 2020; PubMed, 2018).

On the physiology side, the basal ganglia support both reward-based learning and motor tuning—meaning they help the brain learn from outcomes *and* coordinate physical activity. This is one reason that active recovery strategies like walking, cooking, working, volunteering, or helping others are so powerful. These activities engage the same circuits that used to reinforce the addictive loop, but now the loop is being rehearsed in a different direction. You are quite literally asking the brain to practise a new pattern until it becomes familiar (Nature, 2020; PubMed, 2018).

Development and the Striatal "Window"

A 2022 youth imaging study found that higher levels of tissue iron in the striatum—a mineral involved in dopamine function and a marker of neural maturation—were linked to stronger reward responses, particularly during adolescence (PubMed, 2022; Nature, 2020). Tissue iron does not mean rust; it refers to the iron stored inside cells that supports energy use and neurotransmitter activity. This developmental window appears to boost the impact of rewards on learning, making the teenage brain especially responsive to repeated experiences.

This sensitivity is both opportunity and risk. If, during those years, the most powerful "highlights" in a young person's life come from connection, mastery, creativity, sport, or belonging, the basal ganglia learn those patterns and build them into automatic routines. If the main source of relief becomes a bottle, a pill, a pipe, or a digital escape, the same plasticity etches that path instead. The brain is not choosing what is good or bad—it is wiring around whatever is repeated and emotionally charged (PubMed, 2022; Nature, 2020).

The takeaway is simple: the teenage brain is not fragile—it is highly teachable. What it learns most often becomes what it expects, and what it expects becomes what feels normal.

What This Means in Clinic

Here is how you might hear this chapter translated in a consultation room.

"Your brain learned a rule," the clinician says. "It wasn't weak—it was efficient. It did what human brains are designed to do: repeat what worked quickly. That is why this feels so automatic now. The good news is that what was learned can be relearned. Our job is to:

- lower stress so the old rule fires less often
- block the drug's reward where we can
- add new, honest rewards on purpose
- practise until the new habit starts to feel natural"

The message is not about blame but about biology. When people hear that their brain is adaptable—that circuits can change with repetition and support—they often feel relief rather than shame (Nature, 2020; PubMed, 2018).

Medications

Medication for opioid use disorder—such as methadone or buprenorphine—stabilises opioid receptors in the brain and reduces the intensity of cravings and withdrawal. Instead of swinging between sickness and relief, the system levels out, giving the person space to function and to relearn routines. Naltrexone blocks opioid reward and can also reduce heavy drinking by preventing the usual dopamine surge. Acamprosate supports alcohol recovery by helping calm the overactive signalling that develops after long-term alcohol use. For tobacco, nicotine replacement and varenicline reduce the power of cues and make urges less sharp (Nature, 2020; PubMed, 2018).

These medications are not moral compromises; they are tools that quiet a hijacked learning loop so new patterns have a chance to stick. In practice, many people describe medication not as making them feel "drugged" but as making them feel more normal, more stable, and more able to focus on the work of recovery.

Behavioural Work

Behavioural interventions speak directly to the basal ganglia's reliance on timing, repetition, and reward. Cue mapping—literally writing down the people, places, times of day, and emotional states that trigger urges—brings the loop into the light. Once the pattern is visible, it becomes easier to interrupt.

Contingency management adds small, immediate rewards, such as vouchers, privileges, or positive feedback, for drug-negative tests or helpful behaviours. It gives the reward system a clean, honest source of dopamine for healthy actions. It works because it is precise, timely, and consistent—three things the brain responds to extremely well (Nature, 2020; PubMed, 2018).

Therapies like cognitive behavioural therapy, motivational interviewing, and trauma-focused work are not separate from the brain story. They change what the basal ganglia are exposed to and strengthen the circuits that help regulate impulses, especially the prefrontal cortex. Over time, thinking and habit systems begin to work together instead of against each other.

Neuromodulation

In some cases, non-invasive brain stimulation techniques such as repetitive transcranial magnetic stimulation (rTMS) can increase activity in the prefrontal cortex. This region helps with planning, decision-making, and slowing down automatic responses. Boosting its activity does not replace the behavioural work of changing habits, but it can support it—especially when low mood, anxiety, or difficulty with focus are making change harder (Nature, 2020; PubMed, 2018).

Neuromodulation is best understood as strengthening the brain's brakes while the reward system relearns.

Hope, With Science Behind It

The headline is simple: you are not broken; you are trained. The basal ganglia are plastic—they reshape themselves around repeated experience. Remove or reduce the drug. Shrink cues where you can. Add healthy rewards. Practise new routines. Over weeks to months, the loop cools. The cue loses its teeth. The habit shifts. People often say, "I feel like myself again"—that is the system updating (Nature, 2020; PubMed, 2018).

Samuel L. Jackson's trajectory—overdose, rehab, Gator, decades of sobriety—is not proof that recovery is easy. It is evidence that even deeply trained loops can be re-tasked when structure, support, and purpose line up. Recovery is not a miracle; it is learning, repeated until the new pattern becomes the familiar one.

Practical Takeaways You Can Use Today

Treat your brain with respect. It learned exactly what you practised. Practise something different.

- Map your cues: people, places, times of day, emotional states. Create distance where you can.
- Add fast but honest rewards to healthy behaviours: a coffee after a meeting, a favourite song on a walk, a message to someone who gets it.
- Guard sleep, food, and movement; they lower stress signals that make relapse more likely.
- Use medications when they fit; they level the playing field so new habits can take root.
- Do this with others. Recovery is not a solo sport. Connection supplies safe cues and real rewards.

A Night Message to Reward Central

Listen up, night owl. Put the bottle down, breathe.
That thrill is cheap, and it keeps your dreams on mute.
Your brain wants peace; your people want you back.

The fridge can wait, the bar can wait, the ghosts can wait.
Sip water. Call a friend. Lock the door you keep unlocking.

Cravings knock. Let them knock. They do not pay rent.
You do.

Sleep sober.
Wake up with your name clean on your tongue.
Coffee, sunlight, paycheck, pride.
Repeat the quiet wins.

Let tomorrow find you ready and here.

Go the f*ck to sleep,
and keep your life awake.

Hey restless mind that wakes when others sleep,
Put down the drink that keeps your future small;
That quick-hit high won't give you what you seek—
It turns the volume down on every call.

Your brain wants calm, not one more restless round;
Let cravings knock without a place to stay.
They don't pay rent, so walk them off your ground—
You're still the one who gets to choose the day.

Drink water, close the door you open twice;
Let ghosts go quiet on the other side.
The morning pays you back at a fair price—
A name you speak with ease instead of pride.

So close your eyes and let the night run deep;
Wake owning what you saved by choosing sleep.

Closing the Loop

The basal ganglia are Reward Central. They learn what to chase, what to repeat, and what to automate. Drugs flood this system and stamp "urgent" on the wrong target. Cues take over. Habits follow. This is not a story about weak will; it is a story about strong learning pointed in the wrong direction.

That is also why there is hope. A system built to learn can relearn. The same circuits that once pushed Samuel L. Jackson toward the pipe now push him toward the set, the stage, and the family he chose to keep. Your own loops can be redirected in the same way—toward work that matters, people who need you, and a life that fits your values.

Fall seven times, stand up eight. The basal ganglia will notice each time you rise. They will write it down. They will return it to you, one quiet, steady day at a time.

CHAPTER 7

Chasing the High

(Reward Chemicals)

> *When everything seems to be going against you, remember that the airplane takes off against the wind, not with it."*
>
> — HENRY FORD

Introduction

If you grew up watching the 1970s television series *Kung Fu*, you may remember the quiet power of Master Po—the blind monk who trained the young warrior, the hero of the show, his "Grasshopper." His teaching was rarely delivered as instruction. Instead, he asked questions that turned the student back toward his own thinking. The wisdom arrived sideways, not as command but as discovery.

Centuries earlier, Socrates used the same method in the public squares of Athens—guiding students not by delivering answers, but by uncovering what they already believed and did not yet understand. And in a different universe entirely, Yoda sits in the swamps of Dagobah asking Luke Skywalker questions that sound simple until they rearrange his sense of self. Across cultures and eras, the message is similar: real learning happens when a teacher does not hand you the truth but invites you to *see*.

My first years in medicine felt like stepping into that lineage.

In 1998, when I started my combined medicine and psychiatry residency at the University of Virginia program in Roanoke and Salem—not the main Charlottesville campus, but the rural off-shoot Dr. Wilford Spradlin helped build—I did not know I had walked into my own version of the "Grasshopper" apprenticeship. He did not lecture. He did not rush. He asked questions that changed how I thought rather than what I thought. And like every student who has ever stood in front of a quiet master, I didn't realise I was being taught until much later.

What follows is his chapter.

Spud

First Meeting With My Master Po

In 1998 I began my combined medicine and psychiatry residency with the University of Virginia program in Roanoke and Salem. It was not the main campus in Charlottesville, but a branch he had pushed into existence—set miles away in the hills of rural Virginia. The hospitals there drew in people from small towns, mining communities, and forgotten backroads. Many carried early signs of the opioid wave beginning to wash through Appalachia, long before most of the country understood what was coming. That was the landscape where I met Dr. Wilford Spradlin.

He walked the halls with us—quiet, observant, watching young residents try to make sense of hearts, livers, and hijacked minds in a community that had very little and needed almost everything.

I first saw him in the hallway outside the consultation room at the Veterans Affairs Medical Center in Salem, Virginia, in the summer of 1998. Fresh white coat. Raw nerves. A new badge that still felt like costume. An older man stood half in light, half in shadow, leaning against the wall as if he had all the time in the world.

"Spradlin," someone whispered behind me—half respect, half warning.

He watched me introduce myself to the team. No smile. No frown. A slow nod that felt like passing an exam I did not know I was taking.

Later that day, someone added the legend: Chair of Psychiatry in the late seventies. Architect of combined medicine–psychiatry training at UVA. One of the minds behind the vision of psychiatry as an internal medicine subspecialty long before "integrated care" became a buzzword (PubMed, 1982; PubMed, 1981). Emeritus now. Known to residents as the "horse whisperer"—not for horses, but for patients, for trainees, and for frightened young doctors like me.

Rounds

I entered residency in the middle of the War on Drugs era, when addiction meant crime in the headlines and punishment in the courtroom. He had trained through the early years of that war and carried the scars and the questions. His presence made my training feel less like a curriculum and more like an apprenticeship in how to think about hijacked minds.

On rounds, he spoke slowly. He never rushed toward diagnosis. He started from observation.

"Describe what you see," he would say.

I began with vitals, labs, CT scans, liver function—the internal medicine checklist. Heart rate. Blood pressure. AST. ALT. Physical exam. Track marks on the arms. Old ligature scars on the neck.

He listened without interruption. When I finished, he folded his hands and shifted the frame.

"Describe who you see."

Not what. Who.

The team fell silent. The chart no longer felt sufficient. Now I needed to talk about family, work, shame, hope, faith, loyalty, betrayal. I needed to bridge cell to culture. Human Biosociology in real time (SpringerLink, 1994).

Human Biosociology

He never said, "this comes from my book," but the themes became obvious years later when I saw Human Biosociology on his shelf. The text traced how biology, personality, and social systems shape one another (SpringerLink, 1994). He had already been teaching those layers at the bedside.

During those years, addiction patients filled our consult lists—endocarditis on medical floors, overdoses in the emergency department, liver failure from alcohol and hepatitis. He linked every case to three questions:

1. What happened in the body.
2. What happened in the person.
3. What happened in the group around that person.

That structure became my operating system for addiction medicine.

Crazy Horses

One night on call, the pager dragged me from a half-eaten meal. Medical floor. A young man with cellulitis, fever, and agitation. History of intravenous heroin use. Multiple discharges against medical advice. "Drug seeker" stamped between the lines.

I presented the case the next morning. Withdrawal signs. Angry relatives. Staff frustration.

Dr. Spradlin listened without a single interruption. At the end he asked a question that felt out of place.

"Do you ride horses, Dr. Rifai?"

I said no.

He nodded. "You will still understand. A horse never pulls against a rein just for fun. Something hurts. Something frightens. Something feels unfair. Your job is to figure out what the horse thinks the rein means."

The patient became the horse. The rein was the hospital bed, the IV line, the antibiotic, the opioid policy, the probation terms, the family's exhaustion.

He pressed me to map each tug.

"What does the IV mean to him."

"What does withdrawal mean."

"What does the label 'addict' mean when the nurse says it within earshot."

This approach did not excuse behaviour—it decoded behaviour. That distinction shaped my entire practice.

The Uncertainty Principle

His work on educational models for psychiatry inside internal medicine sat quietly in the background (PubMed, 1981; PubMed, 1982). He believed psychiatry should be integratable, not siloed. We were the next iteration of that experiment—combined residents walking the same halls where he proved that idea.

"We fought hard for you to exist as a specialty," he told me once. "Do not behave like a consultant who writes elegant notes and disappears. Behave like a physician who owns both heart and mind."

That line became a mandate. I stopped splitting my identity. Addiction care demanded both at once—veins and values, synapses and stories.

Years later, I found his book The Search for Certainty, with themes that crossed philosophy, religion, and psychiatry (AuthorHouse, 2009). During residency, those ideas lived in the questions he posed.

"How sure are you," he would ask after I delivered a confident diagnosis.

"Ninety percent," I would answer.

"Where did the ninety come from. Why not seventy. Why not ninety-eight."

He cared less about the number and more about the structure behind it. Certainty, he warned, can seduce clinicians into closing their ears.

In a world that criminalised addiction with simple narratives, he trained us to hold uncertainty with discipline.

Creating the Narrative

He loved stories. Not case summaries—narratives. He spoke about the early decades of the War on Drugs, the rise of biologic psychiatry, the enthusiasm for new tests and medications, and the mistakes that followed when biology flattened social context (SciSpace, 1965).

"What do you learn when your model fails," he asked. "That is the only exam that matters."

Those conversations prepared me far more than any board review lecture.

Years later I discovered Cross To Bear, the novel he coauthored—a story about a woman moving through despair toward some form of grace (AuthorHouse, 2009). That novel lived inside the way he taught us to sit with suffering.

A woman admitted with alcoholic pancreatitis and severe depression. Husband gone. Children estranged. The chart screamed "non-compliant."

He asked me to list her crosses—trauma, stigma, economics, culture, gender roles, systems.

"Now ask yourself which crosses belong to her and which belong to us."

He reframed addiction as shared burden. Systems hijack minds before substances do.

Human Biosociology gave language to those systems (SpringerLink, 1994).

On rounds, he turned that chain into questions:

- What happens in the cell.
- What happens in the family.
- What happens in the neighbourhood.
- What happens in the culture.

Addiction no longer looked like personal failure. It looked like a biosocial process.

That frame guided my later work with transcranial magnetic stimulation and digital therapeutics. The biology thrilled me. His teaching reminded me to ask who receives access.

In the Trenches

One supervision session stands out. A young man wanted buprenorphine. Regulations tightened. A colleague refused treatment.

"I feel trapped," I told him.

"Welcome to the modern War on Drugs," he said. "Policy pulls one rein. Ethics pulls another. Fear pulls a third."

He asked me to rank my loyalties—patient, law, institution, colleagues, family.

"You will never escape those conflicts," he said. "Act with awareness, not panic."

That conversation followed me years later when prosecutors entered my own life.

Ecce Homo

Despite his résumé—departments chaired, programs built—he introduced himself simply as "Spud." Nurses trusted him. Patients sensed something different. He treated addiction as tragedy and opportunity, not spectacle.

He often asked:

"Who learns more from this encounter, you or the patient?"

If the answer leaned too far either way, something was off.

He trained in an era of rising biological optimism and hardening drug policy. I arrived carrying internal medicine algorithms. Under his supervision, those algorithms expanded to include uncertainty, culture, systems, and story.

Every time I sit with a patient whose mind feels hijacked, his voice returns.

- "Describe what you see."
- "Describe who you see."
- "Name your certainties."
- "Name your fears."
- "List the crosses."
- "Ask who carries which one."

Chapter 7 belongs to him—not as hagiography, but as acknowledgment. My approach did not arise from guidelines alone. It grew from long walks beside an emeritus professor who treated knowledge as a living relationship between cells and culture, certainty and humility.

The War on Drugs shaped our surroundings. His teaching shaped my response.

In every hijacked mind I meet, some part of him sits beside me—steady, quiet, asking the same hard questions and reminding me to hold the reins with care.

From those quiet hallways in Virginia, the story now shifts to a different corridor entirely—one lined not with clipboards and medical charts, but with cameras, microphones, and a country watching.

Chasing Two Highs in Washington

Dopamine: the ghost you chase

Dopamine lives at the centre of every story I tell about hijacked minds. Think of dopamine as a chemical nudge—a small messenger that moves between nerve cells and pushes you toward rewards: food, sex, victory, applause, relief from pain. When dopamine surges for the first time in a powerful way, the brain takes a snapshot that says, remember this, do this again.

With drugs, alcohol, and high-intensity behaviours, that spike comes fast and high—far beyond everyday life. The brain learns in one night what might normally take months. Soon the person is not chasing pleasure, but chasing the memory of the first high. The memory becomes a ghost. The chase becomes a life (Kennedy & Fried, 2015).

A family built on fire

Patrick Kennedy knows that chase from the inside. He did not grow up in a household where addiction was an abstract concept. He grew up in a family where alcohol and mental illness sat at the dinner table. In his memoir and public talks, he describes depression, bipolar disorder, and substance use moving through generations of the Kennedy family, including himself (Kennedy & Fried, 2015; Patrick J. Kennedy, n.d.-a).

The Guardian later reported that when he told this story publicly, some relatives felt betrayed, and a family rift followed (The Guardian, 2015).

A brain under the lights

Picture a brain wired for high output and high expectation. The youngest child of Senator Ted Kennedy. Raised in a family where public service feels like destiny. Surrounded by grief, alcohol, and silence. Then place that brain on the floor of the United States House of Representatives at age twenty-seven. Cameras track every movement. Every vote, speech, and campaign event offers another jolt of approval and adrenaline (Patrick J. Kennedy, n.d.-a; Patrick J. Kennedy, n.d.-b).

The same dopamine system that responds to OxyContin and alcohol also responds to applause and political combat. The brain does not differentiate. It simply registers the spike.

The elusive high

This is why his story belongs in a chapter about dopamine and the elusive high. Patrick Kennedy was not only chasing euphoria in a bottle or a pill. He chased it in policy victories, in election wins, in the hope that one more achievement would finally quiet the noise inside his mind. Dopamine does not care about the source. The circuit lights up and repeats the same instruction: do that again (Kennedy & Fried, 2015).

The double life

He has told the story many times: the staffer knocking on the hotel room door, the family member begging him to return to treatment, the thin layer of control breaking again. In 2006 he crashed his car into a security barrier near the Capitol and later described an OxyContin addiction that led to another stay in rehab (Kennedy & Fried, 2015; Patrick J. Kennedy, n.d.-a).

From a distance, it looks like a fall from grace. A psychiatrist sees a brain pulled far past its normal settings.

When the brain pulls the plug

When dopamine spikes repeatedly, the receptors in the reward pathway—the tiny locks that dopamine fits into—begin to pull back. This is the brain's attempt to maintain balance. It is known as tolerance or downregulation. The same amount of substance or excitement now produces less effect.

Everyday pleasures flatten. A walk with a friend barely moves the needle. A family dinner feels grey. The person feels half-alive without the substance or the rush. That inner dullness drives another search for stimulation: higher doses, riskier behaviour, more dangerous combinations (Kennedy & Fried, 2015).

The cost of secrecy

Kennedy writes at length about bingeing and blackouts—moments when the substance use overtook the intention, the plan, the self. He describes the shame that came when he realised he was failing not just his own hopes, but the public expectations of a Kennedy, and the family legacy of service and sobriety. In his memoir A Common Struggle, he notes: "OUR SECRETS ARE our most formidable adversaries... the older I get, the more I see secrecy as 'the enemy within,' which blocks recovery not only for individuals but for society itself." (Kennedy & Fried, 2015, p. xx). This isn't just about hiding a drink or a pill; it's a cultural system where suffering was masked to protect reputation, while the damage spread quietly. He writes about how his family turned mental illness and addiction into private problems rather than public facts, thereby escaping shame but also stifling help and healing (Kennedy & Fried, 2015).

When he broke that silence—when he publicly acknowledged bipolar disorder and addiction—some relatives reacted with anger, feeling exposed or betrayed. Journalists documented the fallout, noting a rift in the Kennedy household and the anger of family members at a memoir that turned private pain into public narrative (The Guardian, 2015). Clinically, that pattern is familiar: secrecy has its own reward. When someone hides substance use or mental illness, the act of hiding delivers a tiny surge of control, of autonomy, of "no one else knows." That surge engages the same reward circuits (dopamine pathways) that drive use itself. Over time, the secret becomes part of the loop: cue (shame/fear) → act (conceal) → internal signal (relief/rush) → repeat. When Kennedy replaced that loop with disclosure, advocacy, and purpose-driven action, his brain began to seek reward from connection, transparency, and change, not from hiding, high, and loss.

Clinically, that pattern is familiar. Secrecy has its own reward.

The secret reward

Dopamine also responds to secrecy: hiding pills, lying smoothly, sneaking alcohol, passing through airport security with a concealed supply. Each successful deception generates a small internal victory. The brain labels these moments as wins, teaching the person to live in a hidden world powered by chemical surges and private triumphs.

When someone like Kennedy speaks openly, the brain is forced to seek reward in new places—honesty, solidarity, and relief instead of concealment (Kennedy & Fried, 2015).

From chaos to law

Kennedy's turning point came when he began speaking not only about his struggles, but about the brain itself. He moved from collapse to advocacy. In Congress, he became the lead sponsor and coauthor of the Mental Health Parity and Addiction Equity Act—a law requiring many health plans to cover mental health and addiction treatment on equal terms with physical health (Kennedy & Fried, 2015; The Kennedy Forum, n.d.; Patrick J. Kennedy, n.d.-b).

A man whose brain once drove him into walls wrote legislation that changed national policy.

The brain did not heal instantly. Cravings lingered. But the source of reward shifted—from substances to purpose (Kennedy & Fried, 2015).

Dopamine is not the enemy

This is what I tell my patients: dopamine keeps you alive. Hunger pushes you toward food. Attraction pushes you toward connection. Curiosity pushes you toward learning. Problems arise when chemicals or behaviours hijack this system and shrink it down to only the biggest spikes.

Patrick Kennedy's life shows both the danger of hijacking and the possibility of retraining.

The personal at the podium

When Kennedy says "the personal is political," it does not sound academic. It sounds earned. In hearings on mental health funding, he was not debating abstractions. He was a person with bipolar disorder, in recovery, from a family marked by substance use. His brain chemistry sat at the table with him.

The same circuits that once demanded a drink now fired in response to justice and accountability.

Breaking the family code

Going public had consequences. Families rarely welcome exposure. Some members expressed anger and hurt when the memoir was released (The Guardian, 2015). From the outside, it looked like scandal. From inside addiction medicine, it looked like the moment when secrecy collapses and something new can begin.

Shame floods the room. Then truth follows.

Building new circuits in public

Kennedy channelled that energy into organisations—The Kennedy Forum, One Mind, and others—focused on enforcing parity law and expanding brain research (The Kennedy Forum, n.d.; Patrick J. Kennedy, n.d.-b). He turned his life into a teaching tool for lawmakers and families. He also pointed out how insurers still restrict coverage despite legal requirements.

The fight did not end when the law passed. He kept showing up.

Teaching dopamine to slow down

Neurologically, recovery means training dopamine to respond to slower, steadier rewards: sleep, exercise, meaningful work, real connection. For Kennedy, that meant unlearning decades of pairing self-worth with crisis and applause. He has spoken about therapy, peer support, and medication for mood stabilisation (Kennedy & Fried, 2015; Patrick J. Kennedy, n.d.-a).

In my clinic, I see the same shift at a different scale: a patient who once needed the blast of heroin finds satisfaction in a day of safety, a repaired relationship, or a paycheque earned without self-harm. The dopamine release is smaller, slower, and more sustainable.

Biology does not care about fame. The same rules apply everywhere.

The first rush

The first high often arrives in pain: a teenager with untreated depression discovers alcohol; a young legislator drowning in pressure discovers opioids. The brain stamps that moment as magic. The magic fades, and the person spends years trying to recreate a feeling that never returns.

That chase destroys bodies and lives.

A common message

Kennedy stopped long enough to write *A Common Struggle*. The title reveals the lesson: this is not just one man's story. It describes millions who hide mood swings, trauma, and addiction because they fear judgment. When a former Congressman says "this happened to me," other brains receive a new pattern: truth is survivable (Kennedy & Fried, 2015; Penguin Random House, n.d.; Amazon, n.d.).

The arc is full: turbulence, collapse, and a long climb toward purpose.

Dopamine again and again—first as tyrant, then as ally.

The choice of highs

When Kennedy speaks today, he still carries urgency. He challenges insurers who bend parity law and industries that profit from addiction. He repeats that mental health deserves equal protection (The Kennedy Forum, n.d.; Patrick J. Kennedy, n.d.-b). Those statements activate his own reward circuits—and yours. Human brains fire in response to fairness.

The lesson is simple and hard: your brain wants highs. The question is which highs you will train it to seek.

Substances that shrink your world—or connection, honesty, and purpose that expand it.

Patrick Kennedy ran on the first track for years. Now he runs on the second. The same dopamine flows. The meaning changed.

When I sit with patients whose minds feel hijacked, I often think of him—a man who fought Congress and his own brain at the same time. Someone who moved from secret use to public accountability. A story that reminds all of us that behind every spike of euphoria lies a choice: chase a ghost, or use that same energy to build something that survives the crash.

Patrick Kennedy chose the second path. Your brain can too. Dopamine will respond to what you repeat. That is the hard science—and the hard hope—running through this chapter.

Conclusion

In the end, this chapter is not about a single doctor or a single public figure—it is about what their stories reveal about the brain we all carry. Dr Spradlin taught me that every hijacked mind deserves more than a diagnosis; it deserves curiosity, patience, and the discipline to sit with uncertainty. Patrick Kennedy's life showed the same lesson at a national scale: a brain can be brilliant, high-achieving, and still be pulled off course by chemistry, secrecy, and pain.

Dopamine runs through both stories—not as villain, but as momentum. It pushes us toward what feels important, whether that is a drug, applause, relief, or purpose. When the system learns the wrong lesson, life narrows. When it learns a different one, life expands. The same circuitry that fuels collapse can be trained toward connection, advocacy, and meaning.

Spradlin reminded us to ask: *What happened in the body? What happened in the person? What happened in the group?* Kennedy reminds us that recovery does not require a perfect history—it requires a different direction, repeated often enough for the brain to notice.

So the takeaway is both scientific and human: the loops that bind us are the loops that can free us. A hijacked mind is not a broken mind. It is a trained system waiting for new practice. Whether in a hospital room in rural Virginia or on the floor of Congress, the same truth holds: the brain will follow what you repeat. And when repetition shifts—from secrecy to honesty, from chaos to structure, from the first high to the quiet win—the chemistry follows.

Recovery is not a miracle. It is rewiring. Slow, deliberate, and possible. Every. Single. Time.

CHAPTER 8

Haunted by Emotions

(Amygdala)

> "*Drugs are a waste of time. They destroy your memory and your self-respect and everything that goes along with your self-esteem.*"
>
> — KURT COBAIN

I still hear the sirens from Aleppo.

They sounded different from American sirens—lower, rougher, unfinished, as if the metal of the horn carried the war inside it. The sound grabbed the body before the mind understood. My nervous system learned those frequencies before my cortex—my thinking, reflective brain—had the vocabulary for siege, displacement, or mortality. That is emotional memory: the body remembering what the story has not yet formed.

Decades later, in a quiet Pennsylvania hospital, a patient accidentally dropped a metal tray in the hallway. The sound was nothing like artillery—different pitch, different volume, different meaning. Still, my shoulders jumped. My jaw clenched. My heart raced. For a moment, my body returned to Aleppo. The cortex tried to reason—"this is a hospital, not a battlefield"—but the limbic system had already hit the alarm.

The brain does not always wait for facts.

This is the frame for addiction. Emotional memory and anxiety can drive substance use with the same force they once drove survival. The body remembers threat and relief long after the conscious mind forgets—or rewrites—the origin story. Fear, comfort, danger, safety—these are not abstract concepts. They are patterns burned into neural wiring.

A bottle, a pill, a syringe, a vape pen, a slot machine, a glowing phone screen—each was once paired with relief. The nervous system catalogs the pairing, not the consequences. Long after vows of abstinence, the association waits inside the circuitry, patient and confident, like a reflex rehearsed a thousand times.

How emotional memory works—without neuroscience jargon

To understand addiction, we must understand emotional memory—not as metaphor, but as biology.

The amygdala, an almond-shaped cluster buried deep in the temporal lobe, acts as the brain's threat detector. It responds not only to actual danger but to perceived or remembered danger, which means it can sound the alarm long before the cortex has evaluated the situation. The hippocampus—its closest partner—adds context: where the fear happened, with whom, at what age, in what season, with what smell or sound. Together, they form a memory system built not to intellectualize fear but to survive it.

When the amygdala fires, the stress axis—the hypothalamus, the pituitary gland, and the adrenal glands—floods the bloodstream with cortisol, adrenaline, and other survival chemicals. Heart rate rises. Breathing shallows. Muscles tense. Digestion slows. The immune system shifts into rapid-response mode. The brain narrows its attention to threat, shutting down curiosity, creativity, and long-term planning.

This entire sequence can unfold in less than a second. It does not require language, reflection, or permission.

This is why trauma feels eternal—because the body experiences it in real time, even decades later.

Now add chemistry

Some substances quiet the alarm quickly.

Alcohol slows neural firing and smooths the sharp edge of vigilance. Opioids melt physical and psychic pain. Cannabis lowers hyperarousal and softens the constant scanning for danger. Benzodiazepines press directly on anxiety circuits, slowing racing thought. And all of them, eventually, boost dopamine—especially in the nucleus accumbens, the brain's reward-learning hub.

The brain does not write an essay about coping.

It writes a rule:

threat → substance → relief

And because the nervous system's first job is survival—not wisdom, not morality, not long-term planning—it prioritizes that rule above social expectations, health warnings, family promises, or future consequences.

But for a child of the Middle East, that rule forms in a distinctive emotional climate. Emotional memory there carries extra weight: war, sanctions, dictatorship, corruption, displacement, sectarian tension. The nervous system of a boy in Aleppo, Baghdad, or Tehran learns to scan for risk every second—footsteps in the stairwell, a shift in a soldier's posture, a sudden blackout, a rumor in the market.

And that same nervous system learns something else: relief often arrives in secret.

- A shared cigarette on a rooftop.
- A bottle hidden behind prayer books in a conservative household.
- An opium pipe in the shadows of a bazaar.
- A small white pill slipped across a cafeteria table in medical school.

Relief feels sacred because it is rare. Sacred because it is forbidden. Sacred because it works. The moment repeats. The repetition becomes a shortcut. The shortcut becomes a chain.

I grew up inside those contradictions—faith that condemns intoxication, yet streets where substances still change hands; families that recite Qur'an at dusk, yet uncles who drink alone in the garden; a culture that praises patience, gratitude, and trust in God, yet generates nervous systems ground down by inflation, military checkpoints, surveillance, and sudden loss.

Emotional memory in that setting does not only store fear. It stores secrecy, shame, loyalty, longing, and hypocrisy—a complicated map of forbidden comfort.

So when substances appear, they do not simply mute anxiety. They enter a landscape already primed for rescue, ritual, and silence.

In that context, the brain does not just learn *relief*.

> It learns **identity**—who I can be when the danger turns off.
>
> It learns **belonging**—who shares the secret with me.
>
> It learns **escape**—what it feels like to breathe again.

And once emotional memory pairs a threat with relief, the nervous system—any nervous system—tends to follow the rule without asking permission.

"Do that again" — the brain's simplest lesson

Dopamine does not create pleasure, despite the nickname "the pleasure chemical." It creates *importance*, *relevance*, *salience*. It highlights experiences worth repeating because they improved survival odds. Historically, those experiences included finding food, forming alliances, escaping predators, or identifying safe shelter.

But the brain is not sentimental. It does not distinguish between a tiger and unpaid rent, between starvation and loneliness, between bombs and an abusive parent. If the nervous system interprets something as threat, the emotional memory system responds.

So when a substance brings rapid relief, dopamine delivers the evolutionary equivalent of applause.

Yes. That worked. Remember it. Repeat it.

This is why addiction is not a moral failure. It is a learning process—just one learned too well.

Aleppo is everywhere

People often assume trauma must involve war, disaster, or atrocity. But emotional memory does not require international headlines. A child living with unpredictable parents learns to monitor every footstep in the hallway. A teen bullied at school learns to scan every glance. A spouse living with domestic violence learns to read silence as danger.

The nervous system becomes a historian. It writes its own textbook, annotated in heartbeats, muscle clenching, and shallow breath.

The brain memorizes the world not as a map but as a pattern of alarms.

Addiction medicine did not begin in the West

For most of my medical training, I assumed addiction medicine was a modern invention—something born in fluorescent hospital wings in Boston or Zurich, sometime after methadone protocols and DSM checklists appeared. Then I discovered a detail that rewired my sense of lineage: the first dedicated medical treatise on opium dependence, withdrawal, and treatment was written not in the United States or Europe, but in 16th-century Safavid Iran, by a Persian physician named Imad al-Din Mahmud Shirazi (ScienceDirect, 2018).

A Muslim doctor, living in a culture where intoxicants carried religious, moral, and legal weight, still sat down and produced a full manual on opium. Not a warning. Not a sermon. A physician's handbook.

> *"At first it brings joy and lightness of heart.*
> *With repetition, the joy diminishes and the need grows.*
> *Then the body demands what the soul no longer enjoys."*

His manuscript—*Afyunieh*—was astonishingly comprehensive (Moosavyzadeh et al., 2018). It documented:

- medical indications for opium
- techniques of preparation and dosing
- the pleasurable rush known as *neshaat*
- the gradual slide from relief into compulsion
- tolerance and dose escalation
- physical and psychological dependence
- cravings that override reason
- recognisable withdrawal syndromes
- stepwise tapering rather than sudden cessation
- supportive care for patients and families
- management of side effects
- ethical guidance for patients observing Ramadan
- comparisons with Greek, Arab, and earlier Persian scholars (Academia.edu, 2022)

This was not a list of herbal recipes. This was addiction medicine—centuries before the phrase existed.

Shirazi categorized users by pattern of consumption. He analyzed compulsion. He described physiological withdrawal. He advocated gradual reduction over punitive abstinence. He recognized that addiction was not a moral defect, but a biopsychosocial condition requiring structured, compassionate intervention (Scite, 2020; Wikipedia, n.d.).

In my mind, that makes him one of the first addiction medicine specialists in human history.

And he was not an anomaly. For centuries before and after him, Arab and Persian physicians wrestled openly with opium—admiring its analgesic and anesthetic power, while fearing its capacity to hollow out a life. A physician in Baghdad described daily opium use among laborers seeking relief from heat, exhaustion, and sorrow. Medical teachers across the Islamic world warned that opium was the most potent stupefying substance known, capable of tolerance, cognitive decline, respiratory depression, and death, urging precise dosing and clinical restraint (ScienceDirect, 2018; Scite, 2020).

They also wrote about anxiety, but they used different words—*sadness, tightness of heart, restlessness, spiritual distress.* One physician described patients whose thoughts "rebounded like a trapped bird," who returned to opium day after day seeking peace. They were describing emotional memory without yet naming the amygdala.

A story repeated across manuscripts: a man loses a child. The grief feels unbearable. Someone offers opium. Warmth blooms in the chest, tears slow, breath returns. The suffering becomes tolerable for a moment. The brain records a law: **loss + opium = survival**. Years later, any hint of abandonment—an argument, an empty room, a delayed phone call—pushes the same man back toward the pipe or pellet.

I often picture Shirazi writing by lamplight—ink pot nearby, pages of earlier scholars open beside him. Historical accounts suggest he had personally used opium after surviving a night of freezing punishment, developing a tremor that lasted for life. He knew dependence not as theory, but as embodied truth. Who understands emotional memory better than a man whose own nervous system shakes from trauma, and who finds relief in a bitter resin?

He did not judge. He documented. He treated. He tried to help.

Which means addiction medicine did not begin with neuroscience or psychiatry textbooks. It began with physicians living in societies shaped by war, trade, empire, and faith—watching human beings reach for chemical refuge in a world that offered too little safety, too little rest.

A Middle Eastern physician wrote the first clinical roadmap for addiction. That matters—not for cultural pride, but because it restores an erased truth:

the struggle between anxiety, memory, and chemical relief is ancient, global, and deeply human.

A medical lineage stretching across centuries

Avicenna — Ibn Sina (980–1037, Persia)

In *The Canon of Medicine*, he classified opium as both a therapeutic analgesic and a dangerous intoxicant capable of tolerance, respiratory suppression, cognitive decline, and death. Recommended cautious dosing and recognized the risk of habitual use long before modern pharmacology (Wikipedia, n.d.; Scite, 2020).

> *"Opium may quiet pain and bring sleep, but its nature is cold and harmful. Used often, it darkens the mind, weakens the body, and may stop the breath."*

Abu Bakr al-Razi — Rhazes (865–925, Persia/Iraq)

Practiced clinical medicine in Baghdad, using opium for anesthesia and pain management while warning against chronic consumption. Noted emotional distress, restlessness, and compulsive return to the drug—an early recognition of psychological dependence (Wikipedia, n.d.).

> *"Give opium only when the suffering is great, and never without measure, for the patient who becomes accustomed will seek it beyond need."*

Ibn al-Baitar (1197–1248, Andalusia/Syria)

Compiled extensive pharmacopeias that described opium's sedating properties, its ability to "stupefy," impair judgment, and produce physiological danger at high doses. His catalogues circulated across Islamic medical schools and influenced prescribing caution (Wikipedia, n.d.).

Ibn al-Jazzar (898–980, Kairouan, North Africa)

Recorded opium use for insomnia, intestinal illness, and grief, but emphasized its dangers when used repeatedly for emotional relief—an early articulation of emotional memory driving substance reinforcement (Scite, 2020).

Anonymous Baghdad physicians (13th–15th centuries)

Medical texts from Abbasid Baghdad described daily opium consumption among laborers in hot climates seeking relief from exhaustion and social strain. Documented dose escalation, social withdrawal, and fatal toxicity—mirroring contemporary epidemiology (Academia.edu, 2020).

> *"Among laborers, the poppy became daily bread—taken not for pleasure, but so the troubles of life might loosen their grip for a short time."*

Mamluk-era Cairo physicians (15th century, Egypt)

Chroniclers recorded cases of students overdosing on plant-derived stimulants and opioids used to enhance cognition, resulting in disability, prolonged recovery, and identity change—evidence of neurological and psychosocial harm (Academia.edu, 2020).

> *"A single dose may sharpen the memory for study,*
> *yet too much scatters the wits for a lifetime."*

Safavid court physicians beyond Shirazi (16th–17th centuries, Iran)

Warned political leaders about the growing cultural normalization of opium, linking habitual use to economic instability, family breakdown, and reduced civic functioning. Advocated regulation and moral-medical education (ScienceDirect, 2018).

> *"If the people use it without restraint, the kingdom will weaken.*
> *For a nation depends upon minds that are clear."*

Shared medical themes across the tradition

Across these centuries and regions, physicians:

- recognized tolerance, withdrawal, craving, and relapse
- linked opium use to emotional pain, trauma, boredom, and social stress
- viewed addiction as treatable, not criminal

- recommended gradual tapering rather than abrupt abstinence
- emphasized supportive environments, family involvement, and dignity
- understood addiction as biological, psychological, social, and spiritual

In other words—what modern addiction psychiatry now calls a biopsychosocial model already existed in medieval Islamic medicine (Wikipedia, n.d.; Scite, 2020).

We are not the beginning of the story.

We are the continuation.

Emotional memory in medieval language

Medieval Islamic physicians recognized anxiety but named it differently:

- "restlessness of the heart"
- "melancholic temperament"
- "tightness of the chest"
- "persistent agitation"
- "distress that grows in solitude"

They documented patients who turned to opium daily to calm emotional storms—grief, loneliness, shame, financial desperation, political instability, or domestic conflict. They noted how the relief reinforced the behavior, creating a feedback loop.

They described emotional memory without neural vocabulary. They observed the same pattern we see now in brain scans and clinical interviews.

A man loses a child. Someone offers opium. Warmth spreads. Tears stop. A rule forms.

The drug is not chosen—it is remembered.

The physician who understood from the inside

History contains a detail scholars often overlook: Shirazi reportedly used opium himself after enduring freezing punishment during his medical training, leaving him with lifelong tremor and chronic pain (Academia.edu, 2022). He did not write about addiction as an outsider, judge, or prosecutor. He wrote as a witness—and patient.

He knew what relief felt like. He knew what dependence felt like. He knew what shame felt like.

This matters.

Addiction medicine has always been shaped by those who understood suffering from within.

A straight line from Safavid Iran to small-town America

When I treat addiction today, I feel connected to a lineage—physicians writing treatment plans long before methadone existed, long before urine drug screens, long before DSM criteria. They saw what we see now: emotional memory drives drug use, and anxiety keeps the cycle spinning (ScienceDirect, 2018).

The nervous system has not changed. Only the cultural wardrobe has.

Trauma without headlines

One of my patients grew up in a small American town near coal country. No bombs. No checkpoints. No militias. But trauma does not require artillery. His father's rage arrived like an airstrike—sudden, unpredictable, unavoidable. His mother's depression cast the house into long emotional sieges. Police cruisers appeared often enough that their engines became part of the neighborhood soundscape.

The child learned to hold his breath every time a car pulled into the driveway.

At fourteen, he swallowed his first oxycodone—offered casually by a friend recovering from a football injury. That tiny pill washed years of dread out of his chest. His shoulders dropped. His jaw unclenched. For the first time, he experienced a full breath without bracing for impact.

Emotional memory formed instantly. The nervous system wrote a survival equation:

1. father's footsteps + pill = safety
2. raised voice + pill = quiet
3. panic + pill = survival

The substance did not create addiction. The emotional memory did.

Within a few years, oxycodone came not from teammates but from medicine cabinets, dealers, emergency rooms, and forged prescriptions. By adulthood, his life had crumbled—job losses, legal charges, custody disputes, ruptured relationships, mounting medical crises. He blamed moral weakness. Society blamed lack of discipline. The nervous system blamed nothing—it simply followed the rule it learned at fourteen.

When he reached my clinic, he was exhausted—not from withdrawal, but from living in a brain that had never known safety without a chemical. Waking up sober meant facing an avalanche of old fear and new shame. His amygdala screamed for protection. His cortex whispered about long-term consequences, but the limbic system drowned it out every time.

During one session, I told him about Aleppo—not to compare suffering, but to reveal its shared anatomy. The sirens, the hunger during sanctions, the trembling in my mother's hands each time the news came on. I explained that the body stores those scenes in a language older than English or Arabic. It speaks in heart rate, sweat, jaw tension, shallow breath, stomach knots. Emotional memory does not argue, negotiate, or analyze. It reacts.

He cried—not because he felt exposed, but because, for the first time, he felt understood.

To widen the frame, I told him about the physicians who came before me—Arab, Persian, Andalusian, and Cairene doctors who treated opium dependence centuries before modern psychiatry had a name for it. A medieval physician in

Baghdad described people in hot, impoverished regions using opium daily to ease distress (Academia.edu, 2020). A surgeon in Andalusia used poppy extract for pain relief during procedures but warned rulers about social decay when it spread unchecked (Wikipedia, n.d.). Avicenna urged caution, noting that opium "darkens the mind, weakens the body, and may stop the breath" if used beyond strict need (Wikipedia, n.d.). Imad al-Din Mahmud Shirazi—writing in 16th-century Safavid Iran—catalogued neshaat, the fleeting euphoria after use, and warned that repetition replaced joy with craving, confusion, and collapse (ScienceDirect, 2018; Academia.edu, 2022).

These physicians did not moralize. They observed. They recorded withdrawal, tolerance, craving, and relapse. They recognized that distress—not pleasure—often drove use. They recommended calm environments, supportive families, gradual tapering, community care, and compassion. They practiced biopsychosocial addiction medicine long before the term existed.

I wanted my patient to know that he was not weak, defective, or uniquely broken. He was human—caught in the same ancient loop described in manuscripts from Shiraz, Baghdad, Cairo, and Cordoba. Threat paired with chemical relief becomes survival learning. And survival learning does not surrender easily.

His story and mine—Aleppo and Appalachia—proved the same truth: trauma does not need bombs. Emotional memory does not erase itself. And addiction does not begin with pleasure. It begins with fear.

When craving is actually memory

Emotional memory does not only push people toward substances—it shapes how they respond to treatment. Afyunieh makes this clear long before neuroscience existed. In the chapter on *neshaat*—the brief joy after opium—Imad al-Din Mahmud Shirazi explains that a small dose can soften sorrow, open conversation, and quiet inner storms. But he warns that repetition rewires the nervous system: what begins as comfort becomes confusion, tremor, sexual dysfunction, dependence, and eventually isolation (ScienceDirect, 2018; Academia.edu, 2022). Another chapter catalogues withdrawal—headache, insomnia, diarrhea, sweating, agitation, craving—and recommends targeted remedies for each. Structured tapering. Warm baths. Sleep herbs. Family support. Gentle supervision. Social reintegration.

This is addiction medicine—symptom clusters, pathophysiology, treatment planning, harm reduction—written in the Safavid dynasty.

And yet, Shirazi also understood something modern clinicians still struggle with: people do not simply use opium "for pleasure." They use it because emotional memory demands relief. Because a nervous system taught by war, shame, poverty, humiliation, grief, or silence cannot unclench by willpower alone.

For me, this history changes the room I sit in with patients. Addiction medicine did not originate in Boston or Zurich in the twentieth century. A lineage runs through Damascus, Baghdad, Cairo, Shiraz, and Isfahan. Middle Eastern physicians stocked pharmacies with poppy resins, then watched those same resins hijack minds—and responded with science, ethics, community, and faith (Scite, 2020; Wikipedia, n.d.). They did not shame patients. They observed, documented, and tried to help within their cultural, moral, and political realities.

That history changes the story I tell myself, too. A boy from Aleppo who becomes a psychiatrist in America carries more than trauma. He carries a medical inheritance—physicians who recognized compulsion, tolerance, withdrawal, and craving centuries before Western medicine named them. A doctor like Shirazi faced the social problem of opium use in Iran and wrote a comprehensive system of care. That makes him—not Freud or William Halsted—one of the earliest architects of addiction treatment.

So when I sit across from a patient in opioid withdrawal, I do not only see a modern crisis fueled by pharmaceutical sales, deregulated markets, and economic despair. I see a story that began centuries ago in my own cultural backyard—human brains under threat, emotional memory screaming for relief, opium arriving as both medicine and trap, and doctors trying to help without full understanding or full power.

And anxiety threads through every stage. Anxiety about withdrawal. Anxiety about being without the drug. Anxiety about the next court date, the next shift, the next family conversation. Anxiety about a future that feels empty. Meanwhile, emotional memory loads the body with old terrors—childhood beatings, war zones, parental abandonment, immigration raids, bullying, medical trauma, discrimination, displacement, racism, homophobia, betrayal, shame. Each memory waits in neurons for a cue: a smell, a season, a voice, a slammed door, the first snowfall, the hum of tires in the driveway.

And treatment environments awaken those memories, too. A patient raised under harsh authority may panic when a doctor sets boundaries. Someone shamed through religion may tense in spiritually framed recovery groups. Refugees may distrust clinics with cameras, metal detectors, or intake forms that ask too much. A person who survived chaos may feel safest only when numbed. Emotional memory does not care about therapeutic intent—it cares about survival.

Addiction is not only about what people use.

It is about what their nervous systems expect.

Understanding that truth is not modern. It is ancient. And it still saves lives.

Neuroscience in everyday language

Modern brain science confirms what medieval physicians observed.

When the amygdala is activated, the prefrontal cortex—the part responsible for planning, moral reasoning, perspective-taking, delaying gratification—temporarily loses power. The person can know all the risks, feel all the guilt, rehearse all the promises, and still reach for the substance.

Not because they are selfish, reckless, or irresponsible.

Because survival circuits outrank reflection circuits. The body remembers first.

A snowfall, a relapse, and a buried memory

A patient once told me she relapsed every year during the first snowfall. No overstimulation, no holidays, no social pressure—just snow. Later, in therapy, she remembered that her father left the family in winter. She recalled standing at the window, watching heavy flakes fall in silence as her life changed forever.

Her nervous system paired snowfall with abandonment.

Decades later, her body still braced for loss. Substances offered temporary shelter.

She grew up in Bethlehem—not far from where my grandfather once walked. Trauma travels through centuries effortlessly. Geography changes. The circuitry doesn't.

In my clinic, one of the newest tools on the shelf looks nothing like medication, talk therapy, or detox. It is called Prism—a form of personalized neurofeedback developed first for PTSD. Instead of revisiting traumatic memories, patients sit comfortably while sensors read their brain activity in real time. Software compares those patterns to a "neural signature" associated with distress, then offers gentle visual or auditory feedback whenever the brain drifts toward threat. With repetition, the nervous system learns a quieter rhythm—just as a singer learns pitch by listening. People describe feeling less jumpy, more grounded, better able to sleep and think. Unlike many treatments, Prism does not require verbal trauma disclosure, which makes it especially useful for refugees, veterans, or anyone who struggles to speak about painful events. Research is expanding quickly, with clinical trials now exploring Prism for depression and generalized anxiety, and early data suggesting potential benefit for alcohol and opioid addiction—conditions where stress circuitry and craving often feed each other (van der Kolk et al., 2016). In simple terms, Prism teaches the brain to stop treating ordinary life like an emergency.

When history becomes clinical guidance

Emotional memory does not just pull people toward substances—it shapes how they seek help, how they respond to authority, and how long they stay in treatment. This is not a modern discovery. Medieval Arab and Persian physicians wrote about mizaj—temperament—arguing that some bodies were born more "sensitive to sadness, fear, and worry," and therefore more vulnerable to opium's comfort (Scite, 2020; Wikipedia, n.d.). They linked vulnerability not only to biology, but to climate, childhood experience, family structure, workload, and social shame. In today's language, they were describing what neuroscience now calls amygdala hyperreactivity, stress-system overactivation, and learned alarm responses—the brain behaving as if danger never ended.

History offers vivid examples. Chroniclers in 15th-century Cairo tell of a young legal scholar who overdosed on a plant-based stimulant used to sharpen memory. He survived, but emerged forever changed—trembling, cognitively slowed, unable to return to his studies. He abandoned law and became a poet instead. To medieval observers, this was a moral tale about imbalance and fate. To a modern psychiatrist, it reads like drug-induced neurotoxicity, emotional memory encoded through terror, and a sudden reshaping of reward pathways that redirected a life.

And the pattern continues. A patient raised under a violent parent may feel panic—not safety—when a physician sets boundaries. Someone shamed with religious language may struggle in a recovery group that invokes God. A refugee who once hid from secret police may freeze in a brightly lit psychiatric clinic with surveillance cameras. Their bodies are not "overreacting"—they are remembering. Anxiety becomes avoidance. Avoidance keeps addiction alive. The cycle tightens.

Modern research adds precision but not contradiction. Genetics can influence how strongly dopamine fires in response to reward. Epigenetics—chemical markings on DNA—can carry trauma responses from one generation to the next. The amygdala, a small almond-shaped structure, can become hypersensitive after years of fear. The prefrontal cortex—the brain's calm narrator—may struggle to apply brakes when overwhelmed (Gray & McNaughton, 2000; Nemeroff,

2016). But the core insight remains exactly what Persian and Arab scholars wrote centuries ago: some nervous systems learn fear—and relief—more intensely, and therefore grip substances more tightly.

Which means treatment must honor biography, not just biology. Some patients need quiet rooms, not crowded waiting areas. Some need time before trust. Some need boundaries delivered softly, not sharply. Some need permission to reclaim spirituality without shame. The road to recovery does not begin with willpower. It begins with understanding the emotional maps that guided someone into addiction—and will guide them out.

The physician's own emotional memory

My emotional memory walks into every exam room with me.

When a patient raises their voice—not in violence, just in fear or frustration—my body travels decades and continents in a single heartbeat. I am no longer in a climate-controlled clinic in Pennsylvania. I am sixteen again, standing at a checkpoint outside Aleppo, soldiers shouting, rifles lifted, dust in my teeth. My shoulders tense before I can explain why. My jaw locks. My pulse climbs. The nervous system reacts long before the intellect arrives.

In that moment, I have two choices.

I can follow the old map—tighten, harden, defend.

Or I can pause.

That pause is not poetic. It is mechanical.

One breath.

Feet on the floor.

A glance at the fluorescent ceiling instead of the imagined sky of home.

The cortex catches up to the amygdala. The war dissolves. The patient reappears—afraid, overwhelmed, asking for help, not permission to pass through a border. The pause protects them from becoming a character in my past. It protects me from reliving it.

That same principle shapes addiction care. Emotional memory will fire; anxiety will surge; cravings may follow. The goal is not to erase the reaction—no therapy or medication can sterilize a human nervous system. The goal is to widen the space between trigger and response. Into that space, people can place a phone call to a sponsor, a walk around the block, a shower, a grounding exercise, a whispered prayer, a practiced coping skill from trauma therapy. Each substitution rewires the survival script:

1. panic + phone call = connection
2. shame + honesty = relief
3. craving + delay = safety

Neurons take notes. Over time, the map changes.

I think often of the physicians who came before me—those writing in Arabic and Persian centuries ago. A medieval doctor in Baghdad sitting beside someone in opium withdrawal could not name synaptic plasticity or glutamate receptors. But he understood something modern neuroscience now measures: a calm presence lowers fear. Warm baths loosen the grip of tension. Encouragement steadies the breath. Structure quiets chaos. Treatment was relational before it was biochemical.

Middle Eastern physicians stood at the dawn of addiction medicine. They prescribed opium for pain and insomnia, then documented how people slid from use into compulsion. They wrote guidelines for tapering, warned rulers about rising dependence, described social shame, family collapse, and the aching need for relief. They practiced medicine while navigating religious prohibitions, political scrutiny, and human suffering that looked remarkably like ours today.

I stand on that ground—part Aleppo, part Appalachia, part Western psychiatry, part inherited medical lineage. When I speak about emotional memory and addiction, I speak from two vantage points: the child who internalized sirens and fear, and the clinician who now recognizes that same pattern in others.

- The nervous system remembers.
- Trauma primes circuits for threat.
- Anxiety becomes the background music of life.
- Substances enter as counterfeit peace—fast, reliable, devastating.

Arab and Persian physicians saw this centuries ago. Modern neuroscience simply provided the MRI images and neurotransmitter diagrams to prove it. Emotional memory drives addiction. Anxiety keeps the cycle turning. So treatment must honor both—not just the chemistry, but the story.

Rewiring, one pause at a time

The nervous system can learn new associations. Not quickly. Not painlessly. Not perfectly. But reliably—through repetition. The goal in recovery is not to erase cravings or delete trauma. The goal is to insert a moment between trigger and action.

- craving + phone call
- shame + honesty
- panic + grounding exercise
- loneliness + connection
- flashback + breath
- urge + time

Each interruption weakens old pathways and strengthens new ones. This is neuroplasticity—the brain's ability to modify wiring based on experience—not metaphor, but biology.

Medieval physicians understood this intuitively. They recommended structure, routine, supportive relationships, and gradual change because they saw what helped patients survive and heal (ScienceDirect, 2018; Academia.edu, 2022).

They practiced neuroscience without the word.

Why emotional memory matters

Addiction is rarely about pleasure.

It is about:

- calming the alarm
- softening fear
- slowing the heart
- loosening the chest
- numbing humiliation
- reducing vigilance
- surviving the next hour

People do not use substances to feel "high." They use substances to feel *normal*—to silence a memory the body refuses to forget.

Anxiety keeps the cycle turning

Every step of addiction involves anxiety:

- anxiety about withdrawal
- anxiety about being without the drug
- anxiety about facing relationships
- anxiety about consequences, debt, custody, employment
- anxiety about stigma and judgment
- anxiety about who they would be without the substance
- anxiety about a future they cannot imagine

Recovery requires treating the anxiety—not just the drug use. Medieval physicians treated both. So must we (ScienceDirect, 2018; Academia.edu, 2022; Scite, 2020).

The nervous system remembers—so treatment must too

Trauma teaches the body to prepare for crisis. Substances teach the body to expect relief. The two form a feedback loop powerful enough to override reason, values, promises, and consequences.

Breaking that loop requires more than detox. It requires new emotional memories—moments when safety arrives without chemicals.

We cannot lecture the amygdala into calm. But we can help it learn.

The final inheritance

This chapter belongs to every patient whose body still startles at harmless sounds, whose cravings rise from wounds with no language. And it belongs to every healer—from Baghdad to Shiraz to Bethlehem to Boston—who has steadied a trembling hand and said, in one form or another:

You are not weak.

You are remembering.

The rest of the story—recovery, reconnection, return—gets written in the space created by that pause.

CHAPTER 9

When Impulse Takes Over

(Impulse Control)

> "*Once you learn to quit, it becomes a habit.*"
>
> – VINCE LOMBARDI

The brain that knows better but acts anyway

I think about my own prefrontal cortex every time I do something reckless. That thin strip of gray matter behind the forehead—no thicker than a fingernail—exists to slow the hand, widen the lens, connect present impulses to future consequences, and whisper wait when the limbic system is already screaming yes (Bechara, 2005). It is supposed to weigh options, remember the long term, and say no when every cell in the body chants now.

Under stress, that front region starts to flicker. Under trauma, chaos, and constant threat, it begins to lose authority (Arnsten, 2009). Under repeated drug exposure, sleep deprivation, and withdrawal, the circuits lose even more control; the neural highways lose insulation, signals jitter, and decisions collapse into reflex (Volkow & Fowler, 2000). From the outside, the result looks like moral failure. From the inside, the story feels like one long impulsive storm.

I grew up in Aleppo watching men act first and think later. Arguments at checkpoints. Fights over fuel lines. Sudden rage in grocery queues. A joke that crossed an invisible line and turned into a beating. My young brain stored every scene. The amygdala tagged each moment with red ink: danger, humiliation, unfairness (LeDoux, 2015). The prefrontal cortex tried to keep up—planning, reasoning, taking perspective—but under bombardment, scarcity, and authoritarian pressure, that slow voice never stood a chance. Survival demanded speed, not reflection.

Those early lessons did not vanish when I left Syria. They lived on as invisible reflexes—alarms without sirens.

Years later, in a quiet Pennsylvania clinic with carpeted hallways and ambient music, I met that same conflict in patient after patient. A man looks at me and says, "I do not know why I keep doing this. I swear I will stop in the morning. By evening my hand is on the pill again." A woman cries after another relapse and says, "I watched myself do it, like a movie. I yelled at myself in my head. I did it anyway." They are not being dramatic. They are describing a brain in which ancient circuits push toward quick relief while the front brain tries to hold the line (Koob & Volkow, 2016).

Addiction arrives when stress, trauma, and chemistry weaken that front brain so much that impulses run the show. The person still shows up to work, still loves their children, still makes promises—but inside, the decision system has been rewired around urgency, not intention.

History, cannabis, and the long shadow of impulse

When I read about medieval Arab cultures and the spread of cannabis, I see the same tension written in different clothes. Hashish entered the Islamic world from the east, long after the Qur'an prohibited wine. Greek and Indian texts had described cannabis centuries earlier. Arab scholars in the Abbasid period translated those texts and began to use cannabis in medicine, mixing leaves and resins into prescriptions for pain, inflammation, digestive problems, and anesthesia (Rosenthal, 1971).

At first, cannabis appeared mainly in medical notes and mystical circles. Sufi groups in Persia and Iraq experimented with the plant. Stories speak of dervishes in Nisabur in the twelfth century who used hashish often enough for chronic use to draw attention. During the Seljuk and Mongol periods, refugees and wandering mystics carried hashish from east to west. War, displacement, and political collapse reshaped society; cannabis spread along the same routes.

Some Sufis described hashish as a helper in worship—a plant that softened awareness of hardship, slowed the senses, and opened the heart to music, chant, and contemplation. Other observers detested what they saw. Jurists, chroniclers, and moral writers in Mamluk Cairo and Damascus described groups of poor laborers, fakirs, and marginal men gathering in gardens and courtyards to eat paste balls of hashish. They laughed, ate, moved slowly, and drifted through the day while families starved and markets struggled (Hamarneh, 1966).

Those descriptions point straight to the prefrontal cortex. Medieval Egyptians noted euphoria, increased appetite, relaxation, and spaced-out awareness. A thirteenth-century writer named al-Ukbari even praised these effects—joy, music, friendship. Yet long-term heavy use numbed initiative, slowed thought, and undermined planning. Chronic intoxication blurred the sense of consequence. Old texts describe men who forgot prayer, neglected work, and drifted away from social obligation. The behavior sounds like modern stories of amotivational syndrome and cannabis use disorder (Volkow et al., 2014).

I see a young man from Bethlehem in that history. Not a real patient, but a composite born from many faces. He grows up in a crowded house. Father underpaid. Mother exhausted. Future uncertain. Every adult around him talks about war, borders, corruption, and failure. His prefrontal cortex should help him think about school, apprenticeship, long-term plans. Instead, anxiety sits on those circuits like a weight.

Friends offer hashish in an alley behind a café. The first smoke sends warmth through his chest. Laughter comes easily. Food tastes better. Time slows. For one brief hour, the weight lifts.

The limbic system, hungry for reward, records the moment in bright ink: this helps (Nestler, 2005). Hashish turns down the volume on dread. The prefrontal cortex should whisper, "Careful. This pattern will cost you." But those front circuits already run hot with stress. Sleep is poor. Childhood threats left scars. Social conditions have taught his young mind that planning does not pay off. In that context, the front brain retreats and impulse steps forward. One night of relief becomes a pattern.

Old Arab writers saw this pattern without brain scans. They wrote poems and stories where hashish eaters choose short-term pleasure at the expense of honor, work, and family. Franz Rosenthal, in The Herb, collected those narratives: men gathering in gardens, eating hashish sweets, singing, and forgetting work (Rosenthal, 1971). Chroniclers of the Mamluk period described hashish dens in Cairo as places where the poor escaped hardship and fell deeper into poverty and neglect (Hamarneh, 1966).

Religious scholars argued over legal rules. Some said hashish counted as a full intoxicant and deserved the same punishment as wine. Others classified it as mufsid—a corrupting substance that harmed mind and character without causing full drunkenness—and called for special rulings. Under all those debates lay one observation: large groups of people were choosing a paste ball of crushed leaves over steady effort and hard choices. Stress, hunger, and despair pushed minds toward simple relief. Time under intoxication felt easier than time under responsibility. Fired, shamed, or punished men returned to hashish for comfort, deepening the cycle.

Different names. Same circuitry.

Living inside a brain built for urgency

I sit with patients today who speak the same language without knowing those medieval stories. A twenty-three-year-old tells me, "I always promise myself I'll go straight home after work. On the highway, some part of me turns the car toward the dealer without permission." His words describe loss of prefrontal control. The body moves before the planning brain finishes a sentence.

The prefrontal cortex is the part of the brain that holds two time frames together: a fast reward right now, and a slower reward later (Bechara, 2005; Bickel et al., 2012). When those circuits weaken through trauma, sleep loss, malnutrition, or drug exposure, long-term plans fade. The person senses only the pressure of now. A hit now. Rest now. Silence now. Any thought that points beyond the current hour feels distant and unreal.

My own mind knows that state. During my legal ordeal with federal prosecution, I would stare at the phone and feel a powerful pull toward impulsive statements: call this person and unload; send that email without review; walk into a prosecutor's office and shout. My limbic system overflowed with fear and anger. My prefrontal cortex had to work hard to hold me back—wait, breathe, calculate, consult. Years of psychiatric training helped. So did faith and family. Without those supports, impulse would have ruled (Sinha, 2008).

Many of my patients never learned safe ways to strengthen that front voice. Childhood stress and harsh punishment trained them to act fast and apologize later. Adults around them modeled rage, bingeing, crisis living, and emotional numbing. In that context, substances felt like natural tools for survival. Hashish in medieval Cairo. Cannabis, alcohol, cocaine, or fentanyl in modern Pennsylvania. Different names, same shortcut.

Hashish history in Arab culture also speaks to the stories people tell about themselves. Some medieval writers linked hashish to fakirs—poor wanderers who renounced worldly goods and searched for God. In that frame, hashish became "grass of the poor," a plant of the saints, not the lords. This narrative gave hashish moral cover. A poor man who smoked or ate it did not see weakness alone; the act carried an echo of spiritual rebellion, a refusal to play by elite rules.

Other texts painted hashish eaters as clowns and parasites. Chroniclers described dim tavern rooms where men sat in circles, missed prayer, neglected work, and slid into crime. Mamluk authorities worried about public order and cracked down. Hashish gardens and dens were raided. Punishments ranged from flogging to brutal measures. Those state actions carried their own kind of impulsive energy. Rulers responded to complex social suffering with simple bans and public violence—less planning, more force.

In both directions, impulsivity spread. The individual grabbed a quick high. The state grabbed quick punishment. The prefrontal cortex of society—the part where thoughtful policy and long-term planning should live—remained underdeveloped.

Learning to steer again

I often tell my patients that the prefrontal cortex grows through practice and story. Repeated small acts of delay and consideration strengthen those circuits (Tang et al., 2015). A person puts their phone down instead of firing off an angry text. Walks away instead of swinging a fist. Calls a sponsor instead of a dealer. Each tiny pause is a push-up for the front brain.

Narrative helps as well. When behavior is framed inside a larger story, short-term urges lose some of their grip. Faith traditions understood this long before neuroscience. Tales of prophets, saints, and sinners function as training for the brain. Many medieval Muslim stories about hashish work this way: a man eats hashish, commits shameful acts, then repents. The audience feels the pull of temptation and the relief of return without facing personal ruin. The story exercises moral imagination for the listener.

Middle Eastern doctors watched hashish from a clinical angle too. Treatises describe red eyes, dry mouth, hunger, confusion, mood shifts, and chronic apathy (Hamarneh, 1966). Some manuscripts comment on tolerance and dependence: a small dose once for pain gives way to daily use for every discomfort. The dose rises over time. Patients start to neglect hygiene, work, and social ties. Their world shrinks to the next portion.

Modern research on cannabis use disorder echoes those observations. Neuroscience studies show changes in prefrontal volume and function among heavy users, especially those who begin in adolescence. Delay discounting rises. Risky decisions increase. Emotional control weakens (Volkow et al., 2014). That research gives objective shape to stories those early doctors recorded through ink and careful observation.

As a Middle Eastern psychiatrist, I carry pride and grief together when I read that history. Pride, because Muslim and Arab scientists stood among the earliest to describe psychoactive plants and their dangers in detail. Grief, because some elites, jurists, and rulers used understanding to judge rather than heal. Many users in medieval texts appear as targets for satire and punishment, not patients in need of care.

Chapter 9 of this book belongs to the mind that acts before it thinks:

- the teenager who hits send on a text that burns a relationship;
- the father who screams and throws a plate before he remembers that children are watching
- the woman who buys fentanyl after a month of sobriety because someone cut her off in traffic and old rage erupted;
- the young dervish in twelfth-century Persia who eats hashish to escape loneliness and finds that months disappeared in a fog.

The prefrontal cortex is not a fixed structure. Trauma shapes its growth. Culture shapes its values. Substances shape its connections. Stories shape its sense of what matters. Arab cultures in the medieval period sat at crossroads of trade, conquest, and religious law. Cannabis traveled along those routes. Sufis, merchants, laborers, and criminals used hashish for joy, numbness, and spiritual games. Scholars argued. Rulers punished. Physicians recorded symptoms and advised restraint. The conflict between impulse and reflection, short-term escape and long-term duty, ran through every level.

The long road between urge and action

My own life threads through that same conflict. A child in Aleppo, hungry for safety, learns to act fast and think later. A medical student in the Middle East watches colleagues reach for cigarettes, caffeine, and pills during exams. A resident in Virginia feels his own prefrontal cortex stretched thin by sleepless nights and pager alarms. A defendant in a federal courtroom feels a sudden urge toward reckless speech when prosecutors twist facts. A doctor in Pennsylvania watches a patient torn between a bag of heroin and a long, slow fight for recovery.

Impulse never fully disappears—nor should it. Desire pushes humans toward food, sex, art, invention, faith, movement, survival. The goal is not to kill wanting. The goal is to give the front brain enough strength, support, predictability, sleep, safety, community, and meaning to guide desire into paths that do not destroy the self (Bechara, 2005; Tang et al., 2015). Addiction is what happens when the emotional brain outruns the planning brain—when dopamine fires faster than consequences can form words (Volkow & Fowler, 2000).

Old Arab narratives about hashish give my patients and readers a wider context. Addiction in our communities did not erupt from nothing in the late twentieth century. Cannabis, opium, alcohol, and other agents have moved through Middle Eastern streets for a thousand years. People laughed, sinned, prayed, relapsed, repented, and fought the same inner battles. Medieval cannabis use shows how cultures spin stories around drugs: sacred plant, devil's herb, poor man's friend, civilization's poison. Each label influences the prefrontal calculus inside every user.

Culture shapes chemistry. Narrative shapes neurotransmission.

In your own life, impulse often feels like a stranger who jumps into the driver's seat and jerks the wheel. The science of the prefrontal cortex shows a different picture. That "stranger" grows from a long history of fear, reward, learning, and culture. From Aleppo to Cairo to Nisabur to Bethlehem to Philadelphia, the human brain has struggled to hold the space between urge and action (LeDoux, 2015; Arnsten, 2009).

When you read this chapter, listen for those voices behind you: Sufi mystics in twelfth-century Persia whispering blessings over green leaves; Cairo workers swapping hashish sweets in cramped courtyards; jurists in turban and robe arguing about corruptive herbs; a Persian doctor warning in a manuscript that chronic hashish use destroys resolve; a modern teenager in an American rehab unit, fingers twitching for a vape pen, heart racing, prefrontal cortex firing weakly against waves of craving.

Hijacked minds do not belong to one time or one people. My Arab ancestors wrote early chapters of addiction medicine through their encounters with cannabis and opium. My own life—as a Middle Eastern child of war, a Western-trained physician, a federal defendant, and an addiction psychiatrist—writes another chapter. The struggle with impulse, decision making, craving, fear, opportunity, and a wounded prefrontal cortex ties all those stories together.

The human brain has always tried to hold the small, fragile space between urge and action. Some days we manage it. Some days we don't. Most of a life in recovery is spent learning how to pause.

Conclusion

A hijacked mind is like a ship whose wheel has been seized by wind. The gusts come from childhood, war, loneliness, humiliation, rejection, hunger, grief, or memory—but the drifting still feels like choice. The waves roar, the hull tilts, and the sailor believes he is steering. But somewhere beneath the storm, the compass still exists—buried, but intact. Recovery is not sudden calm. Recovery is the slow reclaiming of the wheel—one knuckle at a time—until the ship turns by degrees so small they seem invisible. Only later does the sailor look back and realize the shoreline has changed.

CHAPTER 10

The Rewired Mind

(Neuroplasticity)

> "*The best time to plant a tree was 20 years ago. The second best time is now.*"
>
> — CHINESE PROVERB

Food as my first sedative

I remember the first time I used food to quiet my brain.

Sirens outside in Aleppo, that cracked, metallic howl that makes adults freeze mid-sentence. Grown-ups whispered the names of people who never came back. I did not understand politics or fronts or ceasefires. I understood the look in my mother's eyes when the radio grew loud and the house fell silent. My small body vibrated like a tuning fork. I went hunting for something sweet. Bread. Sugar. A crust left on the table. Anything.

Chewing became my first sedative. Warm bread in my mouth, soft against my teeth, swallowed into a hollow, churning stomach. The noise outside did not stop, but something inside me softened. Full stomach. Heavy eyelids. Jaw moving in slow, repetitive circles. For a few minutes the war stepped back a few inches, like a wave that did not quite reach my feet. Somewhere deep in my nervous system, circuits fired and linked up. My brain learned a rule so simple it did not need words: fear plus food equals relief. Remember this. Do it again.

At first, the rule looked innocent. A second piece of bread. Extra rice piled "for the growing boy." A hidden chocolate bar found in a cousin's bag. Nobody arrests a child for eating more. No courtroom. No judge. Only a small boy who looks "healthy," cheeks round, plate clean. Aunties praised my "good appetite." Teachers joked I would be "strong like a wrestler." Under that praise, my nervous system rehearsed its first addiction. Not to heroin. Not to alcohol. To comfort delivered on a plate.

Trauma did not arrive once; it came in layers. Explosions that rattled windows. Stories of torture traded in low voices over tea. Streets that used to hold games of football now carved up by checkpoints and armed men. A teenager in that environment learns to live in permanent high alert. Muscles tight. Sleep shallow. Ears tuned for the slightest change in tone outside. Thoughts racing ahead to every possible disaster. The amygdala—that almond-shaped alarm system deep in the brain that screams "danger" before you can think—became a guard that never rested.

Food stepped into that role no human could keep. Food never shouted. Never vanished. Never got taken at a checkpoint. A plate of rice or a late-night sandwich in the kitchen light felt like the only friend who would not betray me or disappear. Each pastry, each extra spoonful stolen in the dark, linked taste with a tiny drop in panic. That is emotional memory: the body storing not just events, but the feelings tied to them. My emotional memory stitched together sirens and sugar, dread and dough, fear and fullness. Long before I could define trauma, my brain had already built its first escape route—the one that started at the refrigerator door.

Trauma, migration, and the quiet rise of food addiction

Years passed. A new country replaced the old skyline. English wrapped around my tongue like a borrowed coat. Medical school, residency, exams, rotations—each milestone stamped proof that I had outrun something. A white coat settled onto my shoulders like armor, and patients sat across from me with their own trembling stories, their own hijacked minds. I listened to them describe urges they didn't trust, cravings they couldn't explain, decisions they couldn't defend. I nodded with clinical understanding. I offered compassion. I wrote treatment plans.

And yet—my own patterns had followed me across oceans, tucked neatly into luggage no customs officer could detect. The war stayed in my nervous system even when my passport changed. Long call nights at the hospital meant long pilgrimages to vending machines. The fluorescent light of a call room mixed with the neon glow of soda dispensers and the plastic shimmer of snack wrappers. Medical charts waited on a desk; processed sugar waited in a glowing metal box.

I knew the science—of course I did. I lectured patients about addiction, reward learning, dopamine loops, emotional triggers, conditioned responses. I drew diagrams on exam table paper explaining how stress hijacks decision-making. And then, at 3:17 a.m., I would find myself tearing open a candy bar like a drowning man grabbing rope. My brain did not care about credentials. It followed the oldest script it had ever memorized: stress plus food equals survival.

Neuroscience explains that script with brutal clarity. Trauma pushes cortisol up, flooding the bloodstream with chemical urgency. When sugar and fat hit the tongue, dopamine sparks in the nucleus accumbens—the brain's reward capital—like a flare in the dark. The reward center learns fast, faster than any lecture or resolution. Neural pathways between the prefrontal cortex—the slow, reasonable planner—and the limbic system—the emotional engine—start to tilt toward short-term comfort, like a road worn smooth by repetition.

The prefrontal cortex still speaks, but its voice grows thin and polite. "Stop," it whispers, like a teacher in a storm. Meanwhile, the craving roars, "Eat now," like an army kicking in the door. The medical part of me observed this process with detached fascination, the way a scientist watches a controlled fire. But the wounded part of me—the child who learned to quiet fear with bread—picked up the fork and obeyed.

When prosecution reactivates old war wiring

Then another wave of trauma hit—colder, quieter, wrapped in legal stationery instead of smoke. Federal prosecution. Indictment. My name printed beneath the words United States of America v. A doctor in a white coat suddenly recast as a criminal defendant. Court dates replaced clinic schedules. Headlines replaced thank-you notes. Agents appeared in offices where patients once wept and healed.

The same body that once ducked from bombs in Aleppo now walked through metal detectors into a federal courthouse. The marble floors were polished, but my nervous system recognized the terrain anyway. Different country. Same threat circuitry. The brain does not check passports before launching a stress response. It reacts first, asks questions later.

During those months and years, food cravings shifted from background hum to blaring siren. Every hearing felt like an air raid. Every legal motion felt like a distant explosion. Every letter from prosecutors sent me into the kitchen like a soldier running to a bunker. The refrigerator became a shelter. The freezer became triage. A young boy in Aleppo had once reached for bread; a middle-aged psychiatrist in Pennsylvania now reached for ice cream, chips, anything dense enough to muffle panic. Different kitchen, same pattern.

The scale crept upward with quiet loyalty. Blood pressure followed. Joints protested. I felt humiliation bloom inside my white coat—prescribing lifestyle interventions to patients while secretly loosening my own belt. In exam rooms, I spoke of balance, moderation, mindful eating. At home, I devoured entire containers while standing over the sink.

And then came the other voice—the one that never blinks. The inner prosecutor.

"You are weak."

"You have no discipline."

"You teach neuroscience and still fail."

That voice carried no badge, yet it handcuffed me more effectively than the government ever could. It fed the cycle with mathematical precision—shame raised anxiety, anxiety sharpened craving, craving sent me back to food, and food delivered temporary relief wrapped in lifelong consequences.

Trauma from war braided itself with trauma from prosecution, two storms roaring through the same neural valley. Food addiction became the bridge between them—the only strategy my body had ever tested that could turn terror into silence, even for a moment.

The body tried to carry unbearable fear the only way it knew how.

The brain did not ask permission.

The brain reached for the fastest relief on the shelf.

This is a story, ultimately of victory, that I covered in my first book, Doctor, Not Guilty.

Watching my brain with compassion

So where does transformation begin?

Not in fireworks. Not in cinematic resolve. Not in a detox montage set to triumphant music.

Transformation begins in a kitchen at 11:47 p.m., fluorescent light buzzing, linoleum cold beneath bare feet. A plastic spoon in one hand, an open container in the other. Heart thudding like footsteps running from something unseen. Jaw clenched so tight it trembles. Tears gathering but refusing to fall—because falling would mean admitting fear.

For years, I believed change required a heroic declaration. But recovery began the first time I didn't spit on myself internally. The first time disgust loosened its grip just enough for compassion to enter.

After a court hearing that scraped raw every nerve in my body, I stood frozen in that kitchen—rage, terror, exhaustion, humiliation, all pulsing under my skin. And then, like a fragile match struck in darkness, a new sentence flared:

"Of course you want this. Your body is trying to protect you."

Not praise. Not permission. Interpretation.

The difference was seismic.

That sentence did not erase the binge. It translated it. It reframed sugar not as sin, but as survival. Trauma had engineered my nervous system toward quick sweetness, quick fullness, quick numbing. Federal prosecution didn't invent the craving—it amplified it to maximum volume. Food addiction became the only survival strategy that never required explanation, insurance authorization, or courtroom consent.

In that moment, I saw my brain not as an adversary sabotaging me, but as a wounded ally—limping, improvising, doing its best.

Neuroplasticity did not walk into the room—it had been there all along, waiting. The same neurons that once memorized the geography of bombed streets in Aleppo or the choreography of federal courtroom intimidation could learn something gentler. Synapses that fired for sugar, panic, and shame could—if given repetition and oxygen—fire for stability, connection, breath.

The biology that built addiction could just as faithfully construct recovery.

But recovery was not a staircase. It was a heartbeat—forward, back, forward, back. Relapses arrived like old friends who never returned your calls but still knew your address. Nights of compulsive eating reappeared—especially after another subpoena, another headline, another attorney email heavy with threat.

Each relapse brought information. Before, I treated every fall like a verdict—proof of moral failure. Later, I treated each fall like evidence.

- What was the first thought?
- What tightened first—the chest, the throat, the gut?
- What time of day?
- What memory resurfaced?
- Who emailed?
- What headline flashed?

Curiosity slipped into the space where condemnation once lived. And curiosity is anesthesia for shame. It lowers cortisol. It quiets the amygdala. A quieter amygdala gives the prefrontal cortex—logic, planning, compassion—a fighting chance.

I began sharing this with patients—not as metaphor, but as anatomy.

- The brain always learns.

- Trauma teaches emergency.
- Addiction teaches shortcuts.
- Recovery teaches alternatives.
- Every repetition lays down myelin like fresh asphalt.
- Every pause between craving and action strengthens prefrontal circuitry.
- Every act of self-compassion loosens shame's chokehold.
- Transformation is not the refusal of craving.
- Transformation is recognizing craving as a messenger rather than a master.
- Recovery does not begin when the spoon drops.
- Recovery begins the moment you stop hating the hand that holds it.

Experience-dependent plasticity and identity

The federal case forced me to confront more than food. Federal prosecution does not simply threaten liberty or career—it attacks the architecture of identity. One day I was a healer, a physician entrusted with suffering. The next, I was portrayed as a thief. A caregiver recast as a criminal. A life devoted to easing pain rewritten as a scheme to cause it. That kind of narrative violence does not stay in legal documents—it burrows into the marrow. It shakes the deepest layers of self, the ones formed long before medical school or licensure. Under that pressure, some people disappear into substances, others into depression, others into rage or resignation. My own mind paced near those cliffs more than once, breathing in their gravity.

And yet, something older and stronger worked beneath the panic. A lineage—not of fame or power, but of endurance. Parents who survived war and refused to surrender dignity. Grandparents who rebuilt life after displacement. Teachers who pushed me across finish lines I didn't believe I could reach. Patients who placed their most fragile truths in my hands. And above all, a God who continued listening even when my own voice fractured into silence. Those forces—human and divine, ancestral and immediate—gave my nervous system experiences of safety and purpose in the middle of legal chaos. Each time I sat with a patient instead of collapsing, some neural pathway for meaning lit up. Each time a jury or judge treated me with basic fairness, some small thread of trust in the world rewove itself.

Neuroscience calls this experience-dependent plasticity—the brain's ability to reshape itself through repeated exposure to safety, support, purpose, relationship, and justice. Every moment of stability grows new dendrites. Every experience of compassion strengthens synapses. Every act of integrity quiets the alarm systems built by trauma. Childhood taught my brain that the world could explode without warning. The courtroom taught my brain that systems can misuse power. Recovery taught my brain that courage, community, and responsibility still bend outcomes. Each chapter left scars—but each chapter also planted seeds.

Slowly, I began treating my food addiction not as an enemy, but as a teacher. Craving became a compass pointing toward unprocessed fear. Binge episodes revealed days when I swallowed grief or humiliation instead of speaking it. Instead of asking, "Why am I so weak?" I began asking, "What pain am I trying to anesthetize right now?" That question moved the focus from the refrigerator to the heart—from self-disgust to self-understanding.

So I built a scaffolding of structure—not perfection, just rhythm. Simple meals eaten without secrecy. Regular times instead of frantic grazing. Honest tracking instead of denial. Prayer or reflection before walking into the kitchen at night, not afterward when the damage was done. Movement—not punishment, but a reminder that my body existed for more than bracing against impact. Sleep, guarded like medication, to give my prefrontal cortex a fighting chance. Each small practice whispered to the brain: you are safe enough to choose differently now.

And the brain listened—not all at once, not forever, but long enough for a new pattern to take root.

Writing as medicine

Writing arrived as another form of medicine—unexpected, unprescribed, but undeniably potent. At first, it felt like punishment. Every sentence dragged me back into rooms I wanted to forget. Aleppo at night. Courtrooms humming with fluorescent indifference. News headlines that carved my name into accusation. Betrayals I swallowed instead of confronting. Kitchens lit only by refrigerator light, spoon in hand, fogged with shame. Writing forced me to sit with memories I had spent decades outrunning.

But somewhere between drafts, a shift occurred. What once felt like reopening a wound began to feel like stitching one. Writing became integration. Traumatic memories stopped floating like shattered glass—cutting, unpredictable, disconnected. They found sequence. Cause met effect. Emotion found language. Moments that once felt random fell into chapter, character, consequence. The narrative brain, tethered to prefrontal cortex and hippocampus, started doing what it evolved to do—organize chaos into meaning, threat into story, survival into purpose. I was no longer drowning in scenes. I was arranging them.

Hijacked Minds did not begin as a book for readers—it began as neural rehabilitation. Every chapter loosened a knot in my history. Food addiction shifted from a source of private humiliation to clinical evidence of a nervous system trying desperately to manage terror. Federal prosecution transformed from a personal injustice into a laboratory of resilience, endurance, and moral injury. War memories stopped being night intruders and became the foundation for a life spent sitting beside other wounded minds. Writing turned symptoms into sentences, sentences into structure.

Transformation rests on one biological truth: the brain never stops learning. Trauma taught my brain vigilance, mistrust, scanning, flinching. Food taught it a rapid-access pathway to numbness. The courtroom taught it that systems can twist truth into weapon. But recovery—through therapy, faith, service, family, and story—now teaches my brain that purpose can outlive panic. Purpose, repeated, rewires.

I still feel cravings. Stress still opens old doors. A smell of cumin and diesel from Aleppo kitchens. A government letter demanding response. A medical billing error implying fault. On those days, my first thought still reaches for food—the oldest comfort my nervous system remembers. But the difference now lies in the second thought. A steadier voice rises: "You survived worse. You do not need to eat this feeling. You can write it. Pray through it. Speak it. Walk it out. Call someone." That voice does not silence the craving—it outvotes it.

And that voice did not arrive by revelation or willpower. It grew the way all neural change grows—slowly, stubbornly, through repetition. Therapy sessions where I told the truth instead of hiding. Prayers whispered when words felt impossible. Family who stayed when shame told them to leave. Patients who unknowingly modeled courage. Pages written when despair said there was nothing left to say. Over years, those repetitions reshaped circuitry. Neural plasticity does not care about ego—it cares about practice. I fed that voice until it became strong enough to speak first.

Writing did not save me. It trained me. It turned pain into instruction, memory into map, survival into story—and story into a way back to myself.

Shared humanity in the consulting room

Transformation also means sharing this journey with others—out loud, without disguise. When I sit with a patient in addiction treatment now, I no longer stand as the clean doctor speaking to the "sick" person across the table. I stand as a fellow traveler who has crawled through his own tunnels. Different substance. Different courtroom. Same nervous system. Same ancient tug-of-war between craving and conscience. And patients feel that. They recognize it in the pauses, the eye contact, the absence of judgment. That shared humanity opens doors no credential ever could. Shame loosens its grip. Hope lifts its head. The room becomes warmer, safer, more possible. Those emotional shifts are not abstract—they form new neural pathways for both of us, teaching our brains that connection, not consumption, brings relief.

From Aleppo to Easton, from kitchen raids to fluorescent courtrooms, from headlines to hospital call rooms, from prosecution to the pages of this book, one theme runs through my story like a spine: the brain bends. The brain scars. The brain heals. Not perfectly. Not quickly. But enough—enough for a life with meaning, for relationships worth keeping, for a purpose that outlasts fear. Enough for a doctor once labeled a defendant to rise again, step into the clinic, and write for others whose minds feel hijacked.

This chapter in Hijacked Minds belongs to that promise. Trauma and addiction are not full stops—they are commas. The sentence continues. The same brain that once reached for bread in panic and sweets in shame now reaches for pen, for patients, for justice, for sunrise after long nights. That transformation rests not on brilliance or purity, but on stubborn perseverance. Neuron by neuron. Breath by breath. Choice by choice. Page by page.

Three Kennedys and a doctor from Aleppo

When I look at recovery now, I see three Kennedys standing beside me like a living family tree of American suffering and resurrection. The father, Senator Robert F. Kennedy, whose life ended before he could tell his own story of grief, trauma, and coping in a language we would recognize today. The son, Patrick, who refused the family tradition of silence—carrying bipolar disorder, addiction, and medication bottles onto the floor of Congress, then channeling that vulnerability into the Mental Health Parity and Addiction Equity Act, shifting national policy with trembling hands. And now the nephew, Robert F. Kennedy Jr, who speaks openly about fourteen years of heroin addiction, spiritual collapse, and long-haul recovery while serving as Secretary of Health and Human Services (Wikipedia, 2025; People, 2025; PBS NewsHour, 2025; Associated Press, 2025).

Three branches of the same dynasty. One murdered in a kitchen after a victory speech, blood spreading across the floor while America watched its future shatter. One crashing into a barricade on Capitol Hill, drowning in OxyContin, antidepressants, secrecy, and shame. One arrested with heroin in his pocket, now taking the oath to lead the nation's health system and renew the opioid public health emergency (Wikipedia, 2025; People, 2025; Associated Press, 2025).

And then there is me. A boy from Aleppo who ran from war, who hid from sirens with bread and sugar, who believed survival depended on chewing fast. A man who stood in American courtrooms as a federal defendant, heart pounding like mortar fire, and now writes a book about hijacked minds—his own included.

On paper, our worlds could not be further apart. Different languages, accents, religions, passports, skin tones, dinner tables, and cultural myths. One raised in the glare of cameras and political prophecy, the other raised in blackout nights under falling shells. One shaped by dynastic expectation, another by rubble and ration lines.

But the brain does not care about zip codes or last names. Trauma talks to neurons in one dialect. Relief talks to dopamine in one dialect. Compulsion speaks the same language in every hemisphere. Recovery—slow, clumsy, stubborn—whispers through plasticity in one dialect. The story repeats, translated but unchanged.

Addiction does not bow to fame. Resilience does not belong to the powerful. Healing does not recognize borders.

The Kennedys prove it on a national stage.

I prove it in the quiet of my kitchen.

We are all—every one of us—one nervous system trying to find its way home.

RFK Jr's heroin story and recovery arc

Robert F. Kennedy Jr stands at the podium in Nashville beneath stage lights that could have belonged to a campaign rally, but instead illuminate confession. The room is quiet—clinicians, sheriffs, paramedics, ministers—people who meet addiction where it bleeds. He tells them that he was a heroin addict for fourteen years. He says the words plainly, without theatrics, as if naming the weather. He describes using in secret bathrooms, in borrowed rooms, in moments when the world believed he was thriving. He recounts spiraling into a darkness so complete that death felt like the only silence available. And then he speaks of a spiritual awakening—an invisible pivot—and a 12-step path that carried him inch by inch into long-term recovery (PBS NewsHour, 2025; Associated Press, 2025; WBUR, 2025).

When I first read that account, my reaction wasn't intellectual or political—it was physical. Something tightened in my ribs. I recognized the tremor beneath his sentences, the cadence of a person who has tasted compulsion and lived long enough to describe it. I know the crack in the voice that only appears when someone says "I should not be alive" and means it. He looks into crowds of young people and tells them they need purpose, community, belonging, meaning—not only medication. He warns that without those anchors, it becomes dangerously easy to reach for heroin, fentanyl, pills, or the bottle, not out of rebellion or pleasure, but out of unbearable emptiness (PBS NewsHour, 2025; Associated Press, 2025).

I say the same thing in my clinic every week. Different vocabulary. Same gospel.

Recovery did not erase his history. Trauma leaves fingerprints. He still carries a nervous system shaped by assassination footage, political dynasty grief, public chaos, and generations of unresolved sorrow. The New York Times describes his life as one of addiction and trauma—an inheritance as real and traceable as the Kennedy jawline. I understand that sentence in my bones. My inheritance of addiction and trauma did not come from a family famous enough for museum exhibits. Mine came from bombs, childhood dread, cultural silence, and a federal indictment that tried to erase my identity as a healer.

So when he sits in Washington as HHS Secretary, and I sit in Pennsylvania writing this chapter, our biographies look incompatible. But our nervous systems rhyme. Both of us learned how fast life can collapse. Both of us learned how the mind reaches for chemicals, food, compulsions, or numbing rituals to quiet the internal alarms. Both of us had to build new pathways—slow, shaky, deliberate—to avoid being swallowed by despair.

He now stands as the nation's health chief, renewing the opioid public health emergency and declaring he intends to "Make America Healthy Again." I stand as a psychiatrist, shaping Hijacked Minds into my own MAHA project—word by word—for patients, colleagues, and communities living in silent crisis (U.S. Department of Health and Human Services, 2025; WBUR, 2025; New York Post, 2025).

His story matters not because he survived addiction—millions do—but because he refused to remain a hidden survivor. He describes how heroin first made him feel normal, how it soothed a restless mind, sharpened academic focus, and quieted an inner storm before slowly taking ownership of his life. Then came the arrest in 1983—police, headlines, shame—a rupture that forced a choice: prison or recovery, self-destruction or surrender. He chose recovery. He walked into meetings. He admitted the truth to strangers. He built new habits the only way any of us do—one unglamorous day at a time (People, 2025; PBS NewsHour, 2025; Associated Press, 2025; Wikipedia, 2025).

My turning point did not involve heroin. It involved food and shame.

As a child in Syria, I used bread to muffle terror. As a resident in Virginia, I used vending machines to numb exhaustion. As a doctor under indictment, I used late-night binges to quiet a heart that beat like artillery. I never collapsed on a bathroom floor with a needle. I collapsed on the inside with a spoon. My body carried weight. My soul carried the rest. When the federal government put me on trial, my oldest coping patterns resurfaced with military precision. Every letter from prosecutors triggered the same survival circuitry that once fired under falling shells in Aleppo.

Recovery began the night I stood in my kitchen, hand trembling over ice cream, and thought, "Of course you want this. Your brain is trying to protect you. You cannot hate yourself out of this." No detox. No paramedics. No cold-turkey dramatics. Just a quiet, unexpected mercy—a small spiritual awakening. Less cinematic than heroin withdrawal. No sirens. No steel cuffs. Still holy in its own way.

When I listen to RFK Jr describe his spiritual awakening, I hear that same recalibration—the shift from self-condemnation to self-recognition. He says God found him at the bottom of hopelessness, that the 12 steps offered a structure for repentance, responsibility, humility, and service. He didn't just stop using. He redirected his life—toward environmental law, public advocacy, and now national health policy (PBS NewsHour, 2025; Associated Press, 2025).

Agree or disagree with him politically—you cannot deny the neurological pattern. Addiction opened a canyon. Recovery pointed him toward purpose.

And purpose is the most powerful medicine the brain has ever known.

Recovery, policy, and the danger of one-story solutions

The brain loves purpose. Purpose reshapes circuits the way rivers reshape rock—slowly, relentlessly, permanently. When people move from addiction to service, something alchemical happens. They often describe cravings loosening, softening, losing their authority. Not because biology vanished. Not because dopamine receptors magically reset. But because the reward system found a new fuel source. Purpose becomes the intoxicant. Standing in a treatment meeting. Visiting a prison on a Saturday morning. Writing legislation instead of prescriptions. Holding the trembling hand of a person who now stands exactly where you once stood. Suddenly dopamine fires for meaning, not only for chemicals. The brain redirects its devotion.

I feel that transformation every time I write these pages. Each sentence becomes a microscopic dose of medicine—not only against relapse, but against despair, isolation, and moral injury. Writing does not replace therapy. Writing does not replace prayer. But it steadies the hand reaching toward the refrigerator. It keeps the nervous system from believing the lie that numbness is the only relief available.

The Kennedy family occupies a unique space in American mythology. Glamour in front of cameras. Devastation behind closed doors. Assassinations broadcast across generations. Plane crashes, whispered affairs, relentless scrutiny. Mental illness, alcoholism, heroin use, silence, shame. Then Patrick Kennedy walks into Congress, names his bipolar disorder and addiction aloud, and refuses the family tradition of secrecy. RFK Jr walks into HHS with his own history of heroin addiction and refuses silence, too (Wikipedia, 2025; The HHR Journal, 2025). The family story shifts—not by miracle, but by testimony.

Their lives deliver a truth many people resist: trauma and addiction do not care about wealth. They do not bow to Ivy League diplomas, marble staircases, Secret Service protection, or Senate seating charts. They cross oceans and borders. They visited my childhood apartment in Aleppo, shaking the window glass with explosions. They visited a Georgetown townhouse where a young Kennedy hid heroin in jacket pockets. They walked into the federal courtroom where I sat at the defense table, pulse racing. They walked into the Senate hearing where RFK Jr explained his views on overdose, involuntary treatment, wellness farms, and national prevention strategies (The HHR Journal, 2025; WBUR, 2025). Different continents, same nervous system response.

In those hearings and speeches, he insists that recovery shaped his vision for the country. He describes taxpayer-funded "wellness farms"—community-based therapeutic environments where people in addiction work the land, rebuild structure, live among peers, and reclaim identity away from the neighborhoods of use. He says treatment should be community, not only clinic. He acknowledges that medications like buprenorphine and methadone matter, but warns that "money alone will not fix this," arguing that young people also need meaning, faith, responsibility, connection, and belonging (WBUR, 2025; New York Post, 2025). Whether or not his blueprint works, the moral argument is unmistakable: humans heal in community.

Experts raise concerns—and they are right to do so. Some ask where medication for opioid use disorder fits, reminding him that the scientific evidence overwhelmingly supports combining medication with therapy, housing, social support, and long-term follow-up. They caution that personal recovery stories, however inspiring or dramatic, cannot substitute for rigorous research, public health infrastructure, and policy evaluation. Science matters. Systems matter. Data matters (The HHR Journal, 2025). And without them, hope becomes theater.

Yet I also see the other side. For decades, America was led by people untouched by addiction—at least publicly. Men who had never sat through a family visitation in rehab lectured the nation about "just saying no." Policymakers who never trembled through withdrawal at 2:00 a.m. called for harsher sentencing. They measured success by arrests instead of recovery. They never felt the humiliation of peeing into a plastic cup under supervision. They never buried a friend from overdose. Policy crafted without lived experience builds prisons, not healing (The HHR Journal, 2025).

So when recovery steps up to the podium, it changes the gravitational pull in the room. A man who used heroin for fourteen years and now swears an oath to protect public health carries an uneasy combination of credibility and risk. Credibility because he understands compulsion—not academically, but viscerally. Risk because personal pathways can become blindfolds. One size never fits all—not in shoes, not in trauma, not in treatment.

I think about that risk every time I walk into court to testify or sit across from a patient desperate for direction. My prosecution taught me that not every investigator seeks truth. My recovery from moral injury taught me to fight fiercely for colleagues under attack. That fierceness can save someone. It can also bias me if I forget caution. My own food addiction makes me exquisitely aware of emotional eating in patients—sometimes helpfully, sometimes excessively. The same wound that gives compassion can distort perception.

RFK Jr brings his own biases into HHS. He has a long public history of promoting unscientific claims about vaccines and other health issues. Addiction specialists now watch his opioid policy decisions with a dual awareness—grateful for his empathy, terrified by his skepticism toward evidence-based medicine. Both reactions are rational. Both are earned (The HHR Journal, 2025; WBUR, 2025).

Recovery after drug use and adversity always lives in this tension. Personal experience saves you. Personal experience tempts you to universalize your salvation. The brain craves simplicity. "This worked for me, so it will work for everyone." But recovery scaled to a nation demands a harder sentence: "This worked for me. You are not me. I will honor both truth and evidence."

That humility—not heroism—is what prevents harm.

Stages of recovery in two lives

In my life, war and prosecution carved trenches through my nervous system—quiet, invisible scars that still pulse under sudden stress. Food addiction did not arrive as a villain; it followed that pain like a loyal shadow, a misguided guardian, offering comfort when the world felt sharp. Recovery taught me humility the hard way. Every patient reminds me that my story is only one map through the wilderness—helpful, but never the territory. So when I hear RFK Jr call for removing smartphones from schools, building wellness farms, banning ultra-processed foods from cafeterias, and framing the overdose crisis as a national security threat, I don't just hear policy proposals. I hear a man trying to protect children from the misery he once carried in his bloodstream (WBUR, 2025; New York Post, 2025).

The scientist in me immediately begins its interrogation. How will this work? Where is the data? What are the unintended harms waiting in the wings? Can rural farms realistically absorb urban overdose epidemics? Will removing processed foods spark underground economies? Will Congress fund buprenorphine, harm reduction centres, and stable housing with the same enthusiasm as tractors and soil (The HHR Journal, 2025)? Evidence-based medicine has been burned before by well-intended idealism.

But the clinician in me hears something different—something softer, something necessary. A man who once shot heroin in secrecy now sits in federal power and tells packed auditoriums, "Kids need hope." He reminds policymakers that addiction is "both a source and symptom of misery," and that effective policy must address loneliness, abandonment, purposelessness—not simply drug supply (PBS NewsHour, 2025; Associated Press, 2025; WBUR, 2025). That language matters. It acknowledges the emotional architecture of addiction, not just the biology.

Because recovery after drug use is not merely abstinence. Recovery is the slow return of meaning—the moment life becomes something you want to remain awake for.

My own recovery unfolded in stages, as if my brain needed chapters to understand its own story.

First came survival. I had to outlive the legal system, the headlines, the humiliation, the urge to disappear. Food still filled the spaces where courage hadn't grown yet. That was the raw, animal stage.

Second came regulation. I learned how to feel distress without sprinting to the refrigerator. I worked with my therapist. I rebuilt sleep like a fragile construction project. I leaned on prayer and breath. I invited family and friends into rooms I once kept locked. My brain discovered—slowly—that terror could be tolerated, not extinguished. That was stabilization.

Third came purpose. I returned to my patients, but with a different heart—less armored, more porous. I began speaking publicly about burnout, physician prosecution, and medical moral injury. I wrote for KevinMD, for colleagues, for strangers, and now for this book. Each sentence rewired synapses. Each published word stitched a torn part of me back into place. My story began entering other bodies, other rooms. Pain became service—the rare alchemy of healing.

RFK Jr describes a similar architecture in his own language. From a desperate young man hiding his heroin use and praying not to wake up, to an environmental attorney filing lawsuits against corporations, to a cabinet member determined to prevent young people from numbing their pain the way he once did (PBS NewsHour, 2025; Associated Press, 2025; Wikipedia, 2025). His recovery—like mine—became directional, not decorative.

Now we both stand in roles sculpted by suffering. He chairs a federal MAHA Commission examining chronic disease and psychiatric prescribing. I run a psychiatric practice for people drowning under substances, medications, trauma, and bureaucratic cruelty. He signs declarations of public health emergencies. I sign FMLA forms for patients who can no longer keep breathing inside capitalism (U.S. Department of Health and Human Services, 2025; WBUR, 2025).

The brain that once sought heroin in a college dormitory now signs orders that shape a nation's health strategy. The brain that once raided the refrigerator at 2:00 a.m. now writes chapters intended to change how doctors and the public understand addiction. That is neuroplasticity in motion—messy, unromantic, miraculous.

But recovery after adversity is never sterile. Old instincts still flicker like pilot lights. RFK Jr sometimes praises heroin in resurfaced clips, saying it "worked" for him academically because it calmed his mind. Those words unsettle many of us in addiction psychiatry. They reveal how seductive relief can remain—even decades later (People, 2025; WBUR, 2025). I hear my own echoes—nostalgic memories of warm fullness, late-night kitchens, sugar silencing panic. Recovery requires ongoing vigilance against romanticizing the substance that almost became destiny.

And yet—those raw admissions are not irresponsible. They are lifelines. They remind people living in active addiction that they are not defective, not cursed, not alone. Their attachment to the drug once made sense. It worked—until it didn't. A person who says, "It saved me before it nearly killed me—and I still had to let it go," can reach hearts no clinical lecture ever will (PBS NewsHour, 2025; Associated Press, 2025).

Because healing doesn't begin with condemnation.

Healing begins with recognition.

Recovery after drug use and adversity

That is what I hope this chapter does. I want you not only to understand my story, but to feel it—taste the metal of fear in your mouth, hear the refrigerator door open at midnight, sense the courtroom oxygen thinning. I want you to feel my cravings, my trembling hands, my legal jeopardy, the way shame can spread through the nervous system like static. I want you to sit beside RFK Jr under Senate lights, watching cameras blink, watching lawmakers lean forward, watching him steady his breath because he knows that a single clumsy sentence could derail his mission, reverse public trust, feed the critics waiting like wolves. I want you to picture Patrick Kennedy pacing the halls of Congress with his medications rattling in his pocket and his private despair hidden beneath a congressional pin. And I want you to see Senator Robert Kennedy's blood spreading across the kitchen floor of the Ambassador Hotel, understand that trauma of that magnitude does not die with the body—it travels, attaches, reshapes descendants, echoes through DNA, culture, family myth (Wikipedia, 2025; The HHR Journal, 2025).

Recovery in the Kennedy family has never been a polished political biography. It has been chaotic, interrupted, nonlinear—just like yours, mine, and every family you know. Some drown quietly. Some fight loudly. Some spend their lives pretending nothing happened. Some turn agony into legislation. Some turn relapse into ministry. Some turn humiliation into testimony. And yes—some write books, trying to make sense of the wreckage. I am one of those.

From heroin in hidden rooms to food in fluorescent kitchens.

From Aleppo to Easton.

From a Nashville podium filled with power to the echoing marble halls of HHS.

From the federal dock under oath to a psychiatrist's office listening for trembling voices.

In every place, one truth remained: the nervous system that once only understood flight, numbness, and survival can—slowly, stubbornly—learn a new pattern.

Feel. Pause. Choose.

It sounds small. It is not. It is a neurological revolution.

That is the core of recovery after drug use and adversity. The feelings do not vanish—they grow wiser. The cravings do not evaporate—they shrink to scale. The memories do not erase—they lose their authority. Instead, the brain—burned, frightened, brilliant—learns to recognize danger sooner, regulate faster, and translate overwhelming emotion into action that protects life instead of destroying it.

RFK Jr uses his story to argue for prevention, community, belonging, connection—structures that cradle the nervous system before crisis hits. I use mine to argue for mercy, proportionality, due process, compassion for physicians and patients caught in the crossfire of flawed policy, prosecutorial theatrics, and public stigma (The HHR Journal, 2025). Different podiums, same plea: treat suffering as suffering—not as crime.

And now, you—reading this page—you have your own version. Maybe quieter. Maybe louder. Maybe private. Maybe still unfolding. Addiction, trauma, compulsion, grief—these forces are democratic. They do not check last names at the door.

Recovery does not belong to one bloodline, one political dynasty, one famous tragedy.

Not even to a family named Kennedy.

Recovery belongs to every person who wakes up—shaking, exhausted, unsure—and still says, "I will use my scars for someone else's safety."

That sentence is not a slogan. It is a vow. It is a nervous system choosing life, again and again.

And that is where transformation truly begins.

CHAPTER 11

Locked in Stress Mode

(Stress Circuit)

> *"It always seems impossible until it's done."*
>
> — NELSON MANDELA

Living inside chronic stress

When you live with addiction, chronic stress does not feel like an abstract medical term, it feels like waking up in the morning already tired, with your chest tight, your jaw clenched, and a quiet sense of dread moving through your day before anything even happens. It is opening your eyes and feeling as if the day has already beaten you. Patients sit in my office and tell me the same line again and again, in slightly different words: "Doctor, I feel as if I ran a marathon in my sleep," or, "It's like my body is on high alert before my feet even touch the floor." They do not talk about cortisol or the hypothalamic–pituitary–adrenal axis, they talk about being exhausted before the day starts, heart pounding in traffic, shoulders never quite dropping, and about a level of anxiety that never fully leaves, even in supposedly "quiet" moments. That is what the chronic release of stress hormones does over time, especially when addiction sits on top of it, turning the body into a battleground where every small decision feels like survival (McEwen, 2007; Sinha, 2008).

Lessons from NIMH: circuits, not character

When I try to understand this, my memory goes back to my early years at the National Institute of Mental Health in Bethesda, Maryland. The campus had tall trees, long corridors, and the quiet intensity of people who spent their lives studying the brain. The air itself felt disciplined—quiet, humming with fluorescent lights and unanswered questions. I walked into that space as a young physician who had survived war in Aleppo and medical training in the United States, and I felt both privileged and humbled, like someone stepping into a cathedral built for human suffering and human possibility. Inside those buildings I listened to Dr Thomas Insel speak about mental illness in a way that rewired my own thinking. He spoke about circuits, about networks, about specific pathways in the brain that govern fear, reward, and control. He insisted that psychiatric conditions were brain disorders—not in the crude sense of a visible lesion on a scan, but in the sense of dysregulated circuits that develop over time under the pressure of genes, early experiences, and ongoing stress. He made it clear that illness was not a moral failure but an adaptation that went too far, a survival response that kept firing long after the threat was gone (Insel, 2015).

In those days, anxiety was not simply an emotion or a personality trait in our discussions. We examined the neural circuits that anticipate danger, at how the amygdala, hippocampus, and prefrontal cortex talk to each other when a person senses threat. We mapped what happens when the alarm system becomes the narrator of someone's life. We studied how repeated exposure to stress changes those circuits so that the brain begins to interpret ordinary situations—grocery stores, phone calls, waiting rooms—as dangerous, and keeps the body on constant alert (LeDoux, 2015; Arnsten, 2009). Later, when I sat across from patients with addiction-induced anxiety, I saw that same story unfold in real time, only now it carried the added weight of substances that had learned to sit in the middle of those circuits and push on them—accelerating fear, numbing connection, and training the nervous system to chase relief at any cost.

When survival never ends

To understand how this works, take the basic stress response. Your brain receives a signal of danger—sometimes a gunshot, sometimes a harsh word, sometimes a memory—and the hypothalamus sends a message to the pituitary, and the pituitary signals the adrenal glands to release cortisol. Within seconds, heart rate increases. Blood flow shifts to muscles. Pupils widen. The body prepares to run, fight, hide, survive. If the danger passes, the system is designed to settle. Cortisol falls, breathing slows, digestion resumes, and the body returns to baseline. That is how evolution intended it to function—a temporary alarm, not a permanent soundtrack.

But in chronic stress, the danger never feels as if it ends. The child who grows up in a war zone, the teenager who lives with daily violence or bullying, the adult who navigates poverty, constant discrimination, unstable housing, or family chaos—each develops a nervous system that learns to treat the world as persistently unsafe (McEwen, 2007). Cortisol stays elevated or fluctuates unpredictably. Muscles remain tense. Sleep becomes shallow and easily disrupted. The immune system begins to fray. Even silence feels suspicious. The sense of vigilance never fades, because the brain has decided vigilance is the only path to survival.

For me, the early template was Aleppo. Sirens that sounded like metal tearing. Explosions that shook the windows. Parents whispering worst-case scenarios when they thought we were asleep. Uncertainty about the next day, the next hour, the next breath. I did not have the language of neuroscience then—no hypothalamus, no amygdala, no cortisol curve—yet my body remembers that level of tension with perfect accuracy. Later, when I learned the science at NIMH, I could finally name what chronic trauma does to the stress circuits: how it sharpens alarms, blunts recovery, and engraves fear into muscle and memory.

So when I meet someone with addiction who grew up in an environment of chaos, their story makes immediate sense to me—not just emotionally, but biologically. Their nervous system was trained to expect danger and to search constantly for the fastest available way to reduce discomfort. In that context, addiction is not mysterious. It is predictable. It is the brain choosing relief over durability, now over later, survival over serenity—because that is the only vocabulary life ever taught it.

Reward, attachment, and the hijack

Once you add substances into that environment, the reward system enters the story—and everything accelerates. At NIMH we talked in simple but precise terms: dopamine, nucleus accumbens, ventral tegmental area, prefrontal cortex.

To most people, those words sound like distant laboratory jargon, the language of textbooks and conference slides. But in reality, they describe the machinery that decides what feels good, what feels worth effort, and what deserves attention—the invisible compass guiding daily life.

Thomas Insel had done elegant, almost poetic, work in animals, especially in small mammals whose pair-bonding behavior could be studied with scientific clarity. In prairie voles, for example, he showed that dopamine in the nucleus accumbens plays a central role in forming and maintaining social bonds. When that circuit is stimulated in a particular pattern, the animal forms a strong attachment to a single partner and stays near that partner. When the signal is blocked, the attachment falters and the pair drifts apart (Insel & Young, 2001). Those experiments were never really about vole romance—they were about the biology of reward, attachment, and devotion in social creatures, including us.

From that work arose a clear and humbling message: the neural circuits that respond to drugs are the same circuits that respond to touch, eye contact, shared meals, care, purpose, and recognition. The so-called "reward center" of the brain is also the "attachment center." Under healthy conditions, dopamine and related signals rise when parents care for their children, when friends reconnect after a long separation, when a person feels chosen, welcomed, or seen. Under the pressure of substances and chronic stress, however, that same machinery adapts in a different direction. Drugs produce a rapid, exaggerated dopamine surge—louder, faster, more intense than anything nature ever intended. Over time, the brain recalibrates its expectations. Natural pleasures weaken. Human connection feels muted. The contrast between the drug-induced signal and everything else grows wider and wider, like a widening canyon between life and aliveness (Koob & Volkow, 2016).

Around the same time that Insel and others were developing this circuit-based model of attachment and reward, Nora Volkow was producing images that made the science undeniable. Her PET scans showed how repeated use of cocaine, methamphetamine, alcohol, nicotine, and opioids alters dopamine receptors in the brain. She demonstrated reduced dopamine receptor availability in the striatum of people with addiction and revealed abnormalities in prefrontal regions responsible for judgment, planning, inhibition, and self-control (Volkow et al., 1997; Volkow et al., 2016). The pictures were not abstract art—they were evidence. They showed, in color and contour, how chronic substance exposure reshapes both the reward system and the control system. And once those circuits change, the person begins to experience intense craving, decreased ability to feel pleasure from ordinary activities, and a fraying capacity to resist urges.

In other words, addiction is not a mystery of character. It is a rewired brain trying—desperately, repeatedly—to return to a moment of relief.

Why relapse makes sense

When you combine Insel's work on social attachment and reward with Volkow's imaging of addiction, a picture emerges of what I call hijacked minds—brains that have not failed, but adapted too well to environments of fear, deprivation, or overwhelm. In a person with addiction and chronic anxiety, stress circuits, reward circuits, and control circuits are not operating as separate departments. They behave like three musicians playing different songs at maximum volume. The stress system pours out cortisol, heightening vigilance, tightening muscles, sharpening fear, and feeding a constant sense of unease. The reward system, once tuned to joy, warmth, belonging, creativity, and ordinary pleasure, now responds most strongly to substances or addictive behaviors and weakly to almost everything else. And the prefrontal cortex—the part of the brain meant to regulate impulses, imagine the future, delay gratification, and choose alignment over relief—loses influence after years of stress, trauma, sleep disruption, inflammation, and exposure to rapid, artificial reward (Arnsten, 2009; Koob & Volkow, 2016).

In daily life, this neuroscience looks heartbreakingly ordinary. You feel anxious from the moment you wake. You spend the day trying to function through restlessness, dread, or mental fog. You find focus only when moving toward the substance, behavior, or ritual that has become central in your emotional economy. And once you engage with it—whether it is alcohol, opioids, cannabis, gambling, binge eating, pornography, work, shopping, social media, or self-harm—you feel a brief exhale, a fragile moment of relief. Then shame returns. Problems return. Stress returns. Cortisol rises again, and the cycle restarts, often stronger than before.

Patients describe this dynamic with heartbreaking clarity. One might tell me, "When I am sober, I feel so nervous and restless that I cannot sit still, and my thoughts race. When I drink or use, for a short time I feel normal—then I feel worse, and my anxiety returns even stronger." Another might say, "I do not experience joy from anything except the drug, and even the drug does not work like before." These are not metaphors or excuses. When you understand cortisol, dopamine, synaptic pruning, and prefrontal inhibition, those statements become neurobiologically precise. They are the human translation of what the scans and circuit diagrams describe.

At NIMH, we did not only study the circuitry in isolation—we confronted how early these patterns begin. We saw that half of all lifetime mental illness starts in youth, often before age twenty-four (Kessler et al., 2005). Anxiety disorders, depression, and substance use disorders frequently overlap like three roots of the same underground tree. A teenager with untreated anxiety and no language for distress might experiment with alcohol or cannabis for relief. A young adult with early trauma, unstable attachment, and genetic vulnerability might discover that opioids quiet emotional pain more effectively than anything else. A child raised in unpredictable environments might learn to soothe themselves with food, screens, or compulsive behaviors long before adulthood.

Over time, repetition becomes wiring. Wiring becomes habit. Habit becomes identity. And by the time a person arrives in an adult psychiatric clinic or addiction program, several circuits have already adapted to years of stress and self-medication—circuits built not out of weakness, but out of survival.

The human cost—and what must change

The way we trained physicians did not always reflect that reality. Medical students and residents often told me they felt uneasy when talking about addiction, trauma, or relentless anxiety. They could recite neurotransmitters, DSM criteria, and medication side effects from memory. They could order labs and adjust dosages.

Yet many felt unprepared—almost tongue-tied—when trying to explain to a patient how chronic stress reshapes the brain, how reward circuitry adapts to survive, or why relapse is not betrayal but physiology. They lacked a coherent narrative that made sense not only to them, but to the person sitting across the room. And without that narrative, treatment conversations remained shallow and transactional. "Stop drinking." "Take this medication." "Go to therapy." When these instructions arrive without a framework, patients rarely hear compassion or collaboration—they hear accusation, disappointment, or abandonment.

My time under Thomas Insel's leadership changed my own approach. He refused to let neuroscience remain trapped in academic journals or conference slides. He reminded us that discoveries mean nothing if they do not reach the street, the clinic, the prison, the shelter, the family dinner table. He often pointed out that we had invested billions in imaging, genetics, and molecular psychiatry while many people with severe mental illness still lacked stable housing, adequate food, and basic continuity of care. Knowledge alone did not reduce suffering—translation did. What mattered was how we turned that knowledge into prevention, diagnosis, and treatment systems that touched real human beings (Insel, 2022). For addiction and anxiety, translation begins with a different kind of clinical conversation—one that sounds like, "Your brain and body adapted to years of stress and substance use in ways that made sense at the time, but now those adaptations cause harm. Together we will work to calm your stress system, retrain your reward system, and strengthen your capacity for self-control, safety, attachment, and meaning."

Cortisol plays a central role in the exhausting cycle that many of my patients describe. In early abstinence, stress-hormone patterns are often chaotic and unpredictable. People report restless sleep, early morning jolts awake, tight chests, buzzing nerves, and racing thoughts—even when they are no longer intoxicated or actively withdrawing. They react intensely to small frustrations, like spilled coffee or a late bus. They feel emotionally thin-skinned, as if the world lost its padding. In that state, the pull of the old substance or compulsive behavior remains terrifyingly strong, not because the person wants to destroy their life, but because the brain vividly remembers that it once brought rapid relief. The nervous system then presents a cruel and urgent choice: endure overwhelming anxiety with no clear end point, or return to the only strategy that has ever worked quickly. Without support—medical, psychological, relational, structural—many return. From the outside, observers label this relapse and assign moral judgment. From the inside, the person experiences it as the only available survival response, the only way to breathe through the next hour (Sinha, 2008)

Healing requires biology and belonging

This is why I speak in this book about the soul as well as the brain. The soul, as I use the term, refers to your sense of self—your internal compass, your capacity for meaning, purpose, and connection. It is the part of you that remembers who you hoped to become before life intervened. When reward circuitry becomes tied to a substance and chronic stress dominates your internal climate, you begin to feel cut off from your own goals and values. You may feel as if you are watching your life from a distance, like a poorly edited documentary about someone who looks familiar but no longer feels like you. You still care about your children, your partner, your work, your faith, your community—those commitments remain intact at the level of belief—yet your daily behavior does not match those loyalties, because your brain has been trained to chase immediate relief despite long-term cost. That mismatch between what you value and what you do produces shame, and shame itself adds a new layer of stress. Cortisol rises, self-blame sharpens, isolation spreads, and the loop tightens again, trapping both body and identity in its grip.

The same biology applies to physicians and trainees, though we rarely acknowledge it openly. During residency and fellowship, I watched colleagues live with chronic sleep deprivation, emotional overload, and the invisible weight of perfectionism. We carried pagers like time bombs, waiting for the next crisis. The hidden curriculum was unmistakable: ignore your own anxiety, push through exhaustion, and treat every symptom of stress as evidence of strength or loyalty to the profession. Some turned to substances—quiet wine, stimulants, leftover opioids from dental surgery. Others turned to compulsive work, over-exercising, or food, or late-night online shopping, anything that offered a few minutes of relief. Their cortisol patterns were likely abnormal, their reward circuits increasingly narrowed around a handful of behaviors that numbed or distracted. When you train a workforce in this way, you end up with clinicians who have learned to disconnect from their own emotions for survival. And a clinician who cannot feel their own fear, sadness, hunger, or longing will struggle to sit fully with patients who speak about anxiety, trauma, and addiction.

The broader statistics reinforce this picture rather than soften it. Rates of burnout, depression, and anxiety in medical students, residents, fellows, and attending physicians remain high. Suicide among young physicians remains an alarming and persistent problem, with heartbreaking stories emerging every year (Rotenstein et al., 2018). When a profession teaches its members to function under chronic stress without meaningful attention to their mental health, the biology we describe in patients—cortisol dysregulation, narrowed reward seeking, emotional numbing—will inevitably appear in clinicians. We then ask those clinicians to care for people whose stress and reward circuits are also dysregulated, whose nervous systems are equally exhausted. The result is a healthcare system where both sides of the encounter sit across from each other depleted, overstimulated, and silently longing for relief.

A healthier future requires change in several layers at once. For patients, we must screen routinely for trauma histories, chronic stress exposure, and substance use—not as afterthoughts, but as foundations of care. We must explain, in accessible human language, how these experiences shape the brain, rather than defaulting to moral judgment or vague reassurance. We must move away from scolding, shaming, or oversimplified instructions, and toward narratives that describe adaptation, learning, survival, and possibility. We need treatments that directly target reward circuitry and stress regulation—medications when appropriate, psychotherapies that teach emotional regulation and cognitive flexibility, neuromodulation techniques like TMS, digital therapeutics that support patients between appointments, and structured routines that strengthen the brain's capacity for predictability and calm. We also need to remember the quieter interventions—sleep, nutrition, movement, safe relationships, nature, faith, creativity—because these experiences directly influence stress hormones and reward systems just as powerfully as pills or procedures.

For clinicians and trainees, we need training programs that integrate neuroscience, lived experience, and self-care rather than treating them as separate domains. We should teach medical students early about dopamine, cortisol, and neural plasticity—not as isolated exam facts, but as frameworks they can use during real conversations with frightened, ashamed, or overwhelmed patients. We should normalize honest discussions about our own stress, anxiety, grief, and coping behaviors, and build institutional cultures where seeking help is treated as professionalism, not weakness. When physicians understand their own stress responses—physiologically, emotionally, relationally—they become more effective, less reactive, and more compassionate when treating patients with addiction-induced anxiety.

Thomas Insel, after leaving NIMH, spoke more urgently about the widening gap between scientific progress and clinical outcomes. He pointed out that people with serious mental illness still struggle with homelessness, incarceration, unemployment, traumatic family environments, and fragmented care systems. He argued that a century of neuroscience will not reduce suffering if patients cannot access housing, coordinated treatment, social connection, and community (Insel, 2022). For addiction, his message aligns with what Nora Volkow has advocated for years—we need less punishment and more treatment, less stigma and more science, fewer prison cells and more integrated care. We need policy that recognizes addiction as a chronic brain disease shaped by social conditions, trauma exposure, genetic vulnerability, and environmental stress—not as a simplistic choice deserving condemnation (Volkow & Koob, 2022).

Your nervous system can learn a new life

When I think about the future of mental health and addiction treatment, I see the influence of both of these leaders in my own work. I see a field that must honor the intricate complexity of reward circuitry and stress biology while staying grounded in the simplest, most ancient human needs: safety, connection, purpose, dignity, belonging. The science gives us language, models, and tools to describe and measure change. But it is the stories—the trembling voice in an exam room, the physician crying after rounds, the silent shame of relapse, the unexpected courage of trying again—that remind us why we entered this field in the first place and why we must continue refining it. Progress is not only data points and journal articles; it is a patient sleeping through the night for the first time in years, a family forgiving one another, a clinician rediscovering compassion after burnout.

If you live with addiction-induced anxiety, I want you to hear one central point clearly, without metaphor or medical jargon: your brain learned to respond to chronic stress in ways that made sense at the time. Your use of substances or addictive behaviors began as a response to pain, fear, isolation, humiliation, or emptiness—not as a desire to sabotage your future or destroy your relationships. The circuits that now feel rigid, automatic, or hopeless are not frozen. They are plastic, alive, capable of change. They respond to new experiences, new relationships, new habits, new stories about who you are. The work, however, is demanding. The early stages of change often feel worse before they feel better, because cortisol remains high while old rewards lose their intensity, leaving a temporary void. That is why support from clinicians, peers, family, community, spirituality, structure, and hope is not optional—it is neurological scaffolding. No one rewires a stressed and hijacked brain alone.

When you and I sit together in my office, our conversation quietly gathers many threads. It carries the echoes of Aleppo—the sirens, the dust, the instinct to survive before understanding. It holds the quiet memory of lecture halls at NIMH, where Thomas Insel taught us to think in terms of circuits, outcomes, and lives rather than labels. It includes the colorful brain images from Nora Volkow's work, showing us how addiction physically reshapes reward systems and decision-making pathways. It incorporates the stories of countless patients whose lives, tragedies, failures, triumphs, and resilience have taught me as much as any textbook, fellowship, or research study. All of that stands behind my simple words when I tell you that your anxiety, your cravings, your shame, and your exhaustion make sense—not morally, but biologically, emotionally, historically—in light of what your brain and body have endured.

You deserve treatment that respects both your biology and your humanity. You deserve a future in which your stress system is steadier, your breathing slower, your nights quieter, your mornings less burdened. A future in which your reward circuitry once again responds to ordinary joys—conversation, kindness, laughter, food eaten without guilt, a walk at sunset, the touch of someone who loves you. A future where your days are not ruled by fear of the next panic or the next relapse, but guided by curiosity, meaning, and agency. The science from NIMH, the work of Insel and Volkow, and the stories from my own practice all point to the same truth. Minds can be hijacked, rewired, shaken by trauma and addiction—and still remain capable of healing, growth, and reinvention.

Your story is not fixed in the circuitry that protected you in the past. It is not confined to dopamine, cortisol, or survival instincts. Together we work to write a new pattern, neuron by neuron, session by session, moment by moment, guided not only by what we know about the brain but also by what your soul tells us about the life you are still reaching for—the life you deserve.

PART TWO

The Drugs That Hijack America

CHAPTER 12

Painkillers and Pills

> *Liberty without virtue would be no blessing to us.*
>
> — DR. BENJAMIN RUSH

Benjamin Rush in a wall in Easton

The day I met Dr Benjamin Rush, he had already been dead for two centuries, and I was standing in a cloud of construction dust on North 13th Street in Easton. My new office at 241 North 13th Street—a weary stone building from the 1800s—had surrendered its walls to electricians and carpenters. Plaster cracked open like old ribs. Wooden lath, dry as bone, fell away in splinters. We were simply trying to run wiring, to bring a bit of the twenty-first century into a nineteenth-century frame.

Then the past rolled out onto the floor.

Behind the lath, the workers uncovered a parchment—browned, brittle, curled tight like a sleeping creature that had forgotten the sound of human hands. When they placed it in mine, dust still rising in the air around us, I felt the weight shift. Not physical weight, but historical gravity.

I unrolled it slowly.

The Declaration of Independence stared back at me.

Not a poster.

Not a reproduction.

A scroll of freedom—folded, hidden, protected—tucked inside a wall by someone who understood what danger and hope looked like in equal measure. Easton was one of only three places where those words were read at noon on July 8, 1776, the same day as Philadelphia and Trenton (Easton, Pennsylvania, n.d.). A river town that heard liberty spoken early and loud.

I did not sell it.

I did not hang it in my waiting room.

Some artifacts demand reverence, not decoration.

I carried it to the Easton Declaration of Independence Museum myself. Now it rests there under glass, under carefully arranged light, breathing across centuries—a covenant between the dead and the living, between the ink of revolution and the dust on my shoes.

And in that moment—an immigrant from Aleppo holding a nation's founding words in an office undergoing renovation—I felt history lean forward, as if to say: Pay attention. You belong to this story more than you know.

The first American psychiatrist

Standing there—still a boy from Aleppo in some part of my soul, plaster dust on my shoes and history in my hands—I thought of the men who had signed that document in Philadelphia. Farmers with calloused palms. Lawyers whose words shaped nations. Merchants who gambled everything on a fragile new idea. And among them, five physicians—men who understood the human mind before the world had a word like psychiatry to describe that terrain (Pennsylvania Hospital History: Stories – Dr. Benjamin Rush, n.d.; Social, Cultural, and Historical Perspectives – Rush, Benjamin, 2015).

Benjamin Rush: signer from Pennsylvania, surgeon general of the Continental Army, educator, reformer, restless architect of American medicine. The man we now call the father of American psychiatry (Benjamin Rush, n.d.; Biography: Benjamin Rush, MD, n.d.; Benjamin Rush and Early American Medicine, n.d.).

While others in his century pointed to demons, curses, or divine punishment, Rush dared to say that madness lived in the mind and the body, not in the wrath of spirits. He spoke of irritated blood vessels—an explanation crude by our standards but revolutionary in his. With that one shift, he cracked open a door that had been sealed for centuries, a door every psychiatrist has walked through since (Biography: Benjamin Rush, MD, n.d.; Stigma in Historical Medical Literature on Alcohol Addiction, 2021). Including a Syrian immigrant who would one day practice a few miles up the Lehigh, holding a parchment that tied him across continents and centuries to that same work.

But Rush did not stop at madness. Long before the word alcoholism entered medical vocabulary, he turned his attention to what he called "habitual drunkenness." In 1784, he published a small treatise with an impossibly long title: An Inquiry into the Effects of Ardent Spirits upon the Human Body and Mind. Within those brittle eighteenth-century pages, he described what we now recognize instantly: a progressive medical condition with craving, loss of control, physical decline, and death (National Prohibition in the United States, 2014; Social, Cultural, and Historical Perspectives – Rush, Benjamin, 2015).

He named the habitual use of distilled spirits an "odious disease." He warned that liquor disordered both body and mind. He drew diagrams of the descent—stages of drunkenness mapped like a slow, predictable collapse. He wrote that the drinker's will erodes over time. He spoke not only of punishment but of cure. Historians now point to that pamphlet as one of the first American articulations of addiction as disease, long before dopamine receptors flickered on PET scans or diagnostic manuals carried numbers and codes (National Prohibition in the United States, 2014; Stigma in Historical Medical Literature on Alcohol Addiction, 2021).

His treatments—bleeding, purging, spinning chairs, tranquilizer devices—strike us now as barbaric. And they were. But beneath those misguided tools lived a belief that still undergirds everything in this book:

That addiction is not a simple failure of morals.

That a mind in trouble deserves science, structure, and compassion.

That a person who drinks or uses despite catastrophic harm is not a villain, but a human being living in a hijacked brain (Benjamin Rush and Early American Medicine, n.d.; Biography: Benjamin Rush, MD, n.d.).

When I read Rush today, I hear the awkward, courageous birth of the language I use in clinics every day. He wrote of "ardent spirits." I write of fentanyl, heroin, oxycodone, benzodiazepines, stimulants—substances whose repeated exposure rewires stress and reward circuits in ways he could never have imagined. He described a slide from casual use, to habitual, to enslaved, to ruined. I describe a shift from social use, to compulsive use, to craving that devours conscience, to a life that narrows into a tunnel.

Different centuries. Different vocabularies.

The grief is the same.

Liberty, democracy, and addiction

Benjamin Rush and the Quiet Tyranny Inside the Bottle

Benjamin Rush sat in a hall in Philadelphia and lifted his pen under the words "We mutually pledge to each other our Lives, our Fortunes and our sacred Honor." He believed in revolt against tyranny, yet he also believed in revolt against the quiet tyranny inside a bottle. He wrote about the way alcohol changes judgment, injures families, and destroys capacity for citizenship. He worried not only about drunk individuals, but about a drunk republic. He saw addiction as a threat to democracy as much as to biology (Pennsylvania Hospital History: Stories – Dr. Benjamin Rush, n.d.; Social, Cultural, and Historical Perspectives – Rush, Benjamin, 2015). For that reason alone, his presence in this chapter matters. Hijacked Minds are not only a clinical problem. They are a constitutional problem.

Two hundred years later, I stood in an Easton office and held a parchment tied to his signature. I practice in a state he served. I treat illnesses he tried to name. In my work, addiction is no longer limited to "ardent spirits." It wears the face of a suburban father whose back surgery led to oxycodone, then to heroin, then to fentanyl pressed into counterfeit pills. It wears the face of a nurse whose first taste of hydrocodone came after an injury on a busy shift, then crept into her breaks and her nights. It wears the face of a teenager who raided a medicine cabinet and found more power than any teenager should hold.

Carrying Rush Into the Exam Room

When I see those patients in my office, I carry Rush in the back of my mind. I hear his rough sketches of brain disease, his insistence that the person in front of him is a patient, not a sinner to be mocked (Stigma in Historical Medical Literature on Alcohol Addiction, 2021). I also carry the document I returned to the museum. The Declaration speaks of life, liberty, and the pursuit of happiness. Addiction erodes all three. Life narrows to survival between doses. Liberty shrinks into a sequence of compulsions and withdrawals. Happiness dissolves into a brief numbness followed by shame. My job in Easton, on North 13th Street, is to stand between that erosion and the person whose brain has forgotten how to choose.

Rush believed mental diseases arose from physical changes in the brain, even if his theory focused on blood vessels and excitability rather than synapses and receptors. In this book I describe how addiction rewires circuits of reward, stress, and executive function. He wrote by candlelight. I watch blood flow in real time with near-infrared light. He heard groans and confessions. I hear those same sounds, and I see their echoes in neuroimaging and in lab values. The spirit of our work is the same. A brain under siege deserves treatment. A person who drinks or uses in a way that destroys health and relationships is not beyond hope.

Freedom, Rediscovered

The scroll in my wall felt like a message. Freedom is not self-executing. Someone has to find the document again in every generation, blow off the dust, and decide to live by it. The same is true for the disease model of addiction. Rush wrote his pamphlet centuries ago, yet in exam rooms and courtrooms I still meet people who believe addiction is nothing but weakness. I still meet systems that respond to a brain disease with handcuffs, ridicule, and neglect. Each time I write a prescription for buprenorphine or naltrexone, each time I recommend residential treatment instead of jail, each time I tell a family their loved one lives with a chronic, treatable illness, I feel I am signing my name under Rush's old argument. Habitual drunkenness, habitual opioid use, habitual cocaine use—these are not simple vices. These are diseases that deserve the full weight of medicine (Substance Abuse and Mental Health Services Administration, 2023).

The Aim We Inherit

Chapter 13 opens in that space between parchment and patient. Between the ink of a Founding Father who saw madness and addiction as diseases of the mind, and the dust of a small office in Easton where an immigrant psychiatrist fights a modern opioid epidemic. Benjamin Rush aimed well, in war and in medicine. My task in this chapter is to pick up that aim. To show you how the disease he tried to describe in an age of rum and whiskey now wears the mask of fentanyl and prescription opioids. To honor his courage and correct his errors. To link his belief in a diseased brain to our current understanding of hijacked neural pathways. And to remember, every time I walk past the museum that holds that scroll, that freedom on paper means nothing if minds remain in chains.

The Opioid Pandemic

I write these words because I carry the memory of what I witnessed between 2013 and 2025 in Pennsylvania. I carry the names. I carry the funerals. I carry the small, improbable victories that kept us from drowning entirely. These years live in me like a shadow that lengthens at dusk—every patient, every family, every attempt at survival etched into its shape.

In 2013, the opioid crisis was no longer a warning on the horizon; it was already rooted in the daily life of the state. Pain pills, once prescribed freely for sprains, fractures, backaches—simple injuries that never deserved such force—had seeded dependencies no one meant to grow. By 2015, overdose deaths began to climb in a curve so steep it felt like watching a graph catch fire. Between 2015 and 2018, drug-related overdose deaths rose by 36 percent. Families who had never imagined addiction in their bloodline found themselves reading toxicology reports and planning interventions instead of birthday parties. By 2019, Pennsylvania's opioid-related mortality rates had surged from roughly 5 per 100,000 to nearly 24 per 100,000—a nearly 475 percent increase in a decade (Centers for Disease Control and Prevention, 2024b; Pennsylvania Department of Health, 2024).

Then came fentanyl—illicit, synthetic, powerful, cheap. It slipped into pills, into heroin, into the veins of people who had no idea the rules had changed. The supply shifted. The risk skyrocketed. The landscape of addiction became unrecognisable. By 2021, more than 5,300 Pennsylvanians died of overdose—fourteen people every day (Pennsylvania Department of Health, 2024). Their stories were devastatingly ordinary. A construction worker with a back injury. A university student sharing pills at a party. A grandmother recovering from knee surgery. A father who fell from prescribed oxycodone into heroin when the refill was denied.

Fentanyl simplified everything except grief. It made overdose quick. It made the margin of error zero. It made relapse lethal. Some families tried for the tenth time to help their loved one get clean. Some surrendered after the third Narcan rescue in their living room. Some found themselves standing beside a grave, holding a small wooden box containing every birthday their child would now miss.

I saw the crisis from inside its marrow. I saw people unravel. I saw futures evaporate. I saw the weight of judgment—police reports, court orders, jail releases, coroners' vans. I saw hallways lined with code blues and families clutching hope like a torn photograph. But I also saw resistance. I saw resilience that defied even biology's cruelty.

Treatment began to evolve under pressure. At first, we offered what we had: detox, oral methadone, sublingual buprenorphine, counselling. We offered hope on difficult terms—show up every day, answer the phone, follow every rule, hold on tighter than the craving holds you. For some, that rope held. For many, it snapped (Substance Abuse and Mental Health Services Administration, 2023).

Then, midway through the decade, injectable medications arrived and changed everything. Monthly naltrexone injections—Vivitrol—blocked opioid receptors and removed the "reward" from opioids. Monthly buprenorphine injections followed—first Sublocade, then in 2023 a new option, Brixadi, offering weekly or monthly dosing (Alkermes, 2023; Indivior Inc., 2017; U.S. Food and Drug Administration, 2023). These medications removed the daily struggle. No more counting pills. No more shame at a pharmacy counter. They gave people something rarely offered in addiction care: time. Time to rebuild trust. Time to reconnect with children. Time to breathe.

By 2023, overdose deaths in Pennsylvania declined to 4,719, and early 2024 estimates fell again. The age-adjusted overdose death rate dropped from 40.9 per 100,000 in 2022 to 37.1 in 2023. Synthetic opioid deaths began to dip. Data, for the first time in decades, allowed cautious hope (Centers for Disease Control and Prevention, 2024b; Pennsylvania Department of Health, 2024; Wilson, 2024).

Hope felt fragile, yes—but hope also felt real. For the first time since 1999, national overdose deaths fell. The sharpest yearly decline in decades (Centers for Disease Control and Prevention, 2024a). Why? More naloxone in homes and purses. More clinics offering MAT. More outreach in rural towns and inner cities. More stories of survival shared across tables, therapy rooms, and recovery halls. Policy shifted—slightly—toward health care and away from punishment (Hedegaard & Spencer, 2021; Substance Abuse and Mental Health Services Administration, 2023).

I remember a family in Allentown: their son in his late twenties, found unresponsive in a gas-station bathroom. Two naloxone doses saved him. His parents arrived in my office hollowed out by fear. After stabilization, we offered monthly buprenorphine injection. He accepted. He stuck with therapy. He rebuilt a relationship with his little girl. He found work stocking supermarket shelves. He called once a month to say thank you. He is alive. The path remains fragile, but alive is a worthy beginning.

I remember a nurse in southern Pennsylvania who nearly died from a fentanyl-tainted pill. Detox after detox. Shame. Guilt. Divorce. Debt. The slow collapse of a once-steady life. She chose extended-release naltrexone. She cried every evening for the first month, terrified the cravings would return. They did not. In her third month, she took her daughter to the park and watched her run under sunlit leaves. "You gave me this moment," she said. "I hope one day she forgets the pills and remembers me."

Across the state, treatment hubs formed. Clinics expanded. Prisons and jails finally began offering medication. Emergency rooms stocked naloxone and referral pathways. Peer recovery specialists walked into living rooms and said what families could not: I understand (Substance Abuse and Mental Health Services Administration, 2023).

Graduations from rehab became solemn but hopeful rituals. A small cake. A photo. A prayer. A breath held—carefully. And for the first time in years, some anniversaries arrived without the weight of an obituary. Some mothers did not bury their children. Some fathers saw their sons graduate. Some children kept their parents.

The crisis is not over. Fentanyl remains. Poverty remains. Trauma, unemployment, chronic pain, despair—they all remain. But the shape of the response changed. It grew less about shame and punishment, more about medicine and care. Recovery became less a gamble and more a process. A difficult process, yes—but a process (Substance Abuse and Mental Health Services Administration, 2023).

I write this section as both warning and promise. Warning that addiction adapts, that drugs evolve, that despair deepens in the soil of economic and emotional hardship. But promise, too. Promise that medicine adapts. That compassionate care spreads. That science continues to build better tools. That a once-monthly shot can open a door to a life a person thought they had already forfeited. That investment in treatment saves lives (Centers for Disease Control and Prevention, 2024a, 2024b).

I write this because I remember the dead. I remember the living. I remember the nearly dead who clawed their way back. I remember the families that collapsed, and the families that healed—just enough. I remember the long road along Riverside Drive in Bethlehem. I remember the hope in the eyes of those who walked out clean. And the grief in the eyes of those who walked out alone.

From 2013 to 2025, we walked through darkness. We lost too many. We treated too few. We battled stigma. We battled policy. We suffered. We learned. We adapted. We built new mechanisms of care. We built systems that might—just might—hold. And still, I believe another world is possible. A world where no prescription for pain becomes a path to death. A world where families do not stand beside fresh graves holding unanswered questions. A world where recovery does not begin on a dead-end road. A world where medicine, psychiatry, compassion, and community stand guard at every doorway.

A world where survival is not rare—where it is expected.

A world where we finally break the chain.

The Rich and the Famous

Many actors and public figures became inadvertent mirrors for the opioid epidemic—reflecting not glamour, but the same quiet unraveling that I saw every week in clinic rooms from Allentown to Bethlehem. Their stories travelled across kitchen tables and car radios, into waiting rooms and late-night conversations. Two of those stories stayed with me more than the others: Rush Limbaugh and Gerard Butler. One spoke daily to millions about politics and culture. The other filled theatres with action and charisma. Yet both were carried to the same desolate place—alone with pain pills and a body that no longer listened to reason.

Rush Limbaugh, the conservative radio titan whose voice rattled America for decades, eventually told his listeners in 2003 that he was addicted to prescription opioids. Severe back pain had led to prescriptions; prescriptions to dependence; dependence to despair. His departure for inpatient treatment left millions stunned. For many in his audience, it was the first time a man who condemned drugs so loudly admitted to being caught in the same chemical net. Court documents later revealed a criminal investigation into large quantities of opioid medication and allegations of doctor shopping. In 2006, Limbaugh turned himself in on a single prescription-related charge and completed a structured agreement involving treatment, random drug testing, and payment toward investigative costs. His record was ultimately expunged. But the story remained: a man who spoke in absolutes about personal responsibility had found himself in the same trap as the patients sitting across from me in Easton (Rush Limbaugh, n.d.).

Gerard Butler stood on a different stage. A Scottish actor known for physical roles and a confident public image, he carried injuries from training and a later surfing accident that left him in chronic pain. Pills followed. Then reliance. In 2012, reports emerged that he had completed treatment at the Betty Ford Center for problems with prescription painkillers. Later he spoke openly about fearing where that dependence would lead. Fans saw him back on red carpets as though nothing had happened; but the truth remained in the background—a reminder that a body chiseled for battle scenes could not protect its owner from the slow erosion caused by a legal prescription (Gerard Butler, n.d.).

These two men walked different political paths, came from different continents, and spoke to different audiences. Yet their journeys revealed the same anatomy of addiction in wealthy societies. Pain began the story. Medication followed. Escalation happened quietly—in private homes, on film sets, in hotel rooms between events. Shame drifted in only after control had vanished. Legal consequences appeared only when neighbors, staff, or media exposed what had been unfolding in silence. For every celebrity whose name appeared in a headline, hundreds of thousands of ordinary Americans lived the same story without witnesses.

Families across the country saw that same pattern unfold. A father hurt his back and filled an oxycodone prescription. A mother took hydrocodone after dental surgery and found she could no longer feel normal without it. A college athlete sprained a knee and accepted a small orange bottle from a trainer. Higher doses followed. Longer courses. A brain slowly rewired to treat a pill as the only rescue. When prescriptions tightened, many turned to whatever source remained. Some found heroin. Others found counterfeit pills pressed with fentanyl, stamped to resemble the medications once dispensed in pharmacies (Centers for Disease Control and Prevention, 2024a).

Stories like Limbaugh's and Butler's illuminated only a sliver of a much larger tragedy. But their visibility mattered. Listeners who trusted Limbaugh heard the word addiction spoken in his own voice. Viewers who admired Butler saw him acknowledge the dangers of prescription medication. That honesty chipped away at destructive myths. Addiction was not a partisan flaw. It did not discriminate by wealth, race, or gender. It moved into homes with swimming pools and private physicians as easily as it moved into apartments above laundromats or trailers near the railroad tracks.

I remember how often patients referenced these stories. A man from a rural county once told me, "If Rush Limbaugh got hooked, what chance did I have?" A young woman who loved action films whispered, "When Gerard Butler went to rehab, I stopped feeling ashamed. If someone like him can need help, maybe I'm not hopeless." Sometimes a famous name opened a door that lectures about willpower and responsibility could never unlock.

Yet these stories also revealed fractures in public compassion. When a beloved actor sought treatment, headlines softened, praising courage and responsibility. When a polarising political figure faced opioid-related charges, the reaction split along party lines—empathy from some, ridicule from others. That divide mirrored the deeper national fault line over addiction treatment: who receives medical care and who receives handcuffs.

Prescription drug misuse tore through American households during the same years. Grandparents raised grandchildren after overdoses. Siblings sent messages swinging between anger and desperation. Parents slept with phones on their pillows waiting for a call from a hospital—or a call from the police. Teenagers learned the names of pills before they learned algebra. Children found adults unconscious on couches and floors. Those children carried love and fear in the same small body.

High-profile stories offered a glimpse of one path forward. Professionals conducted medical assessments. Treatment teams designed detox and stabilization plans. In the last decade, extended-release injectable medications became standard care. Monthly naltrexone injections blocked opioid receptors. Long-acting buprenorphine injections—first Sublocade, then Brixadi in 2023—offered stability without daily dosing (Alkermes, 2023; Indivior Inc., 2017; U.S. Food and Drug Administration, 2023). These medications bought time. Time for therapy. Time for employment support. Time to rebuild trust with families. Time to remember what life looked like without a pill bottle (Substance Abuse and Mental Health Services Administration, 2023).

Famous patients often accessed these tools early. The real test of a society is whether the same treatments reach those without fame: mothers working double shifts, veterans navigating pain and trauma, people sleeping in shelters, teenagers in foster homes, individuals entering courtrooms in handcuffs. All deserve the same chance at recovery.

Rush Limbaugh and Gerard Butler showed two faces of the same illness. One condemned drug use until he was swallowed by it. The other entertained millions while privately fighting pill dependence. Both inhabited a body reshaped by opioid exposure. Both triggered national conversations. Both reminded us that prescription opioids do not touch only "other" people. They sit in millions of medicine cabinets. The risk sits quietly in nearly every extended family.

When I sit with patients, I carry those celebrity stories alongside the thousands of anonymous ones. I have seen how public confession turns shame into something manageable, how a famous person's recovery can create space for someone in a small town to ask for help. I have also seen how legal systems treat defendants differently depending on wealth, race, and fame. This raises a blunt question: will the attention paid to celebrities lead to more compassion and treatment for everyone—or will safety remain a privilege reserved for those with resources and recognition?

Addiction medicine grows through science and through story. Data guide us—dose ranges, relapse rates, mortality curves. Stories move us—faces, children, funerals, small triumphs. The stories of Limbaugh and Butler entered the public square. Families watched. They judged. They cried. They hoped. And sometimes—just sometimes—they acted.

If even one parent called a doctor sooner, or one young person reached for help instead of swallowing another handful of pills, those public admissions saved a life. For a physician who has watched far too many obituaries pile up on a desk, that matters.

CHAPTER 13

Stimulants and Seduction

(Cocaine, Meth, Amphetamines)

> *"It does not matter how slowly you go as long as you do not stop."*
>
> — CONFUCIUS

The Road to Riverside Drive

The first time I drove down Riverside Drive in Bethlehem in 2013, the road felt longer than any map suggested. A narrow two-lane strip shadowed the edge of the Lehigh River, bending and curving as if unsure whether to follow the water or flee from it. Warehouses slouched along the shoulder. Brush pressed inward. The river ran dark on one side, indifferent.

At the very end of that road sat three addresses that told the truth about addiction in America with a bluntness no brochure ever would:

- Lehigh County Center for Recovery.
- Lehigh County jail work release.
- A satellite division of the coroner's office.

Treatment. Jail. Death —Three outcomes arranged like warnings at the end of a dead-end road.

That same year, I became the founding medical director of the Lehigh County Center for Recovery at 1620 Riverside Drive. The county had partnered with CRC Health Group's White Deer Run division to build an adult detoxification and residential rehabilitation program meant to serve as a model for people living with both substance use and psychiatric disorders (PR Newswire, 2013).

On the morning of the grand opening, General Barry McCaffrey, former White House drug czar, stood at the podium flanked by state and county leaders. They spoke about a national model for dual-diagnosis care, about innovation, about closing a widening treatment gap. Behind their speeches, behind the ribbon and the cameras, another truth waited quietly: this building was about to become the place where hope, desperation, and science met every single day.

Entering the Work

Behind the podiums and the ribbon, a different responsibility waited. My responsibility. I did not arrive as a technician assigned to run a detox ward. I arrived as a physician trained in internal medicine, psychiatry, and addiction medicine—three disciplines that rarely live comfortably in one body, yet all of them necessary here. My task was not to manage beds; it was to care for whole people whose hearts, lungs, livers, and brains bore the layered scars of use, withdrawal, trauma, and neglect.

Many came in with psychosis, major depression, panic, or bipolar disorder woven tightly into years of dependence on heroin, prescription opioids, alcohol, benzodiazepines, or stimulants. Others carried diabetes, cirrhosis, heart disease, or COPD alongside their addictions. Every admission represented three specialties at once, sometimes four, sometimes more.

Lehigh County Center for Recovery opened modestly—about three dozen beds, with an eight-bed medically monitored detox unit and a residential wing. On paper, the program promised twenty-four-hour nursing, medical oversight, psychiatric evaluation, and structured therapy (White Deer Run of Lehigh, n.d.). In real time, the work was far less tidy. Patients arrived from emergency rooms, shelters, outpatient clinics, probation offices, and family interventions. Each arrival carried fear that showed itself in different ways—shaking, silence, defiance, tears. Each discharge carried risk, no matter how stable the vital signs looked.

The Opioid Crisis Arrives

From the first month, the center filled against the backdrop of a growing opioid crisis in Pennsylvania. Prescription pain pills had already saturated entire neighborhoods, working their way into medicine cabinets, lunchboxes, backpacks, and glove compartments. Heroin followed those pills like a shadow, cheaper and easier to obtain. Fentanyl waited nearby, invisible at first, then suddenly everywhere—an industrial poison folded into local supplies with ruthless efficiency.

Between 2015 and 2017, drug-related overdose deaths in Pennsylvania jumped more than 60%, reaching 5,456 deaths in 2017 alone, a rate of about 42 deaths per 100,000 residents (DEA, 2018). National data traced the same brutal trajectory, with synthetic opioid deaths rising sharply after 2013 as fentanyl and its analogues spread across the country (CDC, 2019). Every epidemiological curve pointed upward; every headline grew darker. The crisis was no longer a distant warning. It had arrived, fully formed, at our doorstep.

At Riverside Drive, those numbers had faces and names, families and histories. A young father from Allentown arrived with endocarditis and track marks that told the story before he spoke. A nurse from a nearby hospital carried a secret fentanyl habit she could no longer hide. A grandmother who once took oxycodone for back pain slid quietly into heroin when the prescriptions stopped and the pain did not. A college student with ADHD came in shaking, having drifted from stimulant misuse into opioid dependence, the progression so gradual he barely noticed until he could not stop.

They arrived shivering, vomiting, drenched in sweat or wrapped in blankets. Some came in under court pressure, escorted by probation officers or driven by family members who hovered outside the door. Some arrived under the weight of whispered ultimatums—go to treatment or lose your home, your job, your children. And a few walked in on their own, pale and trembling, after one overdose too many, terrified of dying and equally terrified of surviving.

Medical-Psychiatric Complexity

My background in internal medicine shaped the first hours of admission with a clarity I had not fully appreciated until I stood in those rooms. The initial focus was never just on counting pills or confirming the number of bags someone used in a day. It centered on the body as a battlefield: vital signs that whispered danger, cardiac rhythms that hinted at old infections or new arrhythmias, liver enzymes that told quiet stories of years of assault, and the ever-present risk of infectious disease. Many patients needed immediate evaluation for hepatitis C or HIV. Others required stabilization of heart failure that had been ignored in the chaos of addiction, or rapid management of uncontrolled diabetes that placed them at risk before withdrawal even began. Detox without medical oversight would not simply have been inadequate—it would have been dangerous, even lethal.

My psychiatry training guided the next layer of care, the part invisible on lab reports but impossible to ignore in the room. Anxiety, trauma, psychosis, and mood instability arrived as reliably as withdrawal symptoms. Some patients paced hallways, unable to sit still long enough to complete an intake. Others curled into chairs, speaking so quietly that their sentences dissolved into the air before they reached my ears. Detox without acknowledging despair, terror, or disordered thinking would have pushed many straight back to use the moment they crossed the threshold at discharge.

Addiction medicine sat at the intersection of those two worlds—body and mind—rooted in the understanding that substance use disorder is not simply a sequence of bad decisions, but a chronic, progressive, potentially fatal disease shaped by biology, psychology, and social context. That framework allowed us to treat patients not as problems to be solved quickly but as human beings whose suffering required integrated, sustained care.

Medications such as buprenorphine and naltrexone eased withdrawal and craving, giving patients enough stability to sit through groups, to think beyond the next hour, to imagine a future (Vivitrol®, n.d.). Evidence-based therapies—cognitive behavioural therapy, motivational interviewing, relapse-prevention strategies—offered structure to the chaos. They helped patients recognise patterns, name triggers, and plan the fragile architecture of early recovery. Peer support layered in something medicine alone could not provide: the reminder that recovery did not end at discharge and that there were people, alive and working at it, who had walked the same road and survived.

A Day in the Life

A normal day as medical director started before sunrise, in that quiet hour when the river looked almost motionless and the world held its breath. The drive along the water became a kind of ritual—fog lifting off the surface in thin sheets, the sky shifting from blue-grey to pale gold, the old industrial buildings still asleep. By the time I pulled into the parking lot, the nursing staff had already changed shifts. The night nurses handed over reports with the tired efficiency of people who had seen too much darkness and held it together anyway.

Inside, the day unfolded fast. Reports waited on my desk like a stack of unfinished stories: new admissions, patients shaking through withdrawal, complaints of chest pain that might be anxiety or might be the edge of a myocardial infarction, individuals in psychiatric crisis, and others preparing for step-down or discharge, fragile but hopeful. I rounded with nurses, physician assistants, and counselors, moving from detox beds to residential rooms, reviewing labs and EKGs, adjusting medications, and then settling into the small, windowless conference rooms where patients' stories poured out faster than vital signs. Some spoke in torrents; others offered only fragments. Either way, the emotional weight arrived before the clinical details.

During those years, the opioid crisis did not just increase the number of patients—it reshaped who those patients were. Fentanyl had seeped into the drug supply with ruthless speed, raising overdose risk beyond anything we had seen before. Synthetic opioid death rates rose more than tenfold nationally between 2013 and 2019 (CDC, 2019), a statistic that felt abstract until the ambulance bays and emergency rooms filled with bodies we could not revive. Pennsylvania's coroners and medical examiners reported levels that shook entire counties. The phone calls from hospitals became more urgent, the referrals more desperate.

Narcan found its way into homes, cars, school nurse offices, and the pockets of teenagers who never imagined they would need it. Families began speaking a new language—naloxone, Suboxone, MAT—words that had once belonged mostly to clinicians and policy experts. Suddenly they were spoken across kitchen tables, at funeral receptions, and in the hallways of high schools.

In the midst of this, the Center became a regional anchor, a place families, courts, hospitals, employers, and even clergy turned to when they no longer knew what else to do. We were no longer just a treatment facility at the end of a dead-end road. We had become part of the community's emergency response, the place where hope was attempted, where fear landed, and where, on many days, the best we could offer was a safe room, a plan, and our full attention.

The Moral Geography of Riverside Drive

The address at the end of Riverside Drive created an ethical mirror that none of us could avoid. On one side of the parking lot, men and women in work-release uniforms filed through the doors of the jail entrance, shoulders hunched, eyes down, escorted by officers who had walked this route a thousand times. On the other side, vehicles from the coroner's office moved in and out with quiet regularity, their presence a stark reminder of how often addiction ends not in treatment or incarceration, but in a body bag.

And in the middle—our building. A treatment center pinned between two institutions that represented the past and future of so many of our patients. It was impossible not to feel the symbolism. We stood literally and figuratively between confinement and death, trying each day to carve out a third option that remained fragile, uncertain, and easily lost.

Every time a patient stepped outside to smoke or to breathe air that didn't smell like antiseptic, they could see the river running past us, slow and indifferent. And each time they looked out, three options stood within a short walk: recovery, incarceration, death. The geography made the truth unavoidable. Many had already moved between those options more than once—cycles of treatment followed by relapse, jail stays followed by brief sobriety, overdoses followed by frantic resuscitations. The road itself seemed to whisper the stakes: one direction led back to chains, one led to a slab, and one—just one—led toward the possibility of healing.

Systems Collide

My role involved constant translation between systems that rarely spoke the same language. Hospitals sent us patients after their third or fourth overdose in as many months, exhausted nurses calling ahead with a mixture of hope and apology. Probation officers referred clients who stood on the edge of violation hearings, desperate to show a judge that they were trying. Families arrived begging us to keep their loved ones longer, voices trembling from years of fear, pleading for just one more week, one more chance. Insurers, meanwhile, pressed us in the opposite direction, urging shorter stays, fewer days of treatment, fewer billable hours—as though recovery could be timed with a stopwatch.

Inside the building, staff fought their own battles. Burnout crept in quietly, disguised as irritation or numbness. Vicarious trauma settled on people who had once been idealistic, soft-spoken, or relentlessly hopeful. Moral distress became part of the air we breathed—those moments when a patient left against medical advice, relapsed within days, and then appeared in an obituary or a coroner's report. We grieved privately, because the work left no time for ceremony, and yet each loss left an imprint that didn't fade.

Over the decade from 2013 to March 2023, the program transformed. What began as a new county initiative slowly evolved into a regional treatment hub—known, sought after, and, at times, overwhelmed. It merged into a larger network of addiction services (White Deer Run / Acadia, n.d.), expanding our reach but also increasing the weight of expectation. CARF accredited the integrated model, affirming what we already knew: that treating co-occurring disorders required more than a detox bed; it required an ecosystem.

Levels of care grew beyond the original detox and residential units. Day treatment, intensive outpatient programs, and outpatient follow-up were added, creating a continuum rather than a cliff. Patients could move through levels of care at a pace aligned with their progress rather than the limitations of the building.

Meanwhile, the numbers outside our walls continued to rise. Overdose deaths climbed, then plateaued, and only in recent years began to show the faintest signs of decline—a reported 9% drop in fatal overdoses by 2023 (Axios, 2025). It was a fragile victory, and an uneven one, but in a field defined by loss, even a small bend in the curve felt like a breath of relief.

Why This Story Matters

Behind every data point sat human lives—grandmothers who baked for entire neighborhoods, firefighters who once ran into burning buildings, teachers who kept classrooms afloat, people with severe mental illness who had been misunderstood for decades, and others with no psychiatric history at all. Each carried stories far deeper than any diagnosis code could capture. The charts listed substances, dates, vital signs, and lab values, but the real narratives lived in the pauses, in the tears that came without warning, in the pride someone felt after their first night of sleep in weeks, or in the trembling hands of a parent finally willing to ask for help.

This chapter of Hijacked Minds tells the story of that dead-end road and the decade I spent as medical director at the Lehigh County Center for Recovery. It describes patients whose brains and spirits had been rewired by chronic exposure to opioids, alcohol, benzodiazepines, and stimulants—substances that changed not only neurochemistry but identity, relationships, and entire family systems. It shows how treatment teams tried to respond with a blend of science, compassion, and structure inside systems that often valued cost savings, quick discharges, and predictable outcomes over the messy, nonlinear reality of long-term recovery. It captures the small victories—smiles on day five of withdrawal, repaired conversations with loved ones, a patient finishing detox for the first time in years. And it acknowledges the painful losses—the relapses, the overdoses, the names we heard again only through obituary notices. Hope and grief lived side by side in those hallways, often within the same hour.

For some readers, the road to 1620 Riverside Drive may feel familiar. Many communities across the United States have similar clusters where treatment centers stand within sight of jails, morgues, and court buildings, as if the geography itself were underscoring the stakes. For clinicians, this story may echo the moral weight of working during the height of the opioid epidemic—a time when every discharge felt like both a step forward and a risk, when every patient was a reminder of both possibility and fragility.

My work did not end the epidemic. No single clinician, team, or program could shoulder that burden. But the work accomplished something essential: it created a space where thousands of people were told, sometimes for the first time in years, that their lives still mattered—even after overdose, arrest, or deep relapse. That message, repeated day after day, shaped the culture of the building as much as any treatment protocol.

Chapter 13 begins on that narrow road along the Lehigh River. From there, it moves into the clinical rooms, group spaces, and quiet offices where the real work of healing took place. The pages that follow describe how addiction rewires the brain, how chronic stress and despair fuel relapse, and how one community program tried to offer a path forward to people who had been told, in words or actions, that no such path remained.

Cultural Narratives of Stimulant Tragedy

John Belushi: A Hollywood Warning

Hollywood wrote one version of this story in the body of John Belushi. By the early eighties he lived at the centre of American comedy and film, a force of nature whose presence seemed to ignite every room he entered. Saturday Night Live, The Blues Brothers, late-night television—Belushi moved through fame with a kind of volcanic energy that made him unforgettable.

Behind the laughter, though, cocaine use had already woven itself through his long nights on set, and alcohol and heroin soon joined it. The chaos showed itself even during the filming of The Blues Brothers. Crew members would realise he had vanished, leaving cameras and cast waiting. One night, when Belushi disappeared entirely, Dan Aykroyd went out searching for him. He followed a trail of small clues—lights on in a nearby residential neighbourhood, a door left slightly ajar—and found Belushi asleep on a stranger's couch after raiding the refrigerator, a scene both absurd and heartbreaking (Schaefer, 2020; IMDb, n.d.). It became one of the film's most enduring behind-the-scenes stories, a real-time glimpse of a man slipping away from his own career, moment by moment.

On March 5, 1982, staff found Belushi dead in Bungalow 3 at the Chateau Marmont, just thirty-three years old. The coroner listed the cause of death as acute cocaine and heroin intoxication—a speedball overdose (Belushi, 1982). The world mourned a comic icon, but beneath the headlines sat the deeper truth that addiction does not bow to brilliance or fame. It simply takes.

Marion Barry: Power, Crack, and Denial

Public office wrote another version of this story through Marion Barry in Washington, DC. On 18 January 1990, FBI and DC police launched a coordinated sting operation at the Vista International Hotel. Hidden cameras recorded the three-term mayor in room 727, sitting on the edge of the bed, talking casually with a former girlfriend who had agreed to cooperate with investigators. Moments later, the footage showed Barry lighting a crack pipe and taking several drags before agents burst through the door, shouting commands as he tried to stand, stunned and disoriented (Washington Post, 1990a; Washington Post, 2014).

The videotape later became the centrepiece of the prosecution's case. When shown to jurors, it revealed far more than a single lapse in judgment. The recording captured Barry initially refusing to go upstairs — worrying aloud about "nosy rosies" in the hotel — then relenting after repeated pressure, accepting the pipe, and inhaling deeply just before agents stormed the room (Washington Post, 1990b). It was a stark and unforgettable moment in American politics: a sitting mayor, on camera, smoking crack cocaine while federal agents waited outside.

Barry was eventually convicted on a single misdemeanor drug charge, but the scandal seemed certain to end his career. What followed stunned much of the country. Despite the videotape, despite the headlines, and despite months of courtroom testimony, voters in Washington eventually returned him to office. For many residents — particularly those in communities he had championed — Barry's charisma, history of advocacy, and willingness to confront the city's entrenched inequalities outweighed the spectacle of his downfall. The high had seduced him, but it also seemed to seduce supporters who wanted his energy, his fight, and his defiance on their side.

Rob Ford: Toronto's Turbulent Mayor

Toronto lived through its own public reckoning with stimulant addiction in the figure of Mayor Rob Ford. For months in 2013, rumours circulated that a video existed showing the sitting mayor smoking crack cocaine. At first the story sounded like political theatre — an opposition smear, a bizarre urban myth, or a piece of digital gossip destined to fade. But reporters from the Toronto Star and later Gawker insisted the footage was real, describing it in detail and reporting that they had seen it firsthand. Ford denied everything, calling the journalists liars and claiming the allegations were politically motivated.

Then the situation escalated. Police surveillance reports referenced the video, placing Ford in contact with individuals involved in drug distribution. In late October, Toronto's police chief confirmed publicly that investigators had recovered the file, the very video that reporters had described months earlier (People.com, 2023; Wikipedia, n.d.-a). The image of a sitting mayor smoking crack cocaine — once a rumour — became a documented fact.

As the evidence mounted, Ford finally admitted that he had smoked crack cocaine but insisted it had happened "probably in one of my drunken stupors," a phrase that immediately embedded itself in the public imagination. The admission did not quiet the chaos. Instead it revealed a painful mixture of denial, minimisation, and bravado that often accompanies stimulant misuse. Press conferences dissolved into shouting matches. The city council stripped Ford of many of his powers. Late-night television turned him into a global spectacle.

Yet despite the scandal and the relentless media scrutiny, Ford retained a fiercely loyal base. Supporters argued that he spoke plainly, championed the concerns of working-class neighbourhoods, and represented people who felt ignored by traditional political elites. Even after treatment and a leave of absence, crowds still gathered at his rallies, cheering a man whose public struggle mirrored, in some ways, private battles unfolding across the city. Like other figures undone by stimulants, his charisma and his chaos were intertwined — and for many, impossible to separate.

Trey Radel: A Congressional Crash

Congress added another chapter to the story of stimulant seduction through Trey Radel, a freshman representative from Florida whose political career derailed almost overnight. In October 2013, Radel arranged to purchase cocaine from a dealer in Washington, DC. What he did not realise was that the dealer had already been cooperating with the Drug Enforcement Administration. The transaction itself was quick — cash exchanged for a small packet of cocaine — and agents allowed him to walk away without incident. They had a different plan. Later that evening, federal officers visited his Washington apartment, where they found additional drugs and informed him of the pending charges (U.S. Department of Justice, 2013).

The story that unfolded in the days after his arrest echoed patterns familiar to anyone working in addiction medicine. Radel described long hours, heavy stress, and a mounting sense that he could not keep pace with the demands of Congress. Cocaine offered him energy, confidence, and a few moments of escape from the pressure. Over time, the line between "helping him cope" and "controlling his life" dissolved entirely.

In November 2013, Radel stood before a DC Superior Court judge and pleaded guilty to misdemeanor cocaine possession. It was a public act of accountability, but also one of admission: he acknowledged not just the crime, but the addiction driving his behaviour. The court sentenced him to one year of probation and mandated treatment, a decision that signalled a shift in how the justice system viewed substance use — not purely as a moral failing, but as a medical issue requiring intervention.

The political consequences, however, were immediate and unforgiving. Radel took a leave of absence to enter treatment, but pressure from party leadership and constituents intensified. Within months, he resigned, ending a promising career over a handful of grams of cocaine. It was a fall that mirrored so many others — swift, public, and devastating.

In the years that followed, Radel spoke openly about his recovery and the realities of addiction. His honesty offered a rare moment of vulnerability in a political culture built on performance and image. But his story underscored a deeper truth: stimulant addiction does not spare the ambitious. It thrives in high-pressure environments, exploiting insecurity, exhaustion, and the desperate need to appear tireless. And when it brings a person down, it often does so in front of the entire world.

How Stimulants Work on the Brain

These stories show, with painful clarity, what stimulants do to brains chasing achievement, escape, or relief. Cocaine, crack, methamphetamine, and prescription stimulants all operate on the same fragile circuitry: the brain's reward pathways. They flood synapses with dopamine and other neurotransmitters, overwhelming systems that were designed for subtlety, not assault. Under that surge, ordinary sensations become electrified. Music feels sharper, as if someone has removed a filter. Sex becomes urgent and impulsive. Tasks that once felt dull or impossible suddenly feel effortless. Social anxiety dissolves, replaced by a brittle confidence that feels, for a moment, like invincibility.

But the same drugs that create those brief states of euphoria also push the body far outside its safe physiological limits. Stimulants accelerate heart rate and raise blood pressure. They constrict blood vessels, strain the cardiovascular system, and leave the heart working harder than it was built to. Medical literature describes acute cocaine toxicity in three distinct phases: an initial rush of euphoria, followed by dysphoria, agitation, and paranoia, and then — for some — a third phase marked by seizures, dangerous arrhythmias, heart attacks, or strokes (Medscape, n.d.). The transition from exhilaration to collapse can happen within minutes.

Repeated exposure compounds the damage. With continued use, receptors downregulate and neurotransmitter stores deplete, leaving the brain unable to produce ordinary pleasure. The world that once felt too bright now feels muted and washed out. People describe waking each morning with a heaviness in their limbs, irritability that erupts without reason, and a depression that feels carved into the bones. Craving becomes less about getting high and more about trying to feel anything at all. The very circuits designed to keep us motivated, connected, and alive begin to misfire, pulling users back toward the drug that caused the injury in the first place.

Crack Cocaine: The Cycle of Rush and Crash

Crack brought this drama into small rooms and narrow alleys throughout the eighties and nineties, compressing the entire rise-and-crash of cocaine into a brutal, fast-moving cycle. Smoked cocaine reaches the brain in seconds; the surge hits so hard and so quickly that users often describe it as a lightning strike rather than a high. But that rush lasts only minutes. Its brevity is the trap. The high collapses almost as soon as it arrives, leaving behind a hollow crash that feels unbearable. The only immediate relief is more crack, and so the cycle tightens: intense euphoria → abrupt dysphoria → a frantic, grasping return to the pipe.

People caught in that loop often describe it as a form of captivity. Food stops mattering. Children stop mattering. Jobs, relationships, and promises fall away. What remains is the ritual—the pipe, the flame, the inhalation, the seconds of relief before the next wave of desperation. The brain narrows its focus until nothing is left but the pursuit of one more hit. Entire nights disappear into that cycle; then weeks, then months. By the time people realise how far they have fallen, the drug has already stripped away the scaffolding of ordinary life. Only the next flame matters.

Methamphetamine: Damage on a New Scale

Methamphetamine adds another, even more corrosive layer of destruction. Unlike cocaine, which acts quickly and burns out rapidly, meth floods the brain with massive surges of dopamine and norepinephrine and blocks their reuptake. The result is a stimulant that hits harder, lasts longer, and leaves deeper injury in its wake. Whether snorted in a line, inhaled as a cloud from a glass pipe, or injected directly into a vein, each dose strikes the reward pathways with a force that reshapes them. People often describe the first rush as overwhelming — an almost supernatural sense of energy, confidence, and focus — but that intensity comes with a cost the brain cannot sustain.

As use continues, behaviours shift into patterns that become unmistakable: days without sleep, eyes wide and unblinking; relentless jaw grinding that cracks enamel; obsessive skin-picking triggered by hallucinated insects; frantic cleaning or repetitive tasks performed for hours without purpose. Sexual drive often surges to dangerous extremes, pulling people into impulsive encounters and high-risk situations they would never consider sober.

Over time, the body pays a visible price. Severe weight loss leaves faces gaunt and bodies depleted. "Meth mouth" — a combination of dry mouth, acidic fumes, teeth grinding, and poor hygiene — ravages dentition. Skin lesions and infections spread from constant picking and compromised immunity. Cardiovascular strain increases dramatically, raising the risk of heart attacks, strokes, and sudden death.

Psychiatric complications grow just as severe. Many long-term users develop a meth-induced psychosis that can be nearly indistinguishable from schizophrenia: auditory hallucinations, persecutory delusions, violent agitation, and disorganised thoughts that fracture relationships and endanger lives (NIDA/PMC, n.d.). For some, even after prolonged abstinence, these symptoms linger, suggesting that meth does more than disrupt the brain — it can permanently alter it.

The Rise of P2P Meth

From Home Labs to Industrial Chemistry

Meth manufacturing has changed dramatically over the past two decades, reshaping not only the drug market but the clinical picture seen in treatment centres across the country. Older "shake and bake" operations — small, unstable labs hidden in motel rooms, sheds, and rural basements — relied heavily on pseudoephedrine extracted from cold medicines. These improvised labs were dangerous, volatile, and limited in scale. When federal and state regulations tightened access to pseudoephedrine, many expected meth production to decline. Instead, it adapted.

Traffickers shifted toward phenyl-2-propanone (P2P), a chemical precursor that bypassed pseudoephedrine entirely. This method, once obscure, became the dominant route, and it opened the door to large-scale, industrial manufacturing. Reports now describe vast P2P-based superlabs in Mexico using precursor chemicals sourced through commercial supply chains rather than pharmacies (Bright Futures, 2023). Manufacturing moved from improvised home labs to facilities resembling chemical plants.

The shift was so significant that it filtered into the cultural imagination. The television series Breaking Bad built much of its meth-production storyline around the chemistry of the P2P method, consulting real chemists to ensure that the processes — and the shift away from pseudoephedrine — reflected real-world trends (Fresh Air, 2010). Although stylised for drama, the underlying chemistry and the transition in manufacturing routes were grounded in actual practices.

As P2P production expanded, output surged. Purity climbed to levels rarely seen in the pseudoephedrine era. Prices fell. Methamphetamine became cheaper, stronger, and more widely available, reaching rural counties, suburban neighbourhoods, and cities that once saw only sporadic cases. The drug no longer depended on small clandestine labs; it flowed through international distribution networks with the efficiency of any major commodity. The meth now flooding American communities is not only more potent — it is more destructive.

A More Toxic Product

Reporters and clinicians describe far harsher psychiatric outcomes with the modern generation of P2P methamphetamine. The presentation has shifted from the more predictable stimulant effects of earlier eras to something more chaotic and destabilising. Patients arrive in emergency departments with rapid-onset paranoia, fragmented and disorganised thinking, and bursts of violent agitation that seem to erupt without warning. Outreach workers and shelter staff report encounters with individuals pacing for hours, whispering to unseen threats, or barricading themselves in small spaces out of overwhelming fear. Evidence increasingly links heavy meth use with homelessness, psychiatric crises on city streets, and a revolving-door pattern of hospital holds and jail bookings (OPB, 2021).

Front-line clinicians — emergency physicians, psychiatric nurses, addiction specialists — consistently describe this newer meth as feeling different. Many believe that contaminants, solvent residues, and byproducts from industrial-scale P2P synthesis create a compound that interacts with the brain more aggressively than earlier formulations. Research continues, and definitive toxicology is still emerging, but the lived clinical picture is unmistakable: patients deteriorate faster, decompensate more severely, and take longer to return to baseline.

Over time, brains exposed to this chemical assault begin to lose the capacity for stable mood, clear thought, and ordinary pleasure. The ability to sleep, to concentrate, to trust reality, to feel grounded in one's own body — all erode. What begins as a stimulant high ends as a collapse of basic psychological functioning, leaving people stranded in states of fear, confusion, and emotional exhaustion. The drug that once promised energy and confidence ultimately strips away the very systems that make a stable life possible.

High-Functioning Users and the Illusion of Control

Stimulants seduce through productivity and sexual energy as much as through pure euphoria. They appeal not only to people seeking escape, but to people seeking performance — the ones who pride themselves on pushing harder, staying later, producing more. Many high-functioning professionals take their first line at a party after a long shift, during a conference where sleep is optional, or in a back room with colleagues trying to keep the night alive. The motive looks harmless, even justified: stay awake a little longer, impress a client, finish the project that can't wait until morning.

Soon, the rhythm changes.

- a line before a meeting
- a line at lunch
- a line before driving home

The drug becomes a tool, then a preference, then a requirement. Sleep begins to erode. Nights stretch into early mornings, alarms get snoozed, and energy becomes something borrowed rather than earned. Judgment frays. Emotional reactions sharpen or flatten unpredictably. Secrets multiply in small, incremental ways — missed calls, unexplained absences, cash withdrawals, mysterious trips to the bathroom.

Families start to notice irritability replacing patience, and erratic hours replacing predictable routines. Coworkers see bursts of brilliance punctuated by chaos, half-finished tasks, and excuses that don't match the person they once knew. And through all of it, the user sees only the lift — that quick, bright surge that convinces them they are still in control, still capable, still functioning at a level they fear they cannot reach without the drug.

Public Figures and the Dopamine of Leadership

For politicians, the cycle plays out under bright lights and relentless scrutiny. Every misstep is amplified, every relapse becomes a headline, and every attempt at recovery is measured against public expectation.

Marion Barry regained office after prison — a return that stunned much of the country but made perfect sense to voters who felt he had championed them long before his downfall. His charisma, forged in years of community advocacy, did not vanish with his conviction; if anything, it grew more complicated, more mythic.

Rob Ford drew crowds even after admitting he had smoked crack. Supporters packed his rallies, insisting he spoke for them in ways more polished politicians never had. His chaos and charm were intertwined, and even in disgrace, people saw in him a reflection of their own struggles, their own exhaustion with political theatre.

Trey Radel attempted political and media returns post-treatment, leaning into honesty about his addiction as a way to rebuild credibility. His recovery narrative resonated with some, yet the shadow of his arrest followed him, a reminder of how quickly stimulant misuse can unravel a public identity.

These stories illustrate a deeper truth: stimulants operate on the same reward and attention systems that fuel charisma, leadership, and risk-taking. They amplify qualities that politics often rewards — intensity, energy, confidence — until the line between personality and dependency becomes blurred. When sobriety arrives, it can feel to the user like losing not only the drug, but a piece of the very identity that propelled them into the public eye. The brightness dims, the edges soften, and what remains is the quieter, more vulnerable self they had been outrunning for years.

The Cost to Families

Families pay the quiet price — the slow, grinding toll that rarely makes headlines but shapes the lives of everyone caught in the orbit of a stimulant addiction.

spouses listening for a key that never turns, rehearsing the phrases they'll use if their partner walks in at dawn, or if the phone rings instead children watching a parent pace through the house at 3 a.m., eyes wide, jaw clenched, whispering to themselves or rearranging objects that don't need rearranging parents noticing money missing from wallets, purses, or accounts, feeling the sting of worry layered on top of disappointment grandparents taking custody of children because the home their daughter or son once maintained has dissolved into chaos, fear, or neglect

These scenes unfold quietly, room by room, long before a family ever steps into a treatment centre or a courthouse. The transformation is gradual, then sudden. As meth or crack takes control, families face a person who looks familiar but behaves like a stranger — paranoid, aggressive, sleepless, driven solely by craving. Conversations that once felt ordinary become impossible. Trust erodes. Love remains, but it becomes tangled with fear, resentment, and exhaustion.

Families often describe it as living with two versions of the same person: the one they remember, and the one the drug has created. And as the addiction deepens, the second version takes over more days than not, leaving families caught between hope and heartbreak, trying to reach someone who seems just out of reach.

Medical and Psychiatric Fallout

From a medical standpoint, stimulant addiction leaves a signature so distinct that clinicians can often recognise it before a patient even speaks. The damage follows a pattern — sudden, severe, and out of proportion to age or prior health.

- young stroke victims from vasospasm, barely out of their twenties, arriving confused, half-paralysed, or unable to speak
- heart attacks in people with no traditional risk factors, their coronary arteries clamped tight from prolonged catecholamine surges
- emergency presentations marked by chest pain, arrhythmias that dance unpredictably across the monitor, dangerously high body temperatures, or seizures that resist initial treatment
- psychiatric crises dominated by hallucinations, persecutory delusions, violent fear, and an inability to distinguish inner voices from external threats

In emergency rooms, clinicians learn to spot the signs: the trembling hands, the grinding jaw, the darting eyes, the sudden shifts from charming to combative. On psychiatric units, teams brace for nights when half a dozen stimulant-induced psychoses arrive within hours of each other. On medical floors, doctors watch lab numbers unravel and hearts strain under the constant assault of adrenaline and dopamine.

The entire healthcare system bends under the weight of what often began as a "lift" — a momentary boost before a meeting, a little extra energy for a long shift, a small escape from shame or fatigue. What starts as a shortcut ends as a cascade of medical emergencies, each one revealing the profound physiological cost of chasing a chemical high.

Treatment and the Possibility of Recovery

The story does not end in jails or graves. For many people, treatment works — not through a single intervention or dramatic epiphany, but through the slow, disciplined layering of structure, medication support, and sustained therapy. Cocaine and meth remain harder pharmacologic targets than opioids, but a combination of behavioural and integrated approaches offers real, measurable paths to recovery.

- contingency management, which rewards small, consistent steps toward abstinence and has some of the strongest evidence in stimulant treatment
- CBT and motivational approaches, which help patients examine the thoughts and emotions that drive craving, impulse, and relapse
- integrated mental health services, essential for those whose stimulant use is fused with trauma, depression, psychosis, or unstable mood

These tools do not offer quick fixes. They offer scaffolding — something sturdy enough to support a person while their brain recalibrates. And it does recalibrate. Some patients regain weight after months of depletion. Dental work repairs the damage of "meth mouth." Thought processes sharpen. Families re-enter the picture cautiously, then more fully. People return to work, school, or stable housing. With prolonged abstinence, the brain heals partially, rebuilding reward pathways that had been twisted by months or years of stimulant assault.

Yet the seduction remains powerful. Stimulants offer something our culture often glorifies: energy without rest, productivity without pause, confidence without vulnerability. In societies that reward constant motion and treat exhaustion as weakness, the lure of a chemical shortcut can feel almost logical. That is why treatment must be more than detox or therapy sessions — it must offer a different narrative, one in which rest, balance, and ordinary human limits are not signs of failure, but foundations of recovery.

The Cultural Reckoning

Fame amplifies these patterns. It magnifies the highs, accelerates the unraveling, and broadcasts every misstep to a world eager to watch brilliance collide with self-destruction. But fame also exposes consequences in a way that few other arenas can.

- A comedian dead at thirty-three, his talent extinguished long before its natural arc
- A mayor arrested on camera, the moment replayed endlessly until it becomes both tragedy and spectacle
- A congressman standing in court, voice shaking as he confesses addiction before the very public he once vowed to lead

These moments puncture the illusion that intelligence, power, or charisma can shield someone from the pull of stimulants. They reveal the truth that addiction does not discriminate, and that no social status grants immunity. And as painful as they are, these public collapses can open doors. Families use them to start conversations with loved ones who believe they are functioning "well enough." Clinicians reference them gently, to show patients that they are not alone, that their struggle is part of a much larger human pattern.

Fame turns private suffering into cautionary stories, not for the sake of gossip, but for the chance to speak honestly about how quickly stimulants can seduce, how deeply they can wound, and how urgently intervention is needed before the world breaks in to film the ending.

Closing Reflections

In Hijacked Minds, stimulant addiction sits beside opioid, alcohol, and benzodiazepine stories because all of them flow through the same human brain — a brain seeking relief from fear, pain, exhaustion, or the impossible demands of modern life. The chemical paths differ, but the seduction script remains the same:

Faster. Stronger. Smarter. Less afraid.

Then comes the other script, the one people never imagine when they begin: racing heartbeats that feel like alarms, paranoia that turns familiar rooms into threats, families collapsing under the weight of lies and sleepless nights, bodies shutting down in bathrooms, alleyways, or hotel rooms. The arc that begins with a promise ends with a narrowing of the world until nothing is left but the drug and the devastation it causes.

My work is to stand inside these stories — not above them, not outside them — and offer another line for the brain to follow. A line that leads toward sleep instead of sleeplessness, toward nourishment instead of depletion, toward ordinary joy instead of chemically inflated euphoria. A line that says a life does not have to burn itself out chasing one more rush. In that fragile space between collapse and recovery, treatment becomes not just medicine, but a reminder that another path still exists.

CHAPTER 14

AMERICA'S ACCEPTED VICES

(Alcohol, Cannabis, Nicotine)

> *"Quitting smoking is easy. I've done it a hundred times."*
>
> — MARK TWAIN

The Hashish

A Call During the Opioid Epidemic

It was in the middle of the opioid epidemic in 2016 when my phone rang in my Easton office. The crisis had already settled over the Lehigh Valley like a heavy winter fog — visible, chilling, impossible to ignore. On the line was Democratic State Representative Robert Freeman, whose district office sat just a short walk from mine on North 13th Street. He did not call to talk about zoning disputes or school budgets. His voice carried a different weight. He wanted my medical opinion on marijuana — specifically, the bill moving rapidly through Harrisburg that aimed to legalize medical cannabis across Pennsylvania. Senate Bill 3 had momentum. Governor Tom Wolf had already signaled support. The state stood on the edge of becoming the next jurisdiction to endorse medical marijuana, part of a national shift that felt both inevitable and disorienting (The Guardian, 2016).

I remember listening closely as he spoke. His tone was steady but lined with concern, as if he were trying to solve a puzzle with pieces missing. He described the opioid crisis tightening around our communities. Overdose deaths climbed month after month, leaving behind a trail of funerals that blurred together for families in Easton, Bethlehem, and Allentown. Parents buried young adults whose stories were painfully similar — painkillers after an injury, escalation, heroin, fentanyl, collapse. Freeman wondered whether medical marijuana might offer relief or only deepen the chaos. Could cannabinoids reduce opioid prescriptions? Might patients with chronic pain find safer alternatives? Or would we simply add another intoxicant to a culture already drowning in them, another substance to the shelves of a society that had never learned to manage the vices it already embraced?

It was not a theoretical question for him. It was not for me either. It was a moment when policy, medicine, and grief converged, and he wanted to know what the view looked like from my side of the examining room.

The Landscape of Accepted Vices

By that point I had spent years treating addiction and psychiatric illness in the Lehigh Valley, long enough to see patterns repeat with painful consistency. The same substances that filled commercials, store shelves, gas-station counters, and family celebrations filled my detox units and psychiatric beds. Alcohol. Tobacco. And increasingly, marijuana. All legal in some form. All marketed with the smiling confidence of products considered part of ordinary adult life. Yet every day in clinic I saw the other side of that cultural permission — the hospitalizations, the broken relationships, the lost jobs, the hollowed-out futures. What society labeled as "choices," I saw as biochemical traps that closed slowly around people who never imagined they were vulnerable.

The scale of harm dwarfed the public conversation. Alcohol alone killed an estimated 178,000 people in the United States every year, cutting decades off lives that should have stretched into old age (CDC, 2023a). Tobacco remained the quiet giant of preventable death — more than 480,000 Americans lost annually, a number so large it almost ceased to shock because it had become so familiar (CDC, 2023b). Cannabis, marketed as a natural and harmless alternative, was the most commonly used federally illegal drug. More than 52 million Americans used it at least once in 2021, and federal data showed that approximately three in ten users developed cannabis use disorder, a statistic far out of step with its benign public reputation (CDC, 2023c).

These were not fringe substances whispered about in alleyways or traded in back rooms. These were pillars of the American economy, woven into advertising, tradition, and identity. And yet they filled my office with stories of withdrawal, dependence, and despair — the hidden ledger entries of our accepted vices.

The Law Arrives

So when Representative Freeman asked for my view, I answered from that clinical trench, from the long days and longer nights spent treating the fallout of substances our culture had already welcomed with open arms. I told him, honestly, that I believed the decision in Harrisburg was already made. Medical marijuana felt less like a debate and more like a tidal shift — a fait accompli shaped by years of advocacy, patient testimony, national momentum, and shifting public sentiment. The legislature was not so much steering the ship as acknowledging the current.

By April 17, 2016, Governor Tom Wolf signed Act 16 into law (PA General Assembly, 2016). With a single signature, Pennsylvania moved into the ranks of early adopters with a comprehensive medical marijuana framework, joining a growing list of states reshaping their drug policies. The text of the law was straightforward enough: the program would take effect within weeks, but genuine implementation — building infrastructure, training physicians, licensing growers, drafting regulations, establishing dispensaries — would unfold over years. In medicine we call that a "long runway," but in politics it felt more like inevitability. The direction was set. The train had left the station. What remained was to understand, as clinicians and legislators, what would ride along with it.

Clinical Concerns

I still felt an obligation to speak. Even if the political momentum was irreversible, the medical consequences were not. My concern was simple and rooted in years of frontline experience: our society already struggled to manage three allowed vices that systematically damaged the brain, strained the body, and destabilized families. Alcohol, tobacco, and increasingly marijuana had already carved deep grooves into the public health landscape, and we had not yet demonstrated the capacity — or the collective will — to manage them responsibly. Now the

Commonwealth was preparing to endorse another psychoactive substance, complete with a new industry, new lobbying groups, new marketing narratives, and a fresh set of expectations placed on physicians who were already stretched thin.

I told Representative Freeman what I saw in my practice day after day. Patients with alcohol use disorder who insisted that a product purchased from a state-run store must be inherently safe — as if legality offered immunity from harm. Patients with advanced lung disease who continued smoking cigarettes because tobacco greeted them in every gas station, convenience store, and grocery checkout line; the ubiquity became its own endorsement. And patients whose marijuana use, once occasional or social, had quietly evolved into a daily — then constant — companion. Many were using high-potency THC products that bore little resemblance to the marijuana of the 1970s or even the 1990s. Their symptoms rose accordingly: escalating anxiety, creeping paranoia, diminished motivation, and a tightening psychological dependence that caught them off guard.

Recent national data mirrored what I observed in the clinic. Cannabis use among adults climbed from roughly 7 percent to 15 percent between 2013 and 2022, with daily use accelerating sharply — a shift that signaled not just experimentation, but habituation (PMC, 2024). The stories in my office were not outliers; they were early signals of a larger cultural turn.

The Patients Who Needed Something

I also told him something more complicated, something that didn't fit neatly into the categories of caution or endorsement. In my practice, I cared for patients living with severe chronic pain, metastatic cancer, post-traumatic stress disorder, and seizure disorders that defied every standard treatment we offered. These were not abstract clinical cases — they were people whose faces I knew, whose stories I carried home at night. Some had already turned to marijuana outside the law, using whatever forms they could find, and many reported genuine relief: fewer spasms, fewer nightmares, fewer episodes of crushing pain. Their improvements were not dramatic miracles, but they were meaningful in lives narrowed by illness.

And then there were the parents — mothers and fathers of children with intractable epilepsy who had spent years navigating a medical maze with no exits. They sat in front of me with binders of medical records and videos of seizures, pleading for access to cannabis-derived oils they believed could soften their children's suffering. Some had already traveled to other states out of desperation, seeking treatments unavailable in Pennsylvania. Their voices had reached the Capitol long before any committee hearing or floor debate. Pain travels fast; grief travels faster.

I understood that pain deeply. I had no desire to criminalize suffering or turn desperate families into defendants. The question for me was not whether compassion mattered, but how to balance compassion with clarity — how to acknowledge legitimate therapeutic potential without ignoring the patterns of harm I also witnessed daily.

Act 16 and Its Intent

The Medical Marijuana Act attempted to walk that delicate line between compassion and caution. Act 16 established a structured program for patients with "serious medical conditions," a term that was not left to interpretation but defined explicitly in the statute. The list included cancer, HIV, multiple sclerosis, seizure disorders, inflammatory bowel disease, neuropathic pain, post-traumatic stress disorder, and severe chronic or intractable pain when standard treatment had failed or carried unacceptable risks (PA Department of Health, n.d.). In other words, the law was built around the kinds of patients who had already been appearing in hearing rooms and doctors' offices, people for whom traditional medicine had exhausted its offerings.

Administration of the program fell to the Pennsylvania Department of Health, which was tasked with building an entirely new regulatory framework: developing guidelines, overseeing registration, monitoring compliance, and ensuring that the system did not devolve into a free-for-all. Physicians would have to register, complete training, and certify eligible patients — a role that blurred the line between clinician and gatekeeper. Growers and dispensaries would face licensing, inspections, and operational standards more rigorous than many early observers expected. The law initially prohibited smoking the plant, an attempt to separate medical use from recreational imagery, and limited approved forms to oils, pills, liquids, tinctures, and topicals. Later amendments permitted dry leaf but restricted it to vaporization, an effort to maintain a distinction between therapy and combustion.

On paper, it looked like a tightly controlled system, a cautious entry into new territory. But paper and practice, as I had learned repeatedly in addiction medicine, rarely move in perfect harmony.

Caution Meets Commerce

On paper, that looked careful. The language of the statute suggested restraint, structure, and medical intent. But in practice, every allowed vice in American history has started with careful packaging. Tobacco once wore the costume of medicine — sold as a respiratory aid, endorsed by physicians in white coats, advertised as a friend to digestion and calm. Alcohol came wrapped in community and celebration, a cultural permission slip handed out at weddings, ballgames, funerals, and office parties. Marijuana entered the landscape wrapped in compassion, framed as relief for the sick and dignity for the suffering. Each began as a narrow exception, a tightly managed allowance. And then the economic engine followed close behind.

Pennsylvania's program was no different. Within a few short years of implementation, the landscape transformed. The registry grew to nearly a million patients and caregivers. Dispensaries multiplied across cities and small towns. Growers expanded into warehouse districts and rural farmland. Sales climbed into the billions (Compassionate Certification Centers, 2024). What began as a medical accommodation quickly revealed itself as an emerging industry — complete with branding, loyalty programs, marketing strategies, and the quiet but unmistakable presence of investors.

The market grew exactly as one would expect when a psychoactive substance enters the circle of legality: steadily, confidently, and without hesitation. What had been framed as a compassionate narrow channel widened into a commercial river, carrying with it both legitimate therapeutic hope and the familiar currents of normalization.

Two Competing Truths

When I spoke with legislators and staff in those years — in person across conference tables, over hurried phone calls between committee meetings, and through long threads of email — I tried to hold two truths at once. They were not comfortable truths, and they did not always coexist peacefully, but both were real.

The first truth was that prohibition had failed many patients. Criminal records for possession never treated PTSD, neuropathic pain, or multiple sclerosis. Arrests did not soften nightmares or stop seizures. The families who uprooted their lives and moved to Colorado or other early-adopter states so their children could legally access cannabis oils stood as living indictments of our gaps in care. Their stories were not abstract moral arguments — they were reminders that suffering will always outrun bureaucracy, and when systems fail, families find their own path, legal or not. In that sense, legalization offered compassion where old policies had delivered only punishment.

The second truth was equally urgent: legalization without clear limits, rigorous oversight, and honest public education risked unleashing a new wave of harm, especially in young brains still under construction. Neuroscience had already mapped cannabis's impact on development, motivation, and vulnerability to psychiatric illness. If the state opened the door widely without guardrails, the burden would fall hardest on adolescents and young adults — the same populations already struggling under the weight of anxiety, depression, academic pressure, and social instability.

These two truths pulled in opposite directions. But policymaking, like medicine, often lives in the tension between what helps and what harms. My role was to keep both realities visible at once.

Learning From Our Other Vices

I reminded them of our national record with alcohol — a record written not in policy papers but in coroners' logs and emergency room charts. We knew, beyond debate, that alcohol contributed to liver disease, multiple cancers, motor-vehicle fatalities, domestic violence, suicide, and accidental injuries. We knew it eroded families as much as it enlivened celebrations. And yet alcohol sat unquestioned at every wedding, every sports event, every holiday table, every funeral repast. Permission wrapped itself around the product so tightly that its harms became nearly invisible, swallowed by tradition and routine.

Tobacco told a similar story, though with a slower arc. Decades of mounting evidence — lung cancer, emphysema, vascular disease — finally forced cultural change, but only after extraordinary pressure from public health advocates and relentless resistance from a well-funded industry. Even now, tobacco remains the leading preventable cause of death in the United States, a reminder that legality and normalization can outpace common sense by generations.

Cannabis entered that cultural landscape with its own powerful story — one of safety, naturalness, and therapeutic promise. For many people it arrived as the "gentle" alternative, the plant-based remedy that seemed to carry none of the baggage of alcohol or tobacco. But federal data painted a more complex picture: roughly 30 percent of users eventually developed cannabis use disorder, a rate far higher than public perception suggested (AP News, 2023). And emergency departments across the country were seeing the consequences: surges in visits for cannabis-related anxiety, acute psychosis, and cyclic vomiting syndrome. These were not theoretical risks. They were daily presentations in hospitals, carried in by frightened families who had believed the product was harmless.

Cannabis stepped into a landscape already shaped by denial and industry influence. Without caution, it risked repeating that history — not because it was identical to alcohol or tobacco, but because American culture often treats newly accepted vices exactly the same way.

High-Potency Realities

I told lawmakers that the marijuana I encountered in clinic no longer resembled the marijuana of the 1970s — the mild, low-potency plant passed around at concerts or dorm rooms. What I met instead were concentrated oils, vaporized waxes, dabs, shatter, and high-potency flower with THC levels many times higher than anything their generation had seen. These products delivered fast, heavy hits to the brain's reward system, often with consequences that caught patients by surprise.

Patients described withdrawal symptoms once considered rare or nonexistent: irritability sharp enough to fracture conversations, insomnia that stretched into days, marked appetite loss, waves of depression, and a pull toward craving that felt indistinguishable from other addictive substances. These patterns were no longer anecdotal — they were well documented in national research and federal health data (CDC, 2023c).

As use escalated, the ripple effects seeped into every corner of their lives. Work performance faltered; deadlines were missed, mornings became impossible, and motivation eroded. Relationships strained under the weight of secrecy, emotional volatility, and the quiet but relentless prioritization of use over connection. And in individuals with genetic or psychiatric vulnerability, something more frightening appeared: paranoia, hallucinations, and full psychotic episodes that emerged not after decades of use but sometimes within months. For those patients, cannabis was not a soft drug. It was a trigger.

These were the stories I carried into those legislative conversations — not abstractions, not political arguments, but lived clinical realities unfolding every day just a few miles from the Capitol.

A Paradox in Opioid Care

I also explained a paradox that clinicians faced every day, one that rarely made it into legislative hearings or public debates. Some patients with opioid use disorder viewed marijuana not as a recreational substance but as "medicine," a therapeutic shield they believed protected them from relapse. They used it heavily — sometimes all day, every day — while minimizing or outright denying the severity of their opioid dependence. For a few, this shift did reduce immediate overdose risk; replacing fentanyl with cannabis could mean the difference between life and death in the short term.

But for others, the pattern was more complicated. Heavy cannabis use became a smokescreen, masking an untreated opioid disorder that lingered beneath the surface. They told themselves they were "in recovery" because they had stopped injecting heroin or smoking fentanyl, yet their lives remained dominated by intoxication, avoidance, and emotional dysregulation. Cannabis, in these cases, did not heal. It merely displaced the crisis, offering a false sense of stability while the underlying illness continued its quiet progression.

This paradox — harm reduction for some, harmful distraction for others — required nuance that policy rarely accommodates. And it underscored the reality that no psychoactive substance operates in a vacuum; it interacts with vulnerability, trauma, and disease in ways that vary dramatically from person to person.

Mission Creep

Representative Freeman listened. He did not interrupt or push back; he didn't need convincing about the scale of what we were facing. He understood the funerals, the Narcan kits tucked into glove compartments, the vigils on courthouse steps, the grief that rippled through schools and workplaces after another young person died. He had watched these storms pass through Easton and Bethlehem just as I had. His questions about medical marijuana came from a place of wanting to protect his community, not from political fashion or industry talking points.

My own fear — the one I tried to name gently but clearly — was mission creep. In addiction medicine, mission creep is not an abstract policy flaw; it is the predictable arc of every allowed vice. It begins with strict medical criteria, earnest oversight, and careful guidelines. Then slowly, almost imperceptibly, the boundaries widen. Conditions get added. Certifying physicians turn into high-volume mills. Marketing reframes expectations: what starts as a treatment for a narrow set of serious illnesses evolves into a wellness enhancer, a sleep aid, a stress reducer, a product for "everyday living."

Pennsylvania's early data reflected exactly that trajectory. Within a short span, the state registered hundreds of thousands of residents with active certifications and dispensed millions of products through a rapidly expanding network of dispensaries (Compassionate Certification Centers, 2023). This was no longer a program focused solely on childhood epilepsy, metastatic cancer, and intractable pain. It had grown into something far larger — a new, normalized industry layered atop an already strained public health landscape.

And that scale mattered, not because suffering patients didn't deserve relief, but because the larger a vice becomes, the more invisible its risks appear.

Allowed Vices

I kept returning to one phrase: allowed vices. It was the cleanest way to describe the pattern I had seen unfold from the clinician's chair. Alcohol. Tobacco. Marijuana. Substances woven into ordinary American life, treated as benign companions to adulthood. Yet each one interacts with neural reward systems designed for survival — bonding, nourishment, motivation — not for sustained artificial stimulation. When those circuits are repeatedly pushed, the brain adapts, and then it depends.

Each allowed vice exploits the same familiar vulnerabilities: accumulated stress, long-buried trauma, loneliness, boredom, the quiet ache that follows people through their days. These states create openings. Psychoactive substances slip into those openings easily. Relief becomes habit; habit becomes need.

And behind each of these vices stands an industry — polished, well-funded, and extraordinarily adept at shaping public perception — that thrives only when use increases. No example is clearer than the tobacco industry. When early epidemiological studies began linking cigarettes to lung cancer, companies did not step back in concern; they mobilised. They funded research designed to protect profit, not truth.

One of the most notorious cases involved Hans J. Eysenck, a highly influential psychologist whose work, later exposed as deeply flawed and ethically compromised, claimed that there was *no* causal relationship between smoking and cancer. Eysenck, whose research was supported by tobacco-industry funding, used statistical sleight-of-hand to argue that personality traits, not cigarettes, explained elevated cancer rates. His papers were widely circulated, cited by policymakers, and used to delay regulation for years (Pelosi, 2019). While his conclusions echoed the industry's preferred narrative, they bore little resemblance to biological or epidemiological reality.

Allowed vices do not spread by accident. They spread through culture, commerce, and carefully crafted narratives. Alcohol becomes celebration. Tobacco became sophistication — backed by fraudulent science. Cannabis increasingly becomes wellness. And always, the people most affected are not the ones producing the advertisements but the ones showing up in clinic rooms, trying to understand when a choice became a dependency.

What I Asked

I did not ask the legislature to reverse course — no state had done that, and Pennsylvania was not going to become the first. The momentum behind medical marijuana was cultural as much as political, and cultural tides do not turn because a single physician raises a caution flag. What I asked for instead was something more modest and far more difficult: honesty. Limits. Youth protections. And research equal to the scale of the policy shift.

Honesty meant acknowledging both the potential benefits and the very real risks, without bending the truth to fit advocacy or industry narratives. Limits meant drawing boundaries that reflected medical necessity rather than consumer demand, and enforcing them even when pressure mounted to loosen the gates. Youth protections meant recognising that adolescent brains — still under construction, still vulnerable — would bear the brunt of any miscalculation. And meaningful research meant investing in studies that could clarify long-term outcomes, not relying on anecdotes, marketing claims, or early enthusiasm.

I was not asking the state to turn back. I was asking it to look forward with clear eyes.

The Contrast

When I think back on those days, what lingers most vividly is the contrast. On one side sat the detox units and psychiatric hospitals where I spent my days — fluorescent-lit hallways, patients trembling through withdrawal, families gripping Styrofoam cups of vending-machine coffee while trying to make sense of relapse, fear, and exhaustion. These were the places where addiction showed its true face, stripped of political rhetoric and marketing gloss. This was the world of lived consequences.

On the other side were the ribbon cuttings, the polished podiums, the smiling photographs in local newspapers. Economic forecasts circulated with the warm certainty of a rising tide: job creation, new revenue streams, revitalized storefronts, the promise of prosperity threaded through every press release. The same substance that left patients sobbing in exam rooms was being celebrated as an engine of growth only a few miles away. Policy often lives in the glow of optimism; medicine lives in the residue of its aftermath.

The Medical Marijuana Act promised compassion — relief for the suffering, dignity for those failed by other treatments, a progressive step forward. And some of that promise was real. But promises carry costs, and costs fall unevenly. My duty, then and now, is to describe that cost. To place the lived experiences of patients beside the legislative victories. To remind readers that behind every allowed vice is a population that absorbs the unintended consequences quietly, privately, and often invisibly.

That is the story this chapter insists on telling.

The Normalization of Addiction

America's Quiet Vices

America likes to pretend that only "hard drugs" destroy lives. The phrase itself creates a moral buffer — *those* drugs over there, used by *those* people, far from polite company. But in my clinic, I see otherwise. The substances that unravel families most quietly are often the ones that slip through daily life without a second glance. Alcohol poured into crystal glasses at dinner parties. Vape pens tucked into jacket pockets at work. Edibles offered as novelty gifts. Cigarette packs softened by years of habit and carried like old companions.

These allowed vices travel freely through the spaces of privilege and routine. They pass unchallenged through airport lounges, where business travelers sip bourbon at 7 a.m. They sit on linen-draped tables at state dinners, toasted by policymakers who debate drug policy hours later. They ride on tour buses with musicians, executives, and athletes who believe they are immune to consequence because the substance is legal, familiar, or socially endorsed.

The law smiles on them. Culture welcomes them. And because of that, the damage they cause becomes harder to recognize — not less real, simply less visible. In exam rooms and hospital wards, I see their true footprint: liver failing inch by inch, lungs collapsing from decades of smoke, anxiety spiraling after years of high-potency THC, relationships disintegrating under the slow weight of dependence. These are not the dramatic collapses of heroin or methamphetamine. They are the slow erosions that hollow out a life from the inside.

Allowed vices do not need to hide. That is what makes them so powerful — and so dangerous.

George W. Bush

George W. Bush's early life offered an example that still resonates because it unfolded in full view of the American public, yet remained largely unacknowledged until years later. Long before he reached the Texas governor's mansion or the Oval Office, Bush lived what he later described as a life marked by "drinking too much." Friends and reporters painted a picture of heavy, habitual alcohol use woven into social events, political gatherings, and long nights among peers who saw nothing unusual in the pattern. It was the kind of drinking that hides easily inside privilege — the refilled glass at a fundraiser, the extra rounds at a dinner, the loud storytelling that follows a whiskey too many.

But the consequences eventually surfaced. In 1976 he was arrested for driving under the influence while visiting Maine, a moment that could have prompted reckoning but instead slipped almost unnoticed into the background of his biography until his presidential run decades later. The arrest remained a footnote, overshadowed by a cultural assumption that affluent young men drinking heavily was simply part of the landscape. Alcohol dependence hiding in plain sight looks exactly like that — normalized, excused, invisible.

What made Bush's story unusual was the way it ended. On his fortieth birthday he drank hard one last time. The next morning, hungover and unsettled, he stopped. Not with fanfare, not with a public confession, not with treatment or televised redemption arcs. Just a quiet, absolute decision to walk away, later attributed to faith, family, and the recognition that alcohol had begun to crowd out the parts of life he valued most (ABC News, 2010). In that sense his story illustrates both the insidiousness of an allowed vice and the rarity of a clean break. Most patients I see cannot simply decide not to drink anymore. Biology, trauma, habit, and neurochemistry are not so easily dismissed.

Bush's narrative sits at the intersection of denial and privilege — a reminder that addiction does not always look like collapse. Sometimes it looks like a successful man laughing too loudly at a party, driving too fast down a quiet coastal road, and waking up one morning to realize the mirror has been telling the truth for years.

Lady Gaga

Cannabis holds a different cultural slot — younger, cooler, wrapped in the language of creativity and calm rather than danger. For years, Lady Gaga embodied that image: the avant-garde pop icon, the performer whose artistic extremity seemed to blur seamlessly into personal myth. Fans joked about her wild costumes, her late nights, her boldness. Cannabis, in that narrative, fit neatly as a harmless creative companion, a plant that helped her cope with fame, pressure, and the physical toll of touring.

But the story she later revealed told a much darker truth. In a 2013 interview, Gaga admitted she had been smoking as many as twenty marijuana joints a day while recovering from a severe hip injury — not casually, not socially, but compulsively. What had begun as a tool for pain relief slowly morphed into dependence. She described using cannabis to blunt not only physical discomfort but emotional distress, anxiety, and the relentless pressure to perform. The drug became a buffer between her and the intensity of her life, a haze she stepped into to avoid the sharp edges of reality.

Over time, that haze thickened. Her world shrank. She spoke about withdrawal symptoms — irritability, insomnia, a sense of emotional rawness — now well-documented consequences of heavy cannabis use but still surprising to many who believed marijuana to be non-addictive. She described the internal negotiations familiar to any clinician who works with addiction: the justification, the minimization, the quiet fear that the drug no longer served her but was instead steering her. She eventually quit "cold turkey," a decision she framed as necessary to reclaim her life and her voice (People.com, 2013).

Her disclosure punctured the cultural myth that cannabis is categorically harmless. It showed that dependence can grow not only in the shadows of trauma and poverty but also under stadium lights and behind award-show curtains. It revealed that a substance marketed as natural and gentle can still take hold with surprising force, especially when pain — physical or psychological — opens the door.

Gaga's story is not an anomaly. It is a reminder that addiction does not care about fame, talent, wealth, or intention. It follows biology, not public image. And cannabis, despite its reputation, is fully capable of writing its own version of that script.

Barack Obama

Nicotine slides under the radar more than either alcohol or cannabis. It has been part of American life for so long, and its rituals so deeply ingrained, that many people forget it is a psychoactive drug at all. Cigarettes appear in old movies, on front porches, in the hands of construction workers and senators alike. Even as smoking rates declined, nicotine simply changed costumes — now delivered through sleek vape pens, pouches, and devices marketed as lifestyle accessories rather than addictive products. Its grip remains powerful precisely because it hides in plain sight.

Barack Obama's struggle with nicotine dependence made that invisibility visible. During and after his presidency, Obama acknowledged that he had continued smoking — sometimes eight to ten cigarettes a day — even while navigating the most scrutinized job in the world (Washingtonian, 2020). The admission struck many people as surprising, even incongruous. How could a man responsible for nuclear codes, global diplomacy, and national crises be slipping out to smoke behind the White House residence? But that question misunderstands nicotine's pull. Addiction does not care about titles, résumés, or approval ratings.

Obama described his smoking not as rebellion or indulgence but as a battle — one he fought with nicotine gum, private negotiations with himself, and the quiet pressure of a promise to his daughters. He spoke about stress as a trigger, about the comfort of familiar rituals, about the difficulty of quitting while living inside a relentless spotlight. His honesty reframed the narrative: this wasn't about willpower or moral failure. It was about dependence, plain and simple — the same neurochemical leash that binds millions of Americans in far less forgiving circumstances.

What Obama's story underscored, perhaps more than any public health campaign, was that nicotine addiction does not operate at the level of character. It operates at the level of receptors, synapses, stress hormones, and habit loops. If the President of the United States could find himself stepping outside for a cigarette in the midst of national decision-making, then the rest of us can stop pretending that smoking is a matter of choice alone.

Nicotine remains the quietest, most socially camouflaged of America's vices — but its grip is as physiological, as persistent, and as democratic in its reach as any "hard" drug clinicians treat.

The Medical View

Alcohol, THC, and nicotine all hijack the brain's reward circuits, bending systems built for survival into systems that serve the drug. Each substance alters neurotransmission in its own way — dopamine surges, disrupted GABA and glutamate balance, overstimulated cannabinoid or nicotinic receptors — but the outcome converges on the same point: the brain begins to recalibrate around the presence of the drug. What once felt like enhancement becomes the new baseline.

Over time, these changes ripple outward. Stress responses intensify; ordinary frustrations trigger disproportionate agitation or anxiety. Natural rewards — food, conversation, sunlight, accomplishment — lose their shine. The brain's architecture adapts to expect the chemical shortcut rather than the slower, steadier pathways of intrinsic motivation. In this altered landscape, craving doesn't feel like wanting anymore. It feels like needing.

And that is where choice erodes. People do not continue drinking, vaping, or using high-potency THC because they lack discipline or moral backbone. They continue because the circuitry that once guided voluntary behavior has been rewired to interpret absence as threat. The drug stops offering pleasure and starts offering relief — relief from withdrawal, relief from dysphoria, relief from the jolt of stress that now sits closer to the surface.

Craving replaces choice not through weakness, but through neurobiology. And once that shift occurs, the person in front of me — whether a teenager with a vape pen, a middle-aged professional with a nightly bottle of wine, or a celebrity describing withdrawals — is no longer making decisions in the way outsiders imagine. They are negotiating with a brain that has changed the rules mid-game.

Celebrities in recovery earn praise. Poor patients earn punishment. The molecules don't know zip codes. Society does.

Accepted vices often precede illicit drugs. I have yet to treat a fentanyl patient without earlier alcohol, cannabis, or nicotine misuse.

The Target Is Denial

Not prohibition — but denial. That is the real barrier. The denial that masks addiction behind cultural approval, that hides harm inside rituals and traditions so familiar we stop questioning them. Prohibition imagines the problem lies solely in access; denial insists the problem does not exist at all.

Denial is what lets a society pour alcohol into crystal glasses at every milestone while ignoring the hospital beds filled with cirrhosis and withdrawal. It's what allows high-potency cannabis to be marketed as "wellness" while emergency departments treat surges of anxiety, psychosis, and cyclic vomiting. It's what makes nicotine feel like a personal quirk rather than the leading preventable cause of death — a habit people joke about rather than a dependency that reshapes neurochemistry.

And denial is not limited to the public. Families use it to soften fear. Clinicians encounter it every day in the form of minimized drinking, "just on weekends" cannabis use, or vaping "to take the edge off." Legislators and industry leaders use it to frame substances in the rosiest possible light. Even patients who sit in my office, shaking from withdrawal or gasping from emphysema, sometimes cling to it because letting go means facing the full weight of what has happened.

The power of allowed vices rests not only in their legality but in this shared illusion — that if enough people do something, it cannot be harmful; that if a substance is socially accepted, its risks must be exaggerated. Denial doesn't just obscure addiction; it fertilizes it.

One Message

When famous figures admit dependence, they send a message that cuts through the noise: addiction crosses every boundary we pretend protects us. Class, politics, race, wealth, fame — none of it grants immunity. A president struggling with cigarettes, a global pop star withdrawing from cannabis, a former governor confronting alcohol, a comedian lost to speedballs — their stories travel farther than clinical data ever will. They show that dependence is not a moral failure found only in alleyways or shelters. It is a human vulnerability rooted in neurobiology, stress, and the universal desire for relief.

These confessions puncture the myth that addiction belongs to "other people." They reveal the truth clinicians see daily: allowed vices do not discriminate. They wrap themselves around the lives of CEOs and college students, surgeons and factory workers, senators and teenagers. They wear tuxedos at award shows and prison uniforms in county jails. They appear in corner offices, backstage dressing rooms, kitchen tables, and detox wards. The costume changes, but the circuitry — the hijacked reward system, the escalating tolerance, the quiet dread of withdrawal — remains the same.

My work is to strip away the costume. To look past the tailored suits, past the designer gowns, past the cultural permission that obscures the damage. To see the brain beneath the biography. To show that addiction's reach is not a measure of personal weakness but of how powerfully these substances exploit our most basic neural pathways. When we stop mistaking costumes for character, we can finally confront the real problem — and the real people — with honesty rather than judgment.

THE FINALE

> *"What we don't need in the midst of struggle is shame for being human."*
>
> — BRENÉ BROWN

I wrote this book because I have spent my life watching the human mind taken hostage, again and again.

I saw it first as a child in Aleppo — bombs, fear, hunger, parents whispering at night. My nervous system learned early that the world was not safe. Years later I gave this fear a name: hyperarousal, cortisol, dysregulated threat circuitry. As a boy I called it something simpler: survival. As Viktor Frankl wrote, "When we are no longer able to change a situation, we are challenged to change ourselves." The brain began that work long before I understood it.

I saw hijacked minds again in medical training.

In internal medicine I watched bodies collapse after years of alcohol, cigarettes, pills: hearts enlarged, livers scarred, lungs stiffened by decades of smoke. In psychiatry I saw the same destruction from the inside — flashbacks, voices, panic, a mind unable to quiet itself. Then in addiction medicine I stood at the junction. The same people. The same pain. Now with heroin, fentanyl, crack, meth, benzodiazepines, and alcohol wrapped around their brains.

The science of addiction uses careful words — mesolimbic pathways, dopamine firing, glutamate, corticotropin-releasing factor, a prefrontal cortex under stress. We use these terms to describe a simple, brutal pattern: pleasure and relief shift from gift to demand. A substance becomes the fastest route to calm. The brain learns that route, then refuses to surrender it. A patient says "never again" in the morning and uses by evening. Not because of weak character, but because circuits have rewired. As William James wrote, "The hell to be endured hereafter...is no worse than the hell we make for ourselves in this world by habit."

Trauma and stress sit at the center of this rewiring.

A child grows up under war, abuse, neglect, or quiet contempt. A teenager faces bullying, racism, or assault. A worker survives injury, poverty, or relentless pressure. Stress hormones wash through the brain for years. The alarm system stays stuck on high. In that state, a pill, a drink, a line, or a joint does more than entertain — it feels like air after suffocation.

That has been my work: to stand between that history and the next dose.

I practiced on a detox unit on a dead-end road in Bethlehem, next to a jail and a coroner's office. I rounded there for a decade. I adjusted buprenorphine, treated cellulitis, heart infections, psychosis, and withdrawal. I watched families sit in plastic chairs and try to understand how a child with perfect baby pictures now weighed ninety pounds and trembled in a bed they barely recognized.

I opened an office in Easton and hung my degree on a wall that once hid a copy of the Declaration of Independence. That scroll reminded me that a society promising life, liberty, and the pursuit of happiness must confront the ways those promises fail. Addiction is one of those failures. So is the way we punish it.

I saw patients who held power — executives, doctors, nurses, lawyers, clergy. I saw patients who held no power at all — people without housing, insurance, or stability. Their drugs differed. Their stories converged: early pain, unaddressed trauma, easy access to substances, a brain that learned to numb itself. Shame wrapped around all of it.

My own story brushed against that shame from another angle.

I stood accused in a federal courtroom, labeled a criminal for my work as a psychiatrist. I felt the full weight of the government. My nervous system swung back to childhood danger. I learned how easily systems can misread truth. When the jury cleared my name, I returned to my patients with deeper anger at simple stories about "bad choices." As Maya Angelou wrote, "There is no greater agony than bearing an untold story inside you." Too many of my patients carried that agony.

Because of that, this book stayed honest.

I wrote about dopamine, yes. But I also wrote about mothers in waiting rooms and fathers at gravesides. About presidents who quit alcohol, singers who stopped marijuana, citizens who choked on nicotine, patients who tried again after one more relapse.

Biology matters. Addiction lives in synapses and receptors. Trauma reshapes brain architecture. Stress alters immunity and gut function. Emerging tools such as TMS, ketamine, fNIRS, and digital therapeutics let us see and influence circuits in real time. I have sat with patients under a TMS coil and watched depression lift. I have written ketamine orders for people who had lost hope. I now walk into rooms with infrared devices that read cortical blood flow as patients make choices. This is not science fiction. This is Tuesday afternoon in my clinic.

Yet the heart of treatment remains old. A safe room. A steady presence. An honest conversation. A plan that respects both biology and story. Medication without listening is not care. Story without attention to the brain is not enough. People heal when we hold both at once.

If you carry addiction, hear this: your brain adapted to protect you at a time when you needed protection. It learned to reach for something that worked fast. That adaptation has now turned against you. You live with a medical condition that deserves treatment, not contempt. You also hold responsibility for what comes next. Both truths are real.

If you love someone with addiction, you carry your own trauma. You've lived through lies, overdoses, arrests, vanishing acts. You've slept with one ear open. You hold fear and anger in equal measure. You did not cause this. You cannot control it. You still matter. Your boundaries matter. Your healing matters.

If you work in medicine, law, or policy, you hold power over lives like the ones in this book. You write prescriptions. You argue cases. You design formularies, sentencing guidelines, insurance rules. I hope these pages have placed human faces in front of your decisions. A formulary change is not abstract. A sentencing guideline is not academic. A clinic closure is not fiscal housekeeping. Brains and families pay for each of these choices.

I began this journey as a boy in a city at war. I became a doctor who studies and treats brains at war with themselves. I stood in detox units, courtrooms, and quiet offices. I watched people lose everything to substances. I watched people rebuild. I watched my own life torn apart and rebuilt.

The mind can be hijacked. The brain can adapt in destructive ways. That is the hard news. The hopeful news is just as true: the same brain holds the capacity for new learning, new habits, new circuits. Trauma leaves marks, yet recovery writes new lines alongside them. As Leonard Cohen said, "There is a crack in everything. That's how the light gets in." I have seen that light arrive in the eyes of patients for decades.

This book now ends. The work does not.

Somewhere, as you read this sentence, someone takes a first drink, a first pill, a first hit. Somewhere else, someone flushes their drugs, calls for help, or walks into a meeting and sits in a folding chair for the first time. My life has been about standing closer to that second person.

If these pages move you one step closer as well — toward that person, toward yourself, toward the truth — then every story and every late night at my desk has been worth it.

REFERENCES

Abramson, A. (2017). *'He Really Helped Me.' President Trump Says His Brother Kept Him Away From Drugs*. [online] TIME. Available at: https://time.com/4999318/donald-trump-opioid-crisis-brother-fred-trump-jr/?utm_source=chatgpt.com [Accessed 10 Sep. 2025].

Acadia Healthcare (2021). *Acadia Healthcare*. [online] Acadia Healthcare. Available at: https://www.acadiahealthcare.com/locations/white-deer-run-of-lehigh/ [Accessed 2 Dec. 2025].

Alam, M.A., Parks, C. and Mancarella, S. (2016). Long-term Blood Pressure Measurement in Freely Moving Mice Using Telemetry. *Journal of Visualized Experiments*, (111). doi:https://doi.org/10.3791/53991.

Alzet (n.d.). *ALZET® Technical Information Manual*. [online] Available at: https://agnthos.se/img/cms/Catalogue/TIM2008.pdf [Accessed 3 Oct. 2025].

America, G.M. (2010). *Laura Bush Opens Up on George W's Drinking*. [online] Good Morning America. Available at: https://www.goodmorningamerica.com/amp/news/story/laura-bush-reveals-george-stopped-drinking-10552148 [Accessed 2 Dec. 2025].

American addiction centers (2024). *The addiction cycle: Phases of the chronically relapsing disease*. [online] American Addiction

Centers. Available at: https://americanaddictioncenters.org/the-addiction-cycle.

Apple Podcasts (2024). *Marion Barry Caught Smoking Crack (1990).* [online] Apple Podcasts. Available at: https://podcasts.apple.com/us/podcast/marion-barry-caught-smoking-crack-1990/id1502728938?i=1000642368833 [Accessed 2 Dec. 2025].

Arnsten, A.F.T. (2009). Stress signalling pathways that impair prefrontal cortex structure and function. *Nature Reviews Neuroscience*, [online] 10(6), pp.410–422. doi:https://doi.org/10.1038/nrn2648.

Associated Press (2025). *Obama admits occasional cigarette.* [online] Cape Cod Times. Available at: https://www.capecodtimes.com/story/news/2009/06/23/obama-admits-occasional-cigarette/51924537007/ [Accessed 2 Dec. 2025].

Associates, R.W. (2013). *4-Star Gen. McCaffrey, Lehigh County Exec. Hansell, PA Drug Program Sec. Tennis To Lead Grand Opening Of Lehigh County-CRC Health Group/White Deer Run Drug Treatment Center 11AM Monday, April 15, 1620 Riverside Drive, Bethlehem, PA*. [online] Prnewswire.com. Available at: https://www.prnewswire.com/news-releases/4-star-gen-mccaffrey-lehigh-county-exec-hansell-pa-drug-program-sec-tennis-to-lead-grand-opening-of-lehigh-county-crc-health-groupwhite-deer-run-drug-treatment-center-11am-monday-april-15-1620-riverside-drive-bethlehem--202137571.html [Accessed 2 Dec. 2025].

Baertsch, N.A., Bush, N.E., Burgraff, N.J. and Ramirez, J.-M. (2021). Dual mechanisms of opioid-induced respiratory depression in the inspiratory rhythm-generating network. *eLife*, 10. doi:https://doi.org/10.7554/elife.67523.

Barrymore, D. and Gold, T. (1990). *Little girl lost*. New York: Pocket Books.

Beamer, W.G., Shultz, K.L., Coombs, H.F., Horton, L.G., Donahue, L.R. and Rosen, C.J. (2012). Multiple quantitative trait loci for cortical and trabecular bone regulation map to mid-distal mouse chromosome 4 that shares linkage homology to human chromosome 1p36. *Journal of bone and mineral research : the official journal of the American Society for Bone and Mineral Research*, [online] 27(1), pp.47–57. doi:https://doi.org/10.1002/jbmr.515.

Bechara, A. (2005). Decision making, impulse control and loss of willpower to resist drugs: a neurocognitive perspective. *Nature Neuroscience*, 8(11), pp.1458–1463. doi:https://doi.org/10.1038/nn1584.

Berridge, K.C. and Robinson, T.E. (2016). Liking, wanting, and the incentive-sensitization theory of addiction. *American Psychologist*, [online] 71(8), pp.670–679. doi:https://doi.org/10.1037/amp0000059.

Bickel, W.K., Johnson, M.W., Koffarnus, M.N., MacKillop, J. and Murphy, J.G. (2014). The Behavioral Economics of Substance Use Disorders: Reinforcement Pathologies and Their Repair. *Annual Review of Clinical Psychology*, [online] 10(1), pp.641–677. doi:https://doi.org/10.1146/annurev-clinpsy-032813-153724.

Bouton, M.E. (2004). Context and Behavioral Processes in Extinction. *Learning & Memory*, 11(5), pp.485–494. doi:https://doi.org/10.1101/lm.78804.

Brewer, J.A., Elwafi, H.M. and Davis, J.H. (2013). Craving to quit: Psychological models and neurobiological mechanisms of mindfulness training as treatment for addictions. *Psychology of Addictive Behaviors*, 27(2), pp.366–379. doi:https://doi.org/10.1037/a0028490.

Brewer, J.A., Worhunsky, P.D., Gray, J.R., Tang, Y.-Y. ., Weber, J. and Kober, H. (2011). Meditation experience is associated with differences in default mode network activity and connectivity. *Proceedings of the National Academy of Sciences*, 108(50), pp.20254–20259. doi:https://doi.org/10.1073/pnas.1112029108.

Bricker, T. (2025). *Demi Lovato's Heartbreaking Documentary: Rape Allegation, Heroin Addiction and Her Near-Death Overdose.* [online] Eonline.com. Available at: https://www.eonline.com/news/1248887/demi-lovatos-heartbreaking-documentary-rape-heroin-and-her-near-death-overdose [Accessed 3 Oct. 2025].

Bustin, S.A., Benes, V., Garson, J.A., Hellemans, J., Huggett, J., Kubista, M., Mueller, R., Nolan, T., Pfaffl, M.W., Shipley, G.L., Vandesompele, J. and Wittwer, C.T. (2009). The MIQE Guidelines: Minimum Information for Publication of Quantitative Real-Time PCR Experiments. *Clinical Chemistry*, 55(4), pp.611–622. doi:https://doi.org/10.1373/clinchem.2008.112797.

Calcia, M.A., Bonsall, D.R., Bloomfield, P.S., Selvaraj, S., Barichello, T. and Howes, O.D. (2016). Stress and neuroinflammation: a systematic review of the effects of stress on microglia and the implications for mental illness. *Psychopharmacology*, 233(9), pp.1637–1650. doi:https://doi.org/10.1007/s00213-016-4218-9.

Casey, B.J., Jones, R.M. and Hare, T.A. (2008). The Adolescent Brain. *Annals of the New York Academy of Sciences*, [online] 1124(1), pp.111–126. doi:https://doi.org/10.1196/annals.1440.010.

CDC (2019). *Products - Data Briefs - Number 329 - November 2018.* [online] www.cdc.gov. Available at: https://www.cdc.gov/nchs/products/databriefs/db329.htm.

CDC (2023). *Addressing Excessive Alcohol Use: State Fact Sheets.* [online] www.cdc.gov. Available at: https://www.cdc.gov/alcohol/fact-sheets/states/excessive-alcohol-use-united-states.html.

CDC (2024a). *Alcohol Use.* [online] Alcohol Use. Available at: https://www.cdc.gov/alcohol/index.html.

CDC (2024b). *Cigarette Smoking.* [online] Smoking and Tobacco Use. Available at: https://www.cdc.gov/tobacco/about/index.html.

CDC (2024c). *Polysubstance Overdose.* [online] Overdose Prevention. Available at: https://www.cdc.gov/overdose-prevention/about/polysubstance-overdose.html.

CDC (2025). *Cannabis Facts and Stats.* [online] Cannabis and Public Health. Available at: https://www.cdc.gov/cannabis/data-research/facts-stats/index.html.

Center for Drug Evaluation and Research (2019). *FDA Drug Safety Communication: FDA warns about serious risks and death when combining opioid pain or cough medicines with benzodiazepines; requires its strongest warning | FDA.* [online] U.S. Food and Drug Administration. Available at: https://www.fda.gov/drugs/drug-safety-and-availability/fda-drug-safety-communication-fda-warns-about-serious-risks-and-death-when-combining-opioid-pain-or.

Centers for Disease Control and Prevention (2024). *Provisional Drug Overdose Data.* [online] CDC. Available at: https://www.cdc.gov/nchs/nvss/vsrr/drug-overdose-data.htm.

Centers for Disease Control and Prevention (2025). *Drug overdose mortality by state.* [online] Center for Disease Control and Prevention. Available at: https://www.cdc.gov/nchs/pressroom/sosmap/drug_poisoning_mortality/drug_poisoning.htm.

Chang, R. (2021). *Matthew Perry's Addiction Struggle: He Doesn't Remember Three Years of 'Friends'.* [online] Biography. Available at: https://www.biography.com/actors/matthew-perry-addiction-friends.

Chen, C.-H., Kraemer, B.R. and Mochly-Rosen, D. (2022). ALDH2 variance in disease and populations. *Disease Models & Mechanisms,* [online] 15(6). doi:https://doi.org/10.1242/dmm.049601.

Cohen, L. (2021). *Demi Lovato says she suffered three strokes and a heart attack during 2018 overdose.* [online] Cbsnews.com. Available at: https://www.cbsnews.com/news/demi-lovato-2018-overdose-strokes-heart-attack/.

Committee on the Science of Changing Behavioral Health Social Norms, Board on Behavioral, Cognitive, and Sensory Sciences, Division of Behavioral and Social Sciences and Education and National Academies of Sciences, Engineering, and Medicine (2016). *Ending Discrimination Against People with Mental and Substance Use Disorders: The Evidence for Stigma Change.* [online] *PubMed.* Washington (DC): National Academies Press (US). Available at: https://pubmed.ncbi.nlm.nih.gov/27631043/.

Commonwealth of Pennsylvania Department of Health (2025). *ISSUE REPORT Pain in the Nation: The Epidemics of Alcohol, Drug, and Suicide Deaths.* [online] Available at:

https://www.tfah.org/wp-content/uploads/2025/05/TFAH-2025-PainInTheNation-FINAL.pdf.

Cools, R., Roberts, A.C. and Robbins, T.W. (2008). Serotoninergic regulation of emotional and behavioural control processes. *Trends in Cognitive Sciences*, 12(1), pp.31–40. doi:https://doi.org/10.1016/j.tics.2007.10.011.

Covey, D.P., Mateo, Y., Sulzer, D., Cheer, J.F. and Lovinger, D.M. (2017). Endocannabinoid modulation of dopamine neurotransmission. *Neuropharmacology*, [online] 124, pp.52–61. doi:https://doi.org/10.1016/j.neuropharm.2017.04.033.

D'Onofrio, M. and Fitzpatrick, A. (2025). *Fatal drug overdoses are declining in Pennsylvania*. [online] Axios. Available at: https://www.axios.com/local/philadelphia/2025/02/25/overdose-deaths-decline-pennsylvania [Accessed 2 Dec. 2025].

DEA (2017). *DEA Announces 5,456 Drug-Related Overdose Deaths in Pennsylvania in 2017*. [online] Dea.gov. Available at: https://www.dea.gov/press-releases/2018/08/21/dea-announces-5456-drug-related-overdose-deaths-pennsylvania-2017-0.

Deak, J.D., Miller, A.P. and Gizer, I.R. (2019). Genetics of alcohol use disorder: a review. *Current Opinion in Psychology*, 27, pp.56–61. doi:https://doi.org/10.1016/j.copsyc.2018.07.012.

Decker, A.L., Meisler, S.L., Hubbard, N.A., Bauer, C.C.C., Leonard, J., Grotzinger, H., Giebler, M.A., Torres, Y.C., Imhof, A., Romeo, R. and Gabrieli, J.D.E. (2024). Striatal and Behavioral Responses to Reward Vary by Socioeconomic Status in Adolescents. *Journal of Neuroscience*. [online] doi:https://doi.org/10.1523/JNEUROSCI.1633-23.2023.

Dharavath, R.N., Pina-Leblanc, C., Tang, V.M., Sloan, M.E., Nikolova, Y.S., Pangarov, P., Ruocco, A.C., Shield, K., Voineskos, D.,

Blumberger, D.M., Boileau, I., Bozinoff, N., Gerretsen, P., Vieira, E., Melamed, O.C., Sibille, E., Quilty, L.C. and Prevot, T.D. (2023). GABAergic signaling in alcohol use disorder and withdrawal: pathological involvement and therapeutic potential. *Frontiers in Neural Circuits*, [online] 17(17), p.1218737. doi:https://doi.org/10.3389/fncir.2023.1218737.

DiBona, G.F. (2002). Sympathetic nervous system and the kidney in hypertension. *Current Opinion in Nephrology and Hypertension*, 11(2), pp.197–200. doi:https://doi.org/10.1097/00041552-200203000-00011.

digitaldotEditor (2025). *P2P Meth: The Dangerous Shift in Meth Manufacturing*. [online] Bright Futures Treatment Center. Available at: https://brightfuturestreatment.com/p2p-meth-the-dangerous-shift-in-meth-manufacturing/ [Accessed 2 Dec. 2025].

Do, C., Spencer-Hwang, R., Knutsen, S. and Shavlik, D. (2023). Assessing the Potential Impact of Adverse Childhood Experiences on Subjective Cognitive Decline. *Journal of Aging and Age Related Diseases*, [online] 3(1), pp.1–9. doi:https://doi.org/10.47739/1004.

DOJ (2015). *Congressman Trey Radel Pleads Guilty To Misdemeanor Drug Charge-Admits Purchasing Drugs From Undercover Officer-*. [online] Justice.gov. Available at: https://www.justice.gov/usao-dc/pr/congressman-trey-radel-pleads-guilty-misdemeanor-drug-charge-admits-purchasing-drugs [Accessed 2 Dec. 2025].

DOMINGUEZ, J. and HULL, E. (2005). Dopamine, the medial preoptic area, and male sexual behavior. *Physiology & Behavior*, 86(3), pp.356–368. doi:https://doi.org/10.1016/j.physbeh.2005.08.006.

Dwoskin, L.P. (2014). *Emerging Targets and Therapeutics in the Treatment of Psychostimulant Abuse*. Academic Press.

Eccles, J.C. (1966). Conscious Experience and Memory. *Recent Advances in Biological Psychiatry*, [online] 8, pp.235–256. doi:https://doi.org/10.1007/978-1-4899-7313-9_26.

Everitt, B.J. and Robbins, T.W. (2005). Neural systems of reinforcement for drug addiction: from actions to habits to compulsion. *Nature neuroscience*, [online] 8(11), pp.1481–9. doi:https://doi.org/10.1038/nn1579.

Everitt, B.J. and Robbins, T.W. (2016). Drug Addiction: Updating Actions to Habits to Compulsions Ten Years On. *Annual Review of Psychology*, 67(1), pp.23–50. doi:https://doi.org/10.1146/annurev-psych-122414-033457.

Eyewitness News (2018). *'I will keep fighting': Demi Lovato releases first statement after drug overdose*. [online] ABC7 New York. Available at: https://abc7ny.com/post/i-will-keep-fighting-demi-lovato-releases-statement-after-overdose/3889938/ [Accessed 3 Oct. 2025].

Flannery, J.S., Jorgensen, N.A., Kwon, S.-J., Prinstein, M.J., Telzer, E.H. and Lindquist, K.A. (2023). Developmental Changes in Habenular and Striatal Social Reinforcement Responsivity Across Adolescence Linked With Substance Use. *Biological psychiatry*, 94(11), pp.888–897. doi:https://doi.org/10.1016/j.biopsych.2023.04.018.

Frank, M.G., Fonken, L.K., Watkins, L.R. and Maier, S.F. (2019). Microglia: neuroimmune-sensors of stress. *Seminars in cell & developmental biology*, [online] 94, pp.176–185. doi:https://doi.org/10.1016/j.semcdb.2019.01.001.

Franklin, K.B.J., Paxinos, G. and Schmieder, R.G. (2001). *The mouse brain in stereotaxic coordinates*. San Diego, Calif. ; London: Academic.

Fresh Air (2010). *Vince Gilligan: The Man Behind 'Breaking Bad'*. [online] NPR. Available at: https://www.npr.org/transcripts/124475421?storyId=124475421?storyId=124475421 [Accessed 2 Dec. 2025].

G Alan Marlatt and Donovan, D.M. (2005). *Relapse prevention : maintenance strategies in the treatment of addictive behaviors*. New York ; London: Guilford.

Garbarino, S. (2000). *Robert Downey Jr. Speaks From Prison*. [online] Vanity Fair. Available at: https://www.vanityfair.com/hollywood/2000/08/robert-downey-jr-prison.

German, C.L., Baladi, M.G., McFadden, L.M., Hanson, G.R. and Fleckenstein, A.E. (2015). Regulation of the Dopamine and Vesicular Monoamine Transporters: Pharmacological Targets and Implications for Disease. *Pharmacological Reviews*, 67(4), pp.1005–1024. doi:https://doi.org/10.1124/pr.114.010397.

Gilpin, N.W. and Koob, G.F. (2024). Neurobiology of Alcohol Dependence: Focus on Motivational Mechanisms. *Alcohol Research & Health*, [online] 31(3), p.185. Available at: https://pmc.ncbi.nlm.nih.gov/articles/PMC2770186/.

Goodwin, D.W. (1977). Psychopathology in Adopted and Nonadopted Daughters of Alcoholics. *Archives of General Psychiatry*, 34(9), p.1005. doi:https://doi.org/10.1001/archpsyc.1977.01770210019001.

Hamarneh, S. (1972). PHARMACY IN MEDIEVAL ISLAM AND THE HISTORY OF DRUG ADDICTION. *Medical History*, [online] 16(03), pp.226–237. doi:https://doi.org/10.1017/s0025727300017725.

Harrison, D.G., Bader, M., Lerman, L.O., Fink, G., S.A. Karumanchi, Reckelhoff, J.F., M.L.S. Sequeira-Lopez and R.M. Touyz (2024). Tail-Cuff Versus Radiotelemetry to Measure Blood Pressure in Mice and Rats. *Hypertension*, 81(1), pp.3–5. doi:https://doi.org/10.1161/hypertensionaha.123.22329.

Heath, A.C. (2025). Genetic Influences on Alcoholism Risk: A Review of Adoption and Twin Studies. *Alcohol Health and Research World*, [online] 19(3), p.166. Available at: https://pmc.ncbi.nlm.nih.gov/articles/PMC6875767/?utm_source=chatgpt.com.

Hedegaard, H., Miniño, A. and Warner, M. (2020). *Drug Overdose Deaths in the United States, 1999-2018 Key findings Data from the National Vital Statistics System, Mortality*. [online] Available at: https://www.cdc.gov/nchs/data/databriefs/db356-h.pdf.

Hedegaard, H. and Spencer, M. (2021). *Urban-Rural Differences in Drug Overdose Death Rates, 1999-2019 Key findings*. [online] Available at: https://www.cdc.gov/nchs/data/databriefs/db403-H.pdf.

Heifets, B.D. and Malenka, R.C. (2016). MDMA as a Probe and Treatment for Social Behaviors. *Cell*, 166(2), pp.269–272. doi:https://doi.org/10.1016/j.cell.2016.06.045.

Heifets, B.D., Salgado, J.S., Taylor, M.D., Hoerbelt, P., Pinto, D.F.C., Steinberg, E.E., Walsh, J.J., Sze, J.Y. and Malenka, R.C. (2019). Distinct neural mechanisms for the prosocial and rewarding properties of MDMA. *Science Translational Medicine*, [online] 11(522). doi:https://doi.org/10.1126/scitranslmed.aaw6435.

Holt-Lunstad, J., Smith, T.B. and Layton, J.B. (2010). Social Relationships and Mortality Risk: a Meta-analytic Review. *PLoS Medicine*, [online] 7(7). doi:https://doi.org/10.1371/journal.pmed.1000316.

Holtzhausen, L. (n.d.). *Addiction – a brain disorder or a spiritual disorder*. [online] www.oatext.com. Available at: https://www.oatext.com/Addiction-a-brain-disorder-or-a-spiritual-disorder.php.

https://www.facebook.com/peoplemag (2019). *Trump Opens Up About 'Dark Family Secret' of His Older Brother's Death After Years of Alcoholism*. [online] People.com. Available at: https://people.com/politics/donald-trump-talks-older-brothers-alcoholism-death/?utm_source=chatgpt.com [Accessed 10 Sep. 2025].

https://www.facebook.com/peoplemag (2024). *RFK Jr. Says Heroin Made Him a Top-of-Class Student in Resurfaced Clip: 'It Worked for Me'*. [online] People.com. Available at: https://people.com/rfk-jr-heroin-use-top-of-class-student-8752783.

https://www.facebook.com/peoplemag (2025). *What Happened to Rob Ford? All About the Controversial Toronto Mayor's Life After His Crack Cocaine Video Scandal*. [online] People.com. Available at: https://people.com/what-happened-to-toronto-mayor-rob-ford-11758556.

Hunt, E. (2023). 'An alcoholic from the age of 14': Matthew Perry's troubled life and foreshadowed death. *The Guardian*. [online] 29 Oct. Available at: https://www.theguardian.com/tv-and-radio/2023/oct/29/alcoholic-troubled-life-matthew-perry-addicted-substance.

I am Sober (2024). *George W. Bush On Drinking & Sobriety.* [online] I Am Sober. Available at: https://iamsober.com/en/blog/george-w-bush-sober-story.

IMDB (2025). *The Blues Brothers (1980) - Trivia - IMDb.* [online] IMDb. Available at: https://www.imdb.com/title/tt0080455/trivia/ [Accessed 2 Dec. 2025].

Ingolfsland, J. (2020). *That Time John Belushi Randomly Disappeared From The Blues Brothers Set.* [online] Cinemablend. Available at: https://www.cinemablend.com/news/2558772/that-time-john-belushi-randomly-disappeared-from-the-blues-brothers-set?utm_source=chatgpt.com [Accessed 2 Dec. 2025].

Insel, T.R. (2022). *Healing : our path from mental illness to mental health.* New York: Penguin Press.

Insel, T.R. and Cuthbert, B.N. (2015). Brain disorders? Precisely. *Science*, [online] 348(6234), pp.499–500. doi:https://doi.org/10.1126/science.aab2358.

Insel, T.R. and Young, L.J. (2001). The neurobiology of attachment. *Nature Reviews Neuroscience*, 2(2), pp.129–136. doi:https://doi.org/10.1038/35053579.

Isaacson, Jeffry S. and Scanziani, M. (2011). How Inhibition Shapes Cortical Activity. *Neuron*, 72(2), pp.231–243. doi:https://doi.org/10.1016/j.neuron.2011.09.027.

Islas, Á.A. and Scior, T. (2022). Allosteric Binding of MDMA to the Human Serotonin Transporter (hSERT) via Ensemble Binding Space Analysis with ΔG Calculations, Induced Fit Docking and Monte Carlo Simulations. *Molecules*, 27(9), p.2977. doi:https://doi.org/10.3390/molecules27092977.

Kelly, J.F., Hoeppner, B., Stout, R.L. and Pagano, M. (2011). Determining the relative importance of the mechanisms of behavior change within Alcoholics Anonymous: a multiple mediator analysis. *Addiction*, 107(2), pp.289–299. doi:https://doi.org/10.1111/j.1360-0443.2011.03593.x.

Kelly, J.F., Humphreys, K. and Ferri, M. (2020). Alcoholics anonymous and other 12-step programs for alcohol use disorder. *Cochrane Database of Systematic Reviews*, [online] 3(3). doi:https://doi.org/10.1002/14651858.cd012880.pub2.

Kennedy, P.J. (2025). *A Common Struggle by Patrick J. Kennedy, Stephen Fried: 9780399185717 | PenguinRandomHouse.com: Books.* [online] PenguinRandomhouse.com. Available at: https://www.penguinrandomhouse.com/books/317536/a-common-struggle-by-patrick-j-kennedy-stephen-fried [Accessed 24 Nov. 2025].

Kessler, R.C., Berglund, P., Demler, O., Jin, R., Merikangas, K.R. and Walters, E.E. (2005). Lifetime Prevalence and age-of-onset Distributions of DSM-IV Disorders in the National Comorbidity Survey Replication. *Archives of General Psychiatry*, 62(6), pp.593–602. doi:https://doi.org/10.1001/archpsyc.62.6.593.

Khalil, B., Warrington, S.J. and Rosani, A. (2024). *Physiology, Catecholamines.* [online] Nih.gov. Available at: https://www.ncbi.nlm.nih.gov/books/NBK507716/.

Koob, G.F. and Le Moal, M. (2008). Addiction and the Brain Antireward System. *Annual Review of Psychology*, 59(1), pp.29–53. doi:https://doi.org/10.1146/annurev.psych.59.103006.093548.

Koob, G.F. and Volkow, N.D. (2010). Neurocircuitry of Addiction. *Neuropsychopharmacology*, [online] 35(1), pp.217–238. doi:https://doi.org/10.1038/npp.2009.110.

Koob, G.F. and Volkow, N.D. (2016). Neurobiology of addiction: a Neurocircuitry Analysis. *The Lancet Psychiatry*, [online] 3(8), pp.760–773. doi:https://doi.org/10.1016/s2215-0366(16)00104-8.

Kramer, K., Voss, H.P., J.A. Grimbergen, Mills, P.A., Huetteman, D.A., Zwiers, L.M. and Brockway, B. (2000). Telemetric monitoring of blood pressure in freely moving mice: a preliminary study. 34(3), pp.272–280. doi:https://doi.org/10.1258/002367700780384663.

Kranish, M. (2019). *Trump pressured his alcoholic brother about his career. Now he says he has regrets.* [online] The Washington Post. Available at: https://www.washingtonpost.com/politics/trump-pressured-his-alcoholic-brother-about-his-career-now-he-has-regrets-/2019/08/07/58ec2d70-b216-11e9-8f6c-7828e68cb15f_story.html?utm_source=chatgpt.com [Accessed 10 Sep. 2025].

Krege, J.H., Hodgin, J.B., Hagaman, J.R. and Smithies, O. (1995). A Noninvasive Computerized Tail-Cuff System for Measuring Blood Pressure in Mice. *Hypertension*, 25(5), pp.1111–1115. doi:https://doi.org/10.1161/01.hyp.25.5.1111.

Lattuca, V. (2025). *Benjamin Rush and Early American Medicine | Christ Church.* [online] Christ Church. Available at: https://christchurchphila.org/benjamin-rush-and-early-american-medicine/.

LeDoux (2015). *P - The Emotional Brain Revisited.* [online] Scribd. Available at: https://www.scribd.com/document/863171812/P-The-Emotional-Brain-Revisited [Accessed 26 Nov. 2025].

Ledoux, J. (2015). *Anxious.* Penguin Publishing Group.

Lindsay, R., Krege, J.H., Marin, F., Jin, L. and Stepan, J.J. (2016). Teriparatide for osteoporosis: importance of the full course.

Osteoporosis International, 27(8), pp.2395–2410. doi:https://doi.org/10.1007/s00198-016-3534-6.

Liu, Y. (2011). Cellular and molecular mechanisms of renal fibrosis. *Nature Reviews Nephrology*, 7(12), pp.684–696. doi:https://doi.org/10.1038/nrneph.2011.149.

Loller, T. (2025). *RFK Jr. recounts heroin addiction and spiritual awakening, urges focus on prevention and community*. [online] AP News. Available at: https://apnews.com/article/92924f4ca4e445610e3e179142d6ebd7 [Accessed 26 Nov. 2025].

Maxwell, J.C. and Brecht, M.-L. (2011). Methamphetamine: Here we go again? *Addictive Behaviors*, 36(12), pp.1168–1173. doi:https://doi.org/10.1016/j.addbeh.2011.07.017.

McEwen, B.S. (2007). Physiology and Neurobiology of Stress and Adaptation: Central Role of the Brain. *Physiological Reviews*, [online] 87(3), pp.873–904. doi:https://doi.org/10.1152/physrev.00041.2006.

Medscape (2021). Cocaine Toxicity: Practice Essentials, Background, Pathophysiology. *eMedicine*. [online] Available at: https://emedicine.medscape.com/article/813959-overview.

Melton, R.H. and Abramowitz, M. (1990). *BARRY ARRESTED ON COCAINE CHARGES IN UNDERCOVER FBI, POLICE OPERATION*. [online] The Washington Post. Available at: https://www.washingtonpost.com/archive/politics/1990/01/19/barry-arrested-on-cocaine-charges-in-undercover-fbi-police-operation/16e8e950-766a-4962-9dfa-20bc574437ed/ [Accessed 2 Dec. 2025].

Messinger, J.C. and Beletsky, L. (2025). *What's Old Is New Again in Addiction Treatment: The Expansion of Involuntary Commitment in the United States – HHR Journal*. [online]

Hhrjournal.org. Available at: https://www.hhrjournal.org/2025/05/12/whats-old-is-new-again-in-addiction-treatment-the-expansion-of-involuntary-commitment-in-the-united-states/.

Mills, P.A., Huetteman, D.A., Brockway, B.P., Zwiers, L.M., Gelsema, A.J.M., Schwartz, R.S. and Kramer, K. (2000). A new method for measurement of blood pressure, heart rate, and activity in the mouse by radiotelemetry. *Journal of Applied Physiology*, 88(5), pp.1537–1544. doi:https://doi.org/10.1152/jappl.2000.88.5.1537.

Minogianis, E.-A., Lévesque, D. and Samaha, A.-N. (2013). The Speed of Cocaine Delivery Determines the Subsequent Motivation to Self-Administer the Drug. *Neuropsychopharmacology*, 38(13), pp.2644–2656. doi:https://doi.org/10.1038/npp.2013.173.

Moos, R.H. and Moos, B.S. (2006). Rates and predictors of relapse after natural and treated remission from alcohol use disorders. *Addiction*, 101(2), pp.212–222. doi:https://doi.org/10.1111/j.1360-0443.2006.01310.x.

Moosavyzadeh, A., Ghaffari, F., Mosavat, S.H., Zargaran, A., Mokri, A., Faghihzadeh, S. and Naseri, M. (2018). The medieval Persian manuscript of Afyunieh : the first individual treatise on the opium and addiction in history. *Journal of Integrative Medicine*, 16(2), pp.77–83. doi:https://doi.org/10.1016/j.joim.2018.02.004.

Nader, K. and Hardt, O. (2009). A single standard for memory: the case for reconsolidation. *Nature Reviews. Neuroscience*, [online] 10(3), pp.224–234. doi:https://doi.org/10.1038/nrn2590.

Nakamura, R. (2021). *Demi Lovato Reveals She Had 3 Strokes and a Heart Attack After 2018 Overdose in YouTube Doc Trailer (Video).* [online] TheWrap. Available at:

https://www.thewrap.com/demi-lovato-dancing-with-the-devil-trailer-youtube-doc-video/?utm_source=chatgpt.com [Accessed 3 Oct. 2025].

Nast, C. (2021). *'I Was Out of My Mind': How Samuel L. Jackson's Battle With Addiction Inspired His Breakthrough Performance.* [online] Vanity Fair. Available at: https://www.vanityfair.com/hollywood/2021/10/how-samuel-jacksons-addiction-inspired-breakthrough-performance.

National Academies of Sciences, Engineering, and Medicine (2016). *Ending Discrimination Against People with Mental and Substance Use Disorders*. [online] Washington, D.C.: National Academies Press. doi:https://doi.org/10.17226/23442.

National Action Alliance for Suicide Prevention (n.d.). *Patrick J. Kennedy | National Action Alliance for Suicide Prevention.* [online] theactionalliance.org. Available at: https://theactionalliance.org/about/staff/patrick-j-kennedy.

National Institute on Alcohol Abuse and Alcoholism (2023). *Neuroscience: The brain in addiction and recovery*. [online] www.niaaa.nih.gov. Available at: https://www.niaaa.nih.gov/health-professionals-communities/core-resource-on-alcohol/neuroscience-brain-addiction-and-recovery.

National Institute on Drug Abuse (2020). *Drug Misuse and Addiction.* [online] National Institute on Drug Abuse. Available at: https://nida.nih.gov/publications/drugs-brains-behavior-science-addiction/drug-misuse-addiction.

National Institute on Drug Abuse (2021). *Fentanyl.* [online] National Institute on Drug Abuse. Available at: https://nida.nih.gov/research-topics/fentanyl.

National Institute on Drug Abuse (2022). *Naloxone drug facts.* [online] National Institute on Drug Abuse. Available at: https://nida.nih.gov/publications/drugfacts/naloxone.

National Library of Medicine (n.d.). *Diseases of the Mind.* [online] www.nlm.nih.gov. Available at: https://www.nlm.nih.gov/hmd/topics/diseases-of-mind/bio-benjamin-rush.html.

Naugle (n.d.). *Drew Barrymore Says One Thing She's Proudest of Is Breaking Her Family's Cycle of Alcohol Abuse (Exclusive).* [online] Peoplemag. Available at: https://people.com/drew-barrymore-proudest-breaking-family-cycle-of-alcohol-abuse-50th-exclusive-8630719.

Nelson, R.J. (2025). *APA PsycNet.* [online] Apa.org. Available at: https://psycnet.apa.org/record/2011-21085-000.

Nestler, E.J. (2005). Is there a common molecular pathway for addiction? *Nature Neuroscience*, 8(11), pp.1445–1449. doi:https://doi.org/10.1038/nn1578.

Nestler, E.J. (2014). Epigenetic mechanisms of drug addiction. *Neuropharmacology*, 76, pp.259–268. doi:https://doi.org/10.1016/j.neuropharm.2013.04.004.

News, A. (2004). *Hollywood star John Barrymore dies.* [online] Abc.net.au. Available at: https://www.abc.net.au/news/2004-12-01/hollywood-star-john-barrymore-dies/595200 [Accessed 10 Sep. 2025].

News, A. (2010). *Laura Bush Reveals How George W. Stopped Drinking.* [online] ABC News. Available at: https://abcnews.go.com/Politics/laura-bush-reveals-george-stopped-drinking/story?id=10552148.

News, A. (2014). *Robert Downey Jr.'s Son Indio Arrested for Cocaine Possession: Police.* [online] ABC News. Available at:

https://abcnews.go.com/Entertainment/robert-downey-jrs-son-indio-arrested-cocaine-possession/story?id=24364639&utm [Accessed 10 Sep. 2025].

News, F. (2025). *RFK Jr. proposed sending addicts to taxpayer-funded 'wellness farms' to tackle drug crisis.* [online] New York Post. Available at: https://nypost.com/2025/01/26/us-news/rfk-jr-proposed-taxpayer-funded-wellness-farms-to-deal-with-opioid-addiction/.

newsEmailEmailBioBioFollowFollowReporter, J.W.M. closeJustin W.M. covering breaking (2014). *Indio Downey, Robert Downey Jr., Robert Downey Sr.: Three generations on drugs.* [online] Washington Post. Available at: https://www.washingtonpost.com/news/morning-mix/wp/2014/07/01/indio-downey-robert-downey-jr-robert-downey-sr-three-generations-on-drugs/.

NIAAA (2025a). *Alcohol Use Disorder: From Risk to Diagnosis to Recovery | National Institute on Alcohol Abuse and Alcoholism (NIAAA).* [online] Nih.gov. Available at: https://www.niaaa.nih.gov/health-professionals-communities/core-resource-on-alcohol/alcohol-use-disorder-risk-diagnosis-recovery?utm_source=chatgpt.com.

NIAAA (2025b). *Neuroscience: The Brain in Addiction and Recovery | National Institute on Alcohol Abuse and Alcoholism (NIAAA).* [online] Nih.gov. Available at: https://www.niaaa.nih.gov/health-professionals-communities/core-resource-on-alcohol/neuroscience-brain-addiction-and-recovery?utm_source=chatgpt.com.

NIH (2023). *New NIH study reveals shared genetic markers underlying substance use disorders.* [online] National Institute on Drug Abuse. Available at: https://nida.nih.gov/news-events/news-releases/2023/03/new-nih-study-reveals-shared-genetic-markers-underlying-substance-use-disorders.

NIH (2024a). *Drug Misuse and Addiction | National Institute on Drug Abuse*. [online] National Institute on Drug Abuse. Available at: https://nida.nih.gov/publications/drugs-brains-behavior-science-addiction/drug-misuse-addiction?utm_source=chatgpt.com.

NIH (2024b). *Drugs and the Brain | National Institute on Drug Abuse*. [online] National Institute on Drug Abuse. Available at: https://nida.nih.gov/publications/drugs-brains-behavior-science-addiction/drugs-brain?utm_source=chatgpt.com.

OPB (n.d.). *The formulation of meth has changed. It may be contributing to this country's mental health crisis.* [online] opb. Available at: https://www.opb.org/article/2021/11/01/the-formulation-of-meth-has-changed-it-may-be-contributing-to-this-countrys-mental-health-crisis/.

PA Department of Health (2022). *Medical Marijuana*. [online] Pa.gov. Available at: https://www.pa.gov/agencies/health/programs/medical-marijuana.

Pagano, M.E., Friend, K.B., Tonigan, J.S. and Stout, R.L. (2004). Helping other alcoholics in alcoholics anonymous and drinking outcomes: findings from project MATCH. *Journal of Studies on Alcohol*, 65(6), pp.766–773. doi:https://doi.org/10.15288/jsa.2004.65.766.

Pagano, M.E., Post, S.G. and Johnson, S.M. (2011). Alcoholics Anonymous-Related Helping and the Helper Therapy Principle. *Alcoholism Treatment Quarterly*, [online] 29(1), pp.23–34. doi:https://doi.org/10.1080/07347324.2011.538320.

Parr, A.C., Calabro, F., Larsen, B., Tervo-Clemmens, B., Elliot, S., Foran, W., Olafsson, V. and Luna, B. (2021). Dopamine-related striatal neurophysiology is associated with specialization of frontostriatal reward circuitry through adolescence. *Progress in Neurobiology*, 201, p.101997. doi:https://doi.org/10.1016/j.pneurobio.2021.101997.

Pelosi, A.J. (2019). The Hans Eysenck affair: Time to correct the scientific record. *Journal of Health Psychology*, 24(4), pp.409–420. doi:https://doi.org/10.1177/1359105318820931.

Press, A. (2015). Patrick Kennedy memoir about family addiction and mental illness creates rift. *The Guardian*. [online] 7 Oct. Available at: https://www.theguardian.com/us-news/2015/oct/07/patrick-kennedy-memoir-about-family-addiction-and-mental-illness-creates-rift.

Price, R.B., Brenden Tervo-Clemmens, Panny, B., Degutis, M., Griffo, A. and Woody, M.L. (2021). Biobehavioral correlates of an fMRI index of striatal tissue iron in depressed patients. *Translational Psychiatry*, 11(1). doi:https://doi.org/10.1038/s41398-021-01553-x.

Recovery.com (2017). *White Deer Run Lehigh*. [online] Recovery.com. Available at: https://recovery.com/white-deer-run-lehigh-bethlehem-pennsylvania/ [Accessed 2 Dec. 2025].

Renee, S. and Spradlin, W.W. (2007). *Cross to Bear*. [online] Available at: https://www.authorhouse.com/en/bookstore/bookdetails/268472-Cross-To-Bear [Accessed 24 Nov. 2025].

Richardson, K. (2012). Drug overdose, disability and male friendship in fifteenth-century Mamluk Cairo. *postmedieval: a journal of medieval cultural studies*, 3(2), pp.168–181. doi:https://doi.org/10.1057/pmed.2012.12.

Robinson, T.E. and Berridge, K.C. (2008). The incentive sensitization theory of addiction: some current issues. *Philosophical Transactions of the Royal Society B: Biological Sciences*, [online] 363(1507), pp.3137–3146. doi:https://doi.org/10.1098/rstb.2008.0093.

Root, D.H., Melendez, R.I., Zaborszky, L. and Napier, T.C. (2015). The ventral pallidum: Subregion-specific functional anatomy and roles in motivated behaviors. *Progress in Neurobiology*, 130, pp.29–70. doi:https://doi.org/10.1016/j.pneurobio.2015.03.005.

Rotenstein, L.S., Torre, M., Ramos, M.A., Rosales, R.C., Guille, C., Sen, S. and Mata, D.A. (2018). Prevalence of Burnout Among Physicians. *JAMA*, [online] 320(11), p.1131. doi:https://doi.org/10.1001/jama.2018.12777.

Russo, G. (2021). *Demi Lovato's 'Dancing With the Devil' Album: 25 Powerful Lyrics That Inspire Us.* [online] Teen Vogue. Available at: https://www.teenvogue.com/story/demi-lovato-dancing-with-the-devil-album-25-powerful-lyrics [Accessed 3 Oct. 2025].

Sara, S.J. (2009). The locus coeruleus and noradrenergic modulation of cognition. *Nature Reviews Neuroscience*, [online] 10(3), pp.211–223. doi:https://doi.org/10.1038/nrn2573.

Sarkar, P.R. (2021). Spirits From the Past: Stigma in Historical Medical Literature on Alcohol Addiction and Implications for Modern Practice. *American Journal of Psychiatry Residents' Journal*, 16(4), pp.8–10. doi:https://doi.org/10.1176/appi.ajp-rj.2021.160405.

Sata, Y., Head, G.A., Denton, K., May, C.N. and Schlaich, M.P. (2018). Role of the Sympathetic Nervous System and Its Modulation in Renal Hypertension. *Frontiers in Medicine*, 5(82). doi:https://doi.org/10.3389/fmed.2018.00082.

Schultz, W. (2016). Dopamine reward prediction error coding. *Dialogues in Clinical Neuroscience*, [online] 18(1), pp.23–32. doi:https://doi.org/10.31887/dcns.2016.18.1/wschultz.

Shapiro, T. (2014). *Genes Do Not Cause or Maintain Addictions, Says Dr. Gabor Mate - North Atlantic Books*. [online] North Atlantic Books. Available at: https://www.northatlanticbooks.com/blog/genes-do-not-cause-or-maintain-addictions-says-dr-gabor-mate/?utm_source=chatgpt.com [Accessed 10 Sep. 2025].

Shemo, J.P. (1982). A conjoint psychiatry-internal medicine program: development of a teaching and clinical model. *American Journal of Psychiatry*, 139(11), pp.1437–1442. doi:https://doi.org/10.1176/ajp.139.11.1437.

Shemo, J.P., Withersty, D.J., Spradlin, W.W. and Waldman, R.H. (1980). Psychiatry as an internal medicine subspecialty: an educational model. *Journal of medical education*, [online] 55(4), pp.354–61. doi:https://doi.org/10.1097/00001888-198004000-00006.

Sherer, J. (2023). *Actor Matthew Perry's History Of Addiction*. [online] Addiction Center. Available at: https://www.addictioncenter.com/news/2023/11/matthew-perrys-addiction/.

Sinha, R. (2008). Chronic Stress, Drug Use, and Vulnerability to Addiction. *Annals of the New York Academy of Sciences*, [online] 1141(1), pp.105–130. doi:https://doi.org/10.1196/annals.1441.030.

Smith, D. (2008). *The star who came back from the depths*. [online] the Guardian. Available at: https://www.theguardian.com/film/2008/aug/24/robertdowneyjr.usa?utm_source=chatgpt.com [Accessed 10 Sep. 2025].

Sofroniew, M.V. and Vinters, H.V. (2009). Astrocytes: biology and pathology. *Acta Neuropathologica*, [online] 119(1), pp.7–35. doi:https://doi.org/10.1007/s00401-009-0619-8.

Spradlin, W.W. (2008). *Strange Attraction*. [online] Available at: https://www.authorhouse.com/en/bookstore/bookdetails/269504-strange-attraction [Accessed 24 Nov. 2025].

Spradlin, W.W. and Porterfield, P.B. (1979). *Human Biosociology. Heidelberg science library*. Springer Nature. doi:https://doi.org/10.1007/978-1-4612-6148-3.

Sublocade (n.d.). *Patient Information for SUBLOCADE® (buprenorphine extended-release) injection, for subcutaneous use (CIII)*. [online] www.sublocade.com. Available at: https://www.sublocade.com/.

Takuya Seike, Chen, C. and Mochly-Rosen, D. (2023). Impact of common ALDH2 inactivating mutation and alcohol consumption on Alzheimer's disease. *Frontiers in Aging Neuroscience*, 15. doi:https://doi.org/10.3389/fnagi.2023.1223977.

Tang, Y.-Y., Hölzel, B.K. and Posner, M.I. (2015). The neuroscience of mindfulness meditation. *Nature Reviews Neuroscience*, 16(4), pp.213–225. doi:https://doi.org/10.1038/nrn3916.

Taylor, J. (2018). *Fentanyl-laced 'oxy' caused Demi Lovato's overdose; report*. [online] Securingindustry.com. Available at: https://www.securingindustry.com/pharmaceuticals/fentanyl-laced-oxy-caused-demi-lovato-s-overdose-report/s40/a8245/ [Accessed 3 Oct. 2025].

The (1999). *John Barrymore | Biography, Plays, Movies, & Facts*. [online] Encyclopedia Britannica. Available at: https://www.britannica.com/biography/John-Barrymore?utm_source=chatgpt.com [Accessed 10 Sep. 2025].

The Kennedy Forum (2017). *What is Parity? | The Kennedy Forum*. [online] The Kennedy Forum. Available at: https://www.thekennedyforum.org/focus-areas/coverage-parity/parity [Accessed 24 Nov. 2025].

Tori, M.E., Larochelle, M.R. and Naimi, T.S. (2020). Alcohol or Benzodiazepine Co-involvement with Opioid Overdose Deaths in the United States, 1999-2017. *JAMA Network Open*, [online] 3(4), p.e202361. doi:https://doi.org/10.1001/jamanetworkopen.2020.2361.

Trump, M.L. (2022). *TOO MUCH AND NEVER ENOUGH : how my family created the world's most dangerous man.* 出版商： S.L.: Simon & Schuster.

U.S. Department of Health and Human Services (2025). *Secretary Kennedy Renews Public Health Emergency Declaration to Address National Opioid Crisis*. [online] HHS.gov. Available at: https://www.hhs.gov/press-room/secretary-kennedy-opiod-crisis-emergency-declaration.html.

Ungar, L. (2025). *Fewer of those addicted to marijuana seek help than once did*. [online] AP News. Available at: https://apnews.com/article/a40534877ee6fdfe9936d18c222b71a2 [Accessed 2 Dec. 2025].

University of Pennsylvania Health System (2017). *Pennsylvania Hospital History: Stories - Dr. Benjamin Rush*. [online] Upenn.edu. Available at: https://www.uphs.upenn.edu/paharc/features/brush.html.

US Department of Health and Human Services (2016). *THE NEUROBIOLOGY OF SUBSTANCE USE, MISUSE, AND ADDICTION*. [online] Nih.gov. Available at: https://www.ncbi.nlm.nih.gov/books/NBK424849/.

van der Kolk, B.A., Hodgdon, H., Gapen, M., Musicaro, R., Suvak, M.K., Hamlin, E. and Spinazzola, J. (2016). A Randomized Controlled Study of Neurofeedback for Chronic PTSD. *PLOS ONE*, 11(12), p.e0166752. doi:https://doi.org/10.1371/journal.pone.0166752.

Vento, P.J., Burnham, N.W., Rowley, C.S. and Jhou, T.C. (2017). Learning From One's Mistakes: A Dual Role for the Rostromedial Tegmental Nucleus in the Encoding and Expression of Punished Reward Seeking. *Biological Psychiatry*, 81(12), pp.1041–1049. doi:https://doi.org/10.1016/j.biopsych.2016.10.018.

Verhulst, B., Neale, M.C. and Kendler, K.S. (2014). The heritability of alcohol use disorders: a meta-analysis of twin and adoption studies. *Psychological Medicine*, [online] 45(5), pp.1061–1072. doi:https://doi.org/10.1017/s0033291714002165.

Verma, V. (2015). Classic Studies on the Interaction of Cocaine and the Dopamine Transporter. *Clinical Psychopharmacology and Neuroscience*, [online] 13(3), pp.227–238. doi:https://doi.org/10.9758/cpn.2015.13.3.227.

Vivitrol (2019). *VIVITROL® (naltrexone for extended-release injectable suspension).* [online] ALK-VIV. Available at: https://www.vivitrol.com/.

Volkow, N.D., Baler, R.D., Compton, W.M. and Weiss, S.R.B. (2014). Adverse Health Effects of Marijuana Use. *New England Journal of Medicine*, 370(23), pp.2219–2227. doi:https://doi.org/10.1056/nejmra1402309.

Volkow, N.D., Fowler, J.S., Wang, G.-J., Hitzemann, R., Logan, J., Schlyer, D.J., Dewey, S.L. and Wolf, A.P. (1993). Decreased dopamine D2 receptor availability is associated with reduced frontal metabolism in cocaine abusers. *Synapse*, 14(2), pp.169–177. doi:https://doi.org/10.1002/syn.890140210.

Volkow, N.D., Koob, G.F. and McLellan, A.T. (2016). Neurobiologic advances from the brain disease model of addiction. *New England Journal of Medicine*, [online] 374(4), pp.363–371. doi:https://doi.org/10.1056/nejmra1511480.

Volkow, N.D., Wang, G.-J. ., Fowler, J.S., Tomasi, D. and Telang, F. (2011). Addiction: Beyond dopamine reward circuitry. *Proceedings of the National Academy of Sciences*, [online] 108(37), pp.15037–15042. doi:https://doi.org/10.1073/pnas.1010654108.

Volkow, N.D., Wise, R.A. and Baler, R. (2017). The dopamine motive system: implications for drug and food addiction. *Nature Reviews Neuroscience*, 18(12), pp.741–752. doi:https://doi.org/10.1038/nrn.2017.130.

Volkow, Nora D. and Morales, M. (2015). The Brain on Drugs: From Reward to Addiction. *Cell*, [online] 162(4), pp.712–725. doi:https://doi.org/10.1016/j.cell.2015.07.046.

Wakabayashi, K. (2010). *THE SPEED OF INTRAVENOUS COCAINE DELIVERY ALTERS ITS EFFECT ON THE BRAIN AND DRUG-TAKING BEHAVIOR: IMPLICATIONS FOR ADDICTION LIABILITY.* [online] Available at: https://deepblue.lib.umich.edu/bitstream/handle/2027.42/75876/ktwakaba_1.pdf?sequence=1&utm [Accessed 3 Oct. 2025].

Washington Post (2014). *FBI video of undercover sting on Marion Barry.* [online] www.washingtonpost.com. Available at: https://www.washingtonpost.com/video/local/fbi-video-of-undercover-sting-on-marion-barry/2014/11/23/e1e35f00-7336-11e4-95a8-fe0b46e8751a_video.html [Accessed 12 Jun. 2024].

WBUR (2011). *Scientists Develop Drugs That Target Alcoholism Genes.* [online] Wbur.org. Available at: https://www.wbur.org/hereandnow/2011/03/01/gene-alcoholism [Accessed 10 Sep. 2025].

WBUR (2025). *RFK Jr. has deep experience of opioid addiction. His solutions are controversial.* [online] Wbur.org. Available at: https://www.wbur.org/hereandnow/2025/01/29/rfk-jr-opioid-crisis [Accessed 26 Nov. 2025].

White Deer Run Lehigh (n.d.). *Lehigh County's Leading Drug & Alcohol Addiction Treatment and Rehab Center | White Deer Run of Lehigh.* [online] White Deer Run. Available at: https://www.whitedeerrun.com/about/locations/lehigh/.

Wikipedia (2020). *Benjamin Rush.* [online] Wikipedia. Available at: https://en.wikipedia.org/wiki/Benjamin_Rush.

Wikipedia (2025). *History | Easton, PA.* [online] Easton-pa.com. Available at: https://easton-pa.com/354/History [Accessed 1 Dec. 2025].

Wikipedia Contributors (2019). *Rush Limbaugh.* [online] Wikipedia. Available at: https://en.wikipedia.org/wiki/Rush_Limbaugh.

Wikipedia Contributors (2025a). *Gerard Butler.* Wikipedia.

Wikipedia Contributors (2025b). *Robert F. Kennedy Jr.* Wikipedia.

Wikipedia Contributors (2025c). *Sober (Demi Lovato song).* [online] Wikipedia. Available at: https://en.wikipedia.org/wiki/Sober_%28Demi_Lovato_song%29.

Wikipedia Contributors (2025d). *Timeline of Rob Ford crack video scandal.* [online] Wikipedia. Available at: https://en.wikipedia.org/wiki/Timeline_of_Rob_Ford_crack_video_scandal.

wpadmin (2023a). *Pennsylvania Medical Marijuana: A Look at the Latest Program Data*. [online] Compassionate Certification Centers. Available at: https://www.compassionatecertificationcenters.com/news/pennsylvania-medical-marijuana-update/ [Accessed 2 Dec. 2025].

wpadmin (2023b). *The History & Current Status of Medical Marijuana in Pennsylvania*. [online] Compassionate Certification Centers. Available at: https://www.compassionatecertificationcenters.com/news/history-status-of-medical-marijuana-in-pennsylvania/ [Accessed 2 Dec. 2025].

Yager, L.M., Garcia, A.F., Wunsch, A.M. and Ferguson, S.M. (2015). The ins and outs of the striatum: Role in drug addiction. *Neuroscience*, 301, pp.529–541. doi:https://doi.org/10.1016/j.neuroscience.2015.06.033.

York, M. (1990). *EXCERPTS FROM VIDEOTAPE OF BARRY'S ARREST AT THE VISTA HOTEL*. [online] The Washington Post. Available at: https://www.washingtonpost.com/archive/politics/1990/06/29/excerpts-from-videotape-of-barrys-arrest-at-the-vista-hotel/a6b29ad1-7327-4867-ab4e-6cdec3ae2935/ [Accessed 2 Dec. 2025].

www.ingramcontent.com/pod-product-compliance
Lightning Source LLC
LaVergne TN
LVHW052038200926
848481LV00005B/1719